Y0-BUP-130

THE BRITISH EMPIRE IN
THE VICTORIAN PRESS, 1832–1867

THEMES IN EUROPEAN EXPANSION: EXPLORATION,
COLONIZATION, AND THE IMPACT OF EMPIRE
(General Editor: James A. Casada)
VOL. 8

GARLAND REFERENCE LIBRARY
OF SOCIAL SCIENCE
VOL. 389

THEMES IN EUROPEAN EXPANSION: EXPLORATION, COLONIZATION AND THE IMPACT OF EMPIRE
(General Editor: James A. Casada)

1. Robert Heussler, *British Malaya: A Bibliographical and Biographical Compendium.*

2. William J. Olson with the assistance of Addeane S. Caelleigh, *Britain's Elusive Empire in the Middle East: An Annotated Bibliography.*

3. Susan F. Bailey, *Women and the British Empire: An Annotated Guide to Sources.*

4. Edward J. Goodman, *The Exploration of South America: An Annotated Bibliography.*

5. Naomi Musiker with the assistance of Reuben Musiker, *South African History: A Bibliographical Guide with Special Reference to Territorial Expansion and Colonization.*

6. Philip P. Boucher, *The Shaping of the French Colonial Empire: A Bio-Bibliography of the Careers of Richelieu, Fouquet, and Colbert.*

7. Thomas P. Ofcansky, *British East Africa, 1856–1963: An Annotated Bibliography.*

8. E.M. Palmegiano, *The British Empire in the Victorian Press, 1832–1867: A Bibliography.*

THE BRITISH EMPIRE IN THE
VICTORIAN PRESS, 1832–1867
A Bibliography

E.M. Palmegiano

DA
16
.P3x
West

 ASU WEST LIBRARY

GARLAND PUBLISHING, INC. • NEW YORK & LONDON
1987

© 1987 E.M. Palmegiano
All rights reserved

Library of Congress Cataloging-in-Publication Data

Palmegiano, E. M.
The British Empire in the Victorian Press, 1832–1867.
(Themes in European Expansion; vol. 8) (Garland
Reference Library of Social Science; vol. 389)
Includes indexes.
1. Great Britain—Colonies—History—19th century—
Sources—Bibliography.   2. English periodicals—
Indexes.   I. Title.   II. Series: Themes in European
Expansion; v. 8.   III. Series: Garland Reference
Library of Social Science; v. 389.

Z2021.C7P32   1987   [DA16]   016.941081   86-29624
ISBN 0-8240-9802-1   (alk. paper)

Printed on acid-free, 250-year-life paper
Manufactured in the United States of America

For Mimi and Jack

CONTENTS

ACKNOWLEDGMENTS

There is no way to thank all who have contributed to this book but a few deserve special mention.

The staffs of the British Library, London and the New York Public Library showed great patience and skill in locating missing or misnumbered materials. I am especially indebted to Sallie Hannigan and the entire staff of the Newark Public Library where most of the evidence was gathered.

Jean H. Slingerland, Executive Editor of the *Wellesley Index to Victorian Periodicals*, kindly supplied updated lists of the periodicals to be included in volume IV.

The administration of Saint Peter's College awarded me a fellowship which afforded the time and funding for study. Many of my colleagues lent inspiration by virtue of their own commitments to research.

James A. Casada, the series editor, read the first draft with great care and gave generously of his time to improve the quality of the final manuscript.

Lorraine M. Kozar kept my office running smoothly during the many months of the project.

Aidan C. McMullen, S.J., provided ongoing support and criticism.

To all of these people, I am most grateful. Their assistance made possible the completion, though neither the errors nor omissions, of this work.

E.M. Palmegiano

EDITOR'S INTRODUCTION

This volume, *The British Empire in the Victorian Press,
1832-1867: A Bibliography*, forms a welcome addition to the
series "Themes in European Expansion" as well as filling a
significant gap in the existing corpus of reference works on
British imperial history. In it Professor Eugenia Palmegiano
addresses herself to the important task of unearthing the rich
and virtually untapped sources for the study of colonial history provided by the myriad periodical publications which flour-
ished in the early and mid-Victorian period. This was an age
in which the printed word reigned supreme as a form of communication, a fact all too easily forgotten in the world of today
with its dominance by electrically transmitted visual images
and spoken words. The literate Victorian public were avid
readers, and nothing titillated their collective curiosities
more than developments in the far-flung reaches of Empire.
Through the extensive listings of this bibliography--close to
3000 entries drawn from some fifty London-based magazines--we
see the rich and diverse threads which interwove to form the
colorful fabric which was the British Empire at the height of
its grandeur.

The author's focus on London and periodicals published
there is an appropriate one, for the "infernal wen" which was
this massive metropolis not only served as the hub of Empire;
geographically speaking it is the only logical approach to
examining developments in those portions of the globe invari-
ably depicted by cartographers of the period in resplendent
hues of red. She opens with a substantial narrative intro-
duction--a feature of all the volumes in this series--which
explains the process of selection employed in the fashioning of
the bibliography as well as setting the historiographical stage
for the entries which follow. In particular, the variegated
geographical themes touched upon in this essay offer some indi-
cation of the comprehensive nature of this reference work.
Indeed, it is no overstatement to say that what Palmegiano has
done, in essence, is to smooth the path for all future researchers in this period of imperial history. Her study picks
up where the indispensable volumes of the *Wellesley Index to*

Victorian Periodicals leaves off, carrying students of imperial history, together with those in a host of related disciplines and themes, to a point where they have instant access to pertinent references from a vast array of journals.

Today most of these journals are relatively obscure--several of those covered are new to me despite falling directly in my own area of scholarly specialization--but what is of primary significance is the fact that they were viable publications with appreciable lists of subscribers in their Victorian heyday. Accordingly, they offer the researcher access to hundreds of little-trodden avenues leading into the labyrinths of Britain's imperial past. Only when many of these avenues have been explored and charted will we be able to say that we have something approaching a true understanding of that exceedingly complex ethos which was at the heart of Victoria's Empire. From tiger trails in Bengal to idyllic island scenes in Barbados, all that was spectacular, not to mention sordid, in that splendid mid-nineteenth century imperial edifice passes in review. In short, endless gems await the enterprising researcher, and Professor Palmegiano has done most of our work for us.

The qualifications she brings to her task are exceptional. The holder of an A.B. degree in history (*cum laude*) from Georgian Court College, she has earned three postgraduate degrees (M.A., Ph.D., and J.D.) from Rutgers University. A member of the history faculty at Saint Peter's College since 1967, she has risen through the ranks to a full professorship, and presently Professor Palmegiano directs that institution's Faculty Research and Sponsored Programs. In the course of her career she has also had extensive involvement with humanities and honors programs, including a seven-year stint as Director of the Honors Program at Saint Peter's and service in advisory capacities to both the New Jersey Committee on the Humanities and the National Endowment for the Humanities. More significantly, for present purposes, she has a solid track record as a researching and publishing scholar.

She has read numerous papers and authored several articles on various themes connected with Victorian studies, and her 1976 book, *Women and British Periodicals, 1832-1867*, is widely recognized as a pioneering effort in an important area of the still developing field of woman's studies. Indeed, the present volume is, in many senses, the culmination of a decade and a half of research and writing. Wide-ranging, based on first-hand examination of every one of its entries, and replete with all the appropriate bibliographical appurtenances, it is a work which should find users in many disciplines and fields of interest. Historians will be most obvious among these, but specialists in area studies, international relations, anthropology, sociology, political science, ethnology, historical geography, and other branches of knowledge will also find grist for their mills. Quite simply, there is no comparable work in the field. Anyone who has profited from excursions into such disparate reference sources as *Poole's Index* and the *Wellesley Index* will be delighted with and enlightened by its contents.

James A. Casada, Series Editor

PREFACE

The press and the empire were both important institutions in nineteenth-century Britain. Each was viable but the press gave the empire a visibility which could sustain or threaten it. This bibliography shows something of their intriguing interrelationship by presenting, in a single reference work, the volume and varieties of imperial opinion in the news.

In this study, the phrase "British Empire" applies to those regions over which London exercised authority and to those where it had, was seeking, or was being urged to get influence. The reason for this purview is that the so-called "informal" empire received considerable notice from journalists, sometimes more than true dependencies. The dates were selected because they delimit decades when attention to the empire was reputedly negligible. The era between the Reform Acts, especially when compared to the years after 1870, was supposedly a time of disenchantment with imperialism and fascination with industrialism. Although this characterization is not without merit, an examination of the media has revealed that ideas about the empire were myriad and multifarious.

Victorian coverage of the empire seemed born of mixed emotions and mixed intentions. There were expressions of pride about size, of disgust about cost, and of a whole range of other feelings. There were designs to describe, analyze, applaud, and criticize. In papers from the short-lived *Canadian, British American, and West Indian Magazine* to the established *Asiatic Journal*, stress and style were quite diverse. What emerges from the mass of testimony is that the empire and its members were frequent topics. To some writers, it connoted merely the mysterious, the kind of exotica that customarily enthralled Victorians. For others, even staunch opponents, it was, notwithstanding its complexity, an entity worthy of inquiry because they believed that it affected society in crucial ways. From poor emigrants to prominent merchants, from convicts to Commons, from natives' rights to the nation's defense, all could be helped or harmed by imperial policies and practices. Hence, explicit in all columns was the wish to spark interest; implicit in some, to prolong it in order to shape official decisions. Whatever the purpose of commentators, by headlining the empire in so pervasive and persuasive an estate as the press, they certainly popularized Britain's overseas domain. The process of creating an imperial check-list of periodicals is impeded by the nature of the sources and the subject. Nineteenth-century serials are notorious for their resistance to researchers. Anonymous articles, multiple mergers, and cleverly but unclearly captioned articles are typical. Further, a scrutiny of indices quickly confirms that material about the empire is not always easily identifiable. To ensure accuracy, therefore, all magazines have been seen and all citations read by the writer. While the aim is to record a spectrum of views, initial investigation proved that interpretations of the empire, as defined here, are numerous. Thus data has been gathered in only two categories: specialized journals and specific essays in multi-dimensional publications.

For items focusing on the empire (Section I), inclusion has been restricted to those which were London-issued. These have been chosen because they circulated in the capital, the imperial linchpin, and because they covered, exclusively or extensively, imperial matters. The only London titles omitted are those of religious sponsorship (i.e., missionary reports of the churches) and newspapers (as classified by the British Library, London). The former are missing because theological ideas have been amply surveyed in Section II; newspapers because they suffer from even greater evidentiary problems than do magazines. In newspapers, bylines are rare and names of leader writers rarer.

Of the serials in Section I, none dealt with the empire as a whole, although *Fisher's Colonial Magazine* and *Simmonds's Colonial Magazine* were relatively broad in scope. Most of this genre, however, concentrated on particulars. *The Colonial Intelligencer* devoted itself to the protection of the rights of aborigines while *Sidney's Emigrant's Journal* did the same for prospective settlers. *The Australian and New Zealand Monthly Magazine* depicted the world of the Antipodes while *Alexander's East India Magazine* did likewise for that east of Egypt. *Colburn's United Service Magazine* discussed defense while *The Journal of Civilization* talked about values. Some, as *The Canadian Portfolio* and *Australasian Gold Fields*, were responses to events. Others, as *The Anti-Slavery Reporter* and *The Journal of the East India Association*, addressed longstanding concerns. Several of these gazettes lasted just weeks but the few with longevity tended to contain substantial and serious essays.

The second bibliographic component is an inventory of articles with an imperial orientation appearing in reviews with a wider outlook. The journals have been determined on the basis of their historical significance. Accordingly, all those in the *Wellesley Index to Victorian Periodicals* (volumes I-IV), sixteen in *Poole's Index*, and *The Monthly Repository* have been incorporated. All

periodicals, irrespective of supersession or merger, are chronicled independently, except for those related to *The Westminster
Review* and classified under that heading because merged volumes
therein are numbered in the parent sequence. The end dates of
The New Monthly Magazine and *Tait's Edinburgh Magazine* correspond
to those in the *Wellesley Index*. Otherwise, publications have
been checked from 1832 through 1867 or their runs within that
span.

This segment is meant to be a comprehensive calendar but
reprints and summaries (as of the month's politics) have not
been designated. Also excluded have been fiction, poetry, and
peripheral observations (as on fauna and flora). Moreover, the
approach taken with the formal empire has been more catholic
than that with the informal. For the first, an effort has been
made to indicate all references whereas for the second, only
those with an imperial emphasis have been mentioned. To illus-
trate, an assessment of India's ancient literatures would be
listed but those of China or Egypt would not. Nonetheless,
whatever might have contributed to readers' knowledge of British
interaction with people overseas has been documented.

Entries in Section II represent a plethora of thinking about
the empire. Lengthy treatises and brief abstracts were equally
common. Either format could be speculative or practical. Pages
about the empire *qua* empire could, for instance, ponder its
virtues or dissect its commercial operations. Accounts of an
actual or anticipated possession could weigh, philosophically,
Britain's governance or detail, abundantly, native customs.

An introduction highlights the concepts, in the journals
and articles in both sections, of imperial motifs and areas
which were of consequence or were so regarded by writers. The
introduction comprises the following: imperial themes, sea
routes to the East, India, the Indian Ocean, the Far East, the
Pacific Ocean, British North America, the Caribbean and South
America, and Africa.

Thereafter, the first section of the check-list has such
information as dates of run, subtitles, editors, and the like.
The second section is a catalog done alphabetically by review
and then chronologically by essay under the caption of the
issuer. Citations which are not title-indicative are annotated
as are those which have a minimal amount of news about the
empire. The latter are followed by the word "notes" and a
clarification.

Attribution of authorship comes primarily from the *Wellesley
Index* albeit identifications for volume IV were not available
at this writing. Other printed sources were Anne Lohrli,
*Household Words: A Weekly Journal, 1850-59, Conducted by Charles
Dickens* (Toronto, 1973), and Francis E. Mineka, *The Dissidence
of Dissent: The Monthly Repository, 1806-1838* (Chapel Hill,

1944).
The subject index covers territories and topics as well as critical subdivisions of each (e.g., Punjab in India; Canada in British North America; sugar in addition to trade). Geographic regions have been labeled as they were known at the time.

The British Empire in
the Victorian Press, 1832–1867

INTRODUCTION

a. Imperial Themes

Articles about the British Empire, 1832-1867, focused frequently on a dependency. Less prevalent, but usually more analytic, were essays on subjects of broad imperial significance.

Of these topics, the most popular during the era was the retention of the empire. In the 1830s, authors were about evenly divided on the merits of keeping the overseas possessions. Proponents proclaimed numerous advantages. The vast expanses would purportedly absorb much of Britain's surplus population; the natives, British values. Both new and old residents would produce raw materials to exchange for English manufactures. Local economies would provide opportunities for investment as local governments would patronage. The more territory accumulated, the greater would be British prestige and power, military as well as political.

Ideas did not vary much over the years; only emphasis shifted. For example, in the 1840s, journalists stressed emigration and trade. With too many people and too few jobs, Britain, papers said, could only perpetuate its status by matching domestic energy and machines with imperial resources and labor. Responding to calls for dismantling the empire, those against contended that British citizens, at home and abroad, disapproved of separation and that Britain's destiny was to civilize the world.

By the 1850s, the definition of destiny had gone from statements about responsibility to those about superiority. As more and more reporters assumed that the British race was preeminent, they sanctioned both the destruction of non-European cultures and the conquest of non-European lands. For, imperialists argued, God intended the best to rule. Apart from divine determination, the search, in the 1850s and 1860s, for a safe cotton supply may also have influenced the pleas to hold the empire. Not that the earlier apologies disappeared. Justifications based on markets, politics, defense, progress, mission, position, and the redundant all remained. As advocates concluded, to preserve the empire was logical; to abandon it would be a signal to European enemies and a betrayal of imperial inhabitants.

Balancing these views was criticism of the empire, also published throughout the period. At least in the 1830s, opponents were as vocal as supporters. Disparagement, as endorsement, was repetitious. The most common attacks spoke about morals and costs. Writers insisted that the British ruined natives by bringing vice, disease, drink, firearms, or criminals; by allowing exploitation, in land and wages, by colonists; and by introducing alien practices. Moreover, anti-imperialists were certain that the dependencies were too expensive. They required money to maintain and their commerce was no more profitable than that with foreign nations. Worse, new satellites added to the risk of war, and, thereby, to the budget. At mid-century and after, some columnists further declared that the empire conveyed a false sense of rank. While Britain believed that it gained international respect as it gained paramountcy, other countries really regarded it as rapacious.

To escape this unpleasant scenario, London, the press counseled, should relinquish the empire. However, even the most adamant adversaries wanted to be sure that dismemberment would not impair Britain's reputation or interfere with its income. By the 1860s, especially, some were recommending such a long preparation as to make the transition very indefinite. But, by that decade, the tide of opinion had turned against the ending of the empire.

Another motif which contributors explored was how to run the empire for as long as there was one. This investigation concentrated on the roles of Parliament, the Colonial Office, and local assemblies.

Commentators regularly chastised Parliament for being ignorant about even the larger holdings. This apathy, reputedly born of misplaced security, actually may have contributed to unrest when Westminster passed unsuitable laws. To remedy Parliamentary myopia, a recurrent proposal was to assign, at least to the colonies, some seats in Commons. This plan, some hypothesized, would also lead to more economic integration within the empire; to greater colonial loyalty, particularly in wartime; and to less parochialism at home and abroad. Even those who thought that settlers had no right to sit in Parliament, or would have little sway there if they did, wished to see more communication between London and abroad. Suggestions ranged from the formation of a Parliamentary advisory board, composed of colonists, to the circulation, in Britain, of overseas gazettes and the extension of the telegraphy throughout the empire.

Besides Parliament, magazines scrutinized the Colonial Office. Characterized as equally unaware about the dependencies as was Parliament, the Colonial Office was more censured because it had direct responsibility for most imperial holdings. The root of the problem, for reporters, was inconsistency. Since the Secretary was a political appointee, policy changed with parties. Since the Secretary's appointments were ordinarily based first on patronage and then on competence, allegedly misrule followed, crises ensued, and British taxes escalated.

In the circumstances, it was sensible for reviewers, notably colonial reformers, increasingly to request self-government for the Anglo-Saxon settlements. Because persons of other societies were deemed incapable by many journalists, they concurred that despotism was appropriate therein so long as it was somehow tempered by paternalism. By contrast, the possessions peopled by the European should, as they matured, supervise their own internal affairs. This arrangement would end delays, reduce misunderstandings, and lower expenditures. For scribes theorized, in return for the benefit of responsible government, settlers would have the duty to pay their way. While this advice seemed practical, it did not immediately take into account the matter of defense. However, the extent to which colonists should finance a militia or compensate a war did, over time, generate serious controversy. Whatever the source of their salaries, troops, authors agreed, should if possible be recruited from among the natives who would be cheaper and healthier.

In all their words about local assemblies, essayists broadcast few drawbacks. Noteworthy was the remark, made in the 1840s and after, that the colonies could become so self-governing as to be independent. Serials must have discounted this outcome as they scarcely mentioned it. Nevertheless, one prescription to meet such an eventuality was that Britain federate emerging states under a single imperial Parliament. Other worries about self-rule were that the participants would alter the structure of government until it did not

resemble Britain's; and that the voters, without an aristoc-
racy to guide them, would fall victim to the voices of faction
or the pressures of universal manhood suffrage more than might
the British.

Besides retention and regulation, a third preoccupation
of writers was population movements within the empire. The
most commonly noticed was the emigration of Britons. Periodicals more often approved this exodus as they became apprehensive about the potential rebelliousness of the under- or
unemployed masses. The departure of large numbers would surely
result in better wages for those who went and those who stayed.

As to who should go, there were disparate opinions in
the press. Some preferred candidates chosen, and sustained,
by an agency, as the parish; others proposed natural selection. Organizers affirmed that planning was the only way to
guarantee that enough women and paupers, principally children,
left. Adversaries called such a scheme unjust and inappropriate. It would ship the weak to desolate terrains where
they could never achieve success for themselves, their adop-
tive homes, or Britain. Rather, the empire should operate as
did the market, without restrictions. The promise of a better life would induce countless of the able to embark. With
the gold discoveries, the hope of luring large numbers to
the empire intensified. Even before, Edward Gibbon Wakefield
put forward an option which seemed to combine elements of
compulsion and election, an option which came to be known as
systematic colonization.

During the 1830s, articles were already urging the
government to oversee conditions of passage and land distribution on arrival. As Wakefield's notions circulated, magazines began to debate the theory of systematic colonization
which merely encouraged capitalists to emigrate while funding
laborers to do so. Some essays explained that free soil
would only create impoverished owners never capable of buying
much from Britain whereas a high sale price would ensure that
purchasers could develop their acreage and that workers could
be imported.

Few analysts bothered much about the native titles to
realty. Occasionally someone announced that natives should
be asked to consent to any transfer. For the most part,
reporters accepted, as humanitarian as well as expedient, the
right to settle anywhere without prior native assent. Newcomers, readers were assured, would help, not hinder, the

progress of locals. The regions which Britain claimed did not belong to anyone but, even if they did, Britain's need for space took priority over any other lien or usage. To concede anything else would be to coddle the indigenous in order to win their allegiance.

In addition to settlers, columnists talked about convicts. Transportation was universally neither condoned nor condemned. In the 1830s, journalists classified the system as morally bad for prisoners but economically good for colonists. By the next decade, gazettes depicted it as an ineffective but inexpensive punishment whose fellows could be prototypes of diligence for aborigines in outlying places. In the 1850s, as many locales resisted what citizens perceived as an influx of sinners, the press usually extolled the arrival of unpaid toilers as materially advantageous for young communities. So long as felons were not all sent to one dependency, other immigrants, whose standards and behavior might also be reproachable, should not complain. But for many of the papers, transportation was a blemish on Britain's self-fashioned image as civilizer.

As well as the efforts of colonists and convicts, the empire required the exertions of other migrants, some voluntary, some coerced. Among those examined were Africans, Indians, and Chinese. Stories about Africans described their emancipation, its enactment and its effects, especially on the Caribbean. Indians, presented in the late 1830s as replacements for liberated slaves, were thereafter evaluated in the context of their treatment and performance in tropical settings. Chinese, cited as models of industriousness, were tracked as they moved rapidly throughout the empire in the years between 1832 and 1867.

Interestingly, the British made few attempts to compare, cross-culturally, the natives of the empire. Instead, writers tended to discuss locals only in relation to their specific imperial environments. One exception was the coverage of religion. Missionary activity among natives was a frequent, if not always favored, theme during the era. Further, the need for and organization of churches for colonists received more pages as time passed.

While the words on the assets and liabilities of the empire, its governance, and its constituents are central to the study of imperialism, articles about defense and free trade, though collateral, are often relevant. In their

accounts of the army or the navy, reporters typically included some sentences about how the empire would be benefited or burdened. Also, columns on tariffs ordinarily told
how termination would affect imperial exchanges. Sometimes,
as in the case of sugar, probing was lengthy, if specific to
the West Indies. Generally, few observers predicted the
evolution of preferences; almost none prophesied that colonies
would one day erect their own barriers. Nowithstanding this
lack of foresight, authors were overwhelmingly confident that
they could promote appropriate imperial policies and projects.

b. Sea Routes to the East

The sea routes to the East comprised, for nineteenth-
century journalists, the Mediterranean dependencies, a Suez
link, and Aden. Each of these components received about the
same amount of attention from the press, although in different
decades.

Gibraltar

Periodicals first noticed Gibraltar in the 1840s when
they acknowledged it as the key British fortress in the
Mediterranean and a place to which convicts could still be
sent. But the rock was more than an imperial asset: it was
a significant symbol of the empire itself.

According to the media, Gibraltar was not without
problems. Commentators averred that smuggling was common in
the 1840s and 1850s; troops became ill while garrisoned there,
a condition attributed, by the 1860s, to poor sanitation; and
anchorage was unsafe. Moreover, the ethnic variety of inhabitants was cause for some anxiety.

The only time, nevertheless, that apprehension about
Gibraltar appeared serious was in the 1860s. Writers, worried about Spanish opposition to a British Gibraltar, asserted
the advantages of such dominion. To the reviewer, British
sovereignty would secure trade and a British presence would
set good religious and legal examples for the Spanish. In
mid-Victorian magazines, the matter and merits of Gibraltar's
ownership were indisputable.

Malta

Articles about Malta circulated chiefly in the 1830s
and 1840s. In the earlier years, publications referred to

the island as valuable. They recognized Malta to be, as
Gibraltar, a cardinal Mediterranean stronghold, an opinion
which was the only one to persist in paltry later coverage.
Scribes also noted that Malta was useful both as a coal stop
en route to India and as a quarantine station en route back
from the East.

Again, as with Gibraltar, there were some misgivings
about the population. In the 1830s, the Maltese demanded
a free press but essayists believed that the locals were too
disaffected to enjoy this liberty. Rather, papers maintained,
educational, legal, and wage reforms were indispensable pre-
requisites. By the 1840s, when elementary schools had opened,
some Britons bemoaned the limited impact which instruction
seemed to be having. Perhaps because of this apparent result,
there were fewer calls for other improvements. The request
for changes in the law was not repeated; the concern about
salaries was replaced by a suggestion that workers be dis-
patched to Jamaica's sugar fields. This proposal, which gave
Malta a greater imperial dimension, was the last to do so in
the age.

Ionian Islands

Of all the Mediterranean holdings, the Ionian Islands
most captured the imagination of columnists. Discussion was
always contentious as people debated whether Britain should
keep the islands which it had gotten at Vienna in 1815.

In the 1830s, advocates of retention declared that the
territories had good potential for trade and land for English
settlers; and that the British had already fashioned substantial public works to support commerce and colonists.
Additionally, the government had an obligation to advance the
locals and to make their region politically powerful. Alternatively, foes were convinced that the British had so mis-
managed affairs as to be extremely unpopular. Since most
inhabitants wanted to join Greece and since Crete was strategically preferable, perhaps, observers prompted, Athens and
London could arrange an exchange.

By the 1840s, the complaints against British rule were
more specific. The government had reputedly deprived the
islanders of fundamental rights and damaged their economy by
tariffs. But as disapproval deepened, so too did determination to continue British administration. Even though journalists increasingly asserted that the chain was worthless

to the empire, they professed that London had a responsibility
to prepare its subjects for a free press and a representative
assembly.

Reviewers reiterated the ethical arguments in the 1850s
and early 1860s when local pleas to combine with Greece became strident. Imperialists insisted that British bureaucrats specifically insured justice and deterred crime, provided the shield of the British navy, organized finances,
and responded to grievances, as by the recent conferral of
civil liberties; and generally practiced paternalism. Therefore, to contributors of this persuasion, Ionian annexation-
ists were demagogues, unappreciative of the blessings that
Parliament had dispensed and unaware that many citizens spoke
Italian; and English unionists were disciples of Cobden-
Bright economics who would sacrifice the empire in order to
save money.

As sponsors strengthened their position, adversaries
did so with equal force. The latter denounced as selfish
British motives for controlling the islands. The government
stayed to prevent others from taking these well-situated
places. It filled lucrative local jobs with its pawns and
cared nothing about the welfare of the Ionians who resented
its language and customs. The only fair solution was to give
the territories to Greece. However, even promoters were not
really anti-imperial for they counseled that Corfu be reserved
for defense and that no transfer be completed until calm
returned. To concede under pressure would surely detract
from British prestige.

Notwithstanding all the controversy about their status,
once the Ionian Islands were assigned to Greece in 1864, they
vanished rather abruptly from periodicals.

Suez

The notion of a link between the Mediterranean and Red
Seas was already in the gazettes by the 1830s. Essays speculated then and throughout the 1840s about the rewards of
both a canal and a railroad. In these decades, either seemed
feasible to construct, possibly using convicts otherwise
bound for Australia. If the railroad had a slight edge, it
was because writers thought that it would be cheaper and
easier to build and, at least at first, was more acceptable
to Mehemet Ali who viewed it as an instrument to enlarge
Egypt's markets. Whichever the option, many articles

predicted that Britain could secure its suzerainty in India
and the Antipodes by commanding this route, irrespective of
statements that the Euphrates Valley might be a less expensive passage with better weather. Interestingly, a
contributor occasionally suggested that the British take the
whole of Egypt in order to safeguard their Eastern trade, to
assist the natives, to relocate their surplus population, or
to deter Russian expansion. More typical was the advice that
Parliament should buy a tract for the connection.

By mid-century, canal enthusiasts were quite vocal.
If a waterway might be costly to create and precarious to
maintain, it would certainly speed soldiers, goods, and
emigrants eastward. To forestall French hegemony, magazines
counseled Parliament to supervise a canal or, better, to
possess it outright. To achieve either, Britain should seek
the approval of an international congress or, minimally, of
France. Gallic blessings might be obtained if Britain were
to accept French jurisdiction in North Africa. In any event,
Britain must augment its navy to defend its canal or against
a French one.

Rather suddenly, if unsurprisingly, in the 1860s, many
journals turned against a canal. The actual grounds were
probably Palmerston's opposition and de Lessep's concession
but the papers discoursed more about physical hazards than
about political maneuvers. Serials once again advertised
the Euphrates as a bargain, a fast alternative that could
counteract Russia by controlling Asian markets. Only a few
people theorized that the Suez waterway could profit the
British; none, that it would soon be theirs.

Aden

The acquisition of a coaling station in 1839 caused
the initial publicity about Aden. With a good harbor, the
district looked to become an affluent emporium once British
merchants arrived. In the 1840s, authors added to this hope
another, that Aden would emerge as a major outpost against
French, Egyptian, and even Yankee imperialism. Likewise,
Britain should guarantee personal freedom, thereby aiding
current dwellers and luring the oppressed of East Africa.
The facts that Aden had a limited water supply, Arab inhabitants who disliked their British masters, and a sepoy
force that withered because of prolonged separation from
home escaped the comprehension of most scribes.

Opinion about Aden did not alter much in the 1850s and 1860s. Its shops, somewhat bigger as buyers came from postal steamers stopped for coal, were never as successful as its harbor would allow. Even with the new roads constructed by the sepoys, the heat and the Arabs restricted contacts with the interior. Lack of water was always a hardship, for, although there were ancient tanks, the British had apparently done nothing about reserves or reservoirs. If Aden's mixed population of Jews, Somalis, and Arabs could somehow work together and if Suez became a reality, then Aden, writers postulated, would one day play a crucial imperial part.

c. India

India was without doubt the topic of more articles in nineteenth-century periodicals than any other segment of the British Empire. Fascination with the subcontinent was evident early in the 1830s when the charter of the East India Company came up for renewal. Ensuing essays revealed a pattern which would be true of accounts about India for the next thirty-five years: for every positive opinion published, a contrary one soon followed. Although the Company at first dominated reports, the press explored many other Indian matters.

In the 1830s, attackers of the Company outnumbered its defenders. Still, its champions consistently praised its performance as salutary for the governance of India and the affluence of Britain. Particularly, they congratulated Company officials for sacrificing their health without reaping the monetary rewards of their predecessors in order to help natives whom they knew and respected.

Others contradicted this assessment. They characterized griffins and their seniors as a haughty clique, nominated by Directors and loyal only to them. Moreover, without Parliamentary supervision, the East India Board seemed to set policies which hurt Britain and contravened its ideals. For example, the Company's resistance to colonists purportedly limited trade opportunities, restricted the influence of British law, and prevented the exposure of bureaucratic abuses. Many analysts also disapproved of the Company's relations with the local creeds which, arguably, went well beyond toleration. Yet another issue which stirred a fervent outburst was the Company's decision to halt financial aid for the study of native literatures. For its conviction that learning English would provide access to some jobs, as well

as integrate the population, the Company was accused of
degrading the vernacular to no avail since token English
would hardly serve anyone.

In all of these evils, anti-Company writers were sure
that the Board of Control connived while Parliament was un-
concerned about India and most governors were inept. Thus,
gazettes lodged many complaints against the Double Government generically. The overall picture was one of exploitation by oppressive taxes, ineffectual justice, resource
depletion, inadequate public works (when compared to the
Moghuls), and exclusion of most inhabitants from power.

Chief among these grievances were those about the law
and the economy. Reviewers charged the rulers with maintaining a system of justice which was slow and expensive;
procedurally as well as linguistically incomprehensible; and
substantively irrelevant. The major economic handicaps
reputedly derived from very high imposts on land and salt.
Because of the first, peasants apparently had no incentive
to improve cultivation, irritating to authors who saw India
as a future source of much raw cotton. With the latest
agricultural techniques, fewer internal tariffs, and a safe
steam route, India could sell more of the plant to Britain,
hence transferring less specie when buying Manchester cloth.
If only, some hypothesized, Parliament would grant Indian
cotton the same protection as West Indian sugar, new wealth
would reduce the disasters wrought by frequent famines. Only
a few pointed out that starvation was a logical outcome when
many residents grew opium instead of food and most spent
substantial amounts of meager incomes to pay for salt. Until
change came, the only relief which commentators could offer
to impoverished Indians was the army or emigration to one of
the sugar islands.

There were, of course, papers which endorsed the
Double Government. They judged its behavior as honorable
and its programs as progressive for the natives. The British
had brought order and prosperity. Next they would introduce
education and Christianity which would overcome the concepts
of caste inhibiting modernization. Without England, imperialists surmised, there would only be misery. Therefore, it
was Albion's duty to stay until India was ready, intellectually and fiscally, for independence. In the meantime, the
British would accrue power and riches.

Besides their extensive pages on the government,

magazines were preoccupied with security. Principally in
dispute was whether Russia was likely to invade. Russophobes
warned that the Czarists would have assistance from within
India. Muslims would consort with the enemy because their
British sovereigns were infidels; Hindus, because they were
deprived of office; the princes, because they chafed at being
English puppets, even corrupt ones; the sepoys, because their
allegiance was to their paycheck or their Brahminism; and all
others, because they resented the Double Government as an
interloper. For this group of writers, the proper course for
Britain was to guard its frontiers by accumulating territories, either those strategically vital, as the banks of the
Indus; or those controlled by families reckoned to be dangerous, as the house of Oudh. So long as the British incorporated these areas into the empire, with all of its peripheral
advantages, they were serving India and themselves fairly.

Challengers, discounting Russia as a real threat,
interpreted annexation as an excuse to undermine neighbors'
and natives' rights. Instead, Britain should court the
princes for their military support and their sway over the
masses. As for the sepoys, they were good soldiers whose
dedication was eroded by the sight of drunken commanders or
the loneliness of distant assignments. Indians of all genres
would be more sympathetic if the revenue wasted on external
adventures was put to internal improvements. Otherwise,
some guessed, India would be lost, not by war but by rebellion.

The first test came in Afghanistan. Some narrators had
long cautioned that the Romanovs were infiltrating Persia in
order to win the markets of Central Asia and to raise an
attack against India. At first, counteracting this intrigue
indirectly, by developing a Euphrates route, or even directly,
by lending military officers as advisors to the Persians,
seemed adequate. Yet, as it became clear, at least to Lord
Auckland, Governor-General of India, that Persian-Russian
ties were too close, he decided to take stronger measures.
When the ruler of Afghanistan, Dost Mohammed, signed an alliance with the Persians, after allegedly being rebuffed by the
British, Auckland ordered an invasion of the country. The
British averred that they were only restoring the rightful
sovereign, Shah Sujah, in place of a usurper, but the war
touched off a furor in the press.

Whigs quickly painted Dost Mohammed as an illegal chief
and a Russian pawn. They sermonized that the people of
Afghanistan might resent the return of Sujah, previously

ousted, but that there would be no real resistance to him. Moreover, by removing Dost Mohammed, the British were eliminating tyranny and establishing a barrier for India.

Tories and others were soon to reply, branding the conflict wrong on philosophical and pragmatic grounds. How, they inquired, could the British ever again censure Romanov expansion if they overran Asia. The campaign, costly in prestige, troops, and money, would only be the beginning: it would cost even more to retain Afghanistan. Besides, geography impeded Russia and the locals hated the Russians. The best course was to admit a mistake, withdraw, and negotiate with Dost Mohammed and/or the Persians. Although later followed, this direction was for the moment ignored.

In all their words about India, journalists penned little about the people themselves. There was a flurry when thuggee was exposed. Occasional pieces expressed Britons' horror about the Juggernaut or their enchantment with the Hurdwar fair. Stories also delineated the customs of a tribe or the plight of the Anglo-Indians. But the daily lives of their imperial siblings scarcely intruded on the consciousness of most reporters.

By the 1840s, awareness was not much greater. To their paragraphs on thuggee, the papers added new ones on dacoitry; and the pages on natives' looks and traits became more extensive, if stereotyped. Nonetheless, some of the media realized that the Indians had had, long before the British, sophisticated literatures and philosophies, both evidence of a mature society. In spite of this history, columnists encouraged colonization as useful, ideologically and commercially: natives, instructed in English language and habits, would surely be more enlightened, at least about the value of British sovereignty; and settlers, irrespective of the heat which felled officers and officials, would have that energy indispensable for lucrative production.

Among the most prized crops were indigo and opium. The indigo planters, equated to slave drivers by some, represented to others the industriousness which the peasants were imagined to lack, although ancient tanks and canals belied this deficiency. Opium was not only profitable but seemingly without the overt element of duress applied to indigo ryots. Of anticipated new goods, tea, which grew wildly in Assam, was being advertised but cotton was not much publicized. By the 1840s, experiments had shown that

the soil was incompatible with seed from the United States.
In addition, essayists identified numerous handicaps to
cotton cultivation, such as inland tolls, primitive transportation, and Indians' purported resistance to technology.
Yet, optimism persisted that if the East India Company would
build railroads and Parliament would legislate preferences,
enough cotton would be reaped to supply English mills and,
incidentally, to destroy slavery in the United States.

The ongoing concern about cotton led to a larger investigation about the conditions of land cultivation throughout the subcontinent. Authors regularly questioned whether
the land tax was detrimental. There was some testimony that
ryots were the victims of their brothers' usury and fraud;
and that zemindars, without the right of land redemption, had
no motivation to try new methods and machines. Absent inno-
vation, Indians would be doomed when famines struck. These
outbreaks, allegedly caused by authorities' failure to create
either grain storage facilities or a speedy means to move food
around India, were devastating for people barely subsisting.
But, given Parliament's insensitivity to Indians' well-being
or even India's worth, columnists could but repeat their
advice that inhabitants emigrate, once that activity carried
legal safeguards.

As in past years, in the 1840s, the economy shared
space with defense. And, as before, the main fear was Russia,
whose assault Britons expected to be accompanied by a Muslim
uprising. This expectation, based on a presumed nexus among
these Indians, Persia, and Russia, went unfulfilled. However, the Afghans' rebellion against Shah Sujah and his British backers fueled apprehension about the Romanovs. After a
disastrous defeat, the British demolished Kabul. But a new
government did not attempt to retake the area and Dost Mohammed
resumed his seat. Nonetheless, these events reawakened the
quarreling about British aims.

Since the whole episode seemed to be a fiasco, critics
had an easy time denouncing it. The British had apparently
misunderstood everything about the situation: Russia's goals,
Sujah's reputation among his subjects, Dost Mohammed's
friendship, the Afghans' willingness to fight for their
governmental integrity, and Afghanistan's terrain. Because
of their miscalculations, the British had lost much. As
aggressors they flaunted morality and forfeited their good
name, revealed their insecurity to all outsiders and the
discontented within India, and offended many sepoys by

forcing them to cross the Indus. These consequences were dangerous for the empire, especially in the unsettled politics of Asia.

Those who undertook the justification of Auckland's decision had a more difficult task. Some accused Sujah of gross ineptitude but could not comprehend why his actions should reflect on his British benefactors. Others, more realistically, conceded that the expedition might have been unpopular among the Afghans but excused it as expedient. If the Tories had not chosen to quit the region, and thereby conveyed a sense of weakness to the world, Afghanistan would have become a major emporium and fortress. Command of it would have meant access to buyers there and throughout Central Asia as well as room for British emigrants who would have disseminated Western values. All of these results would have hindered not only Russian but princely ambitions.

Again magazines tried to inspire the conquest of princely states, particularly those close to the Indus. Since the motive, if not its accomplishment, was covert, the rajahs had to be discredited on other bases, such as treason or cruelty. Reviewers decried princely manipulation of unhappiness about rapid social reforms into insurrection against the reformers and categorized the princes as autocrats to whose subjects Britain owed liberation. The duty to rescue was underlined in the takeovers of Sind and the Punjab as well as those projected in Oudh and Hyderabad. While to some the triumph in Sind signaled more trade and greater safety for India, others saw few markets, popular animosity, and proximity to an Afghanistan which hated the English. Contributors even more hotly debated the subjugation of the Sikhs. Claims of local disorder, Russian deterrence, British prestige, and a terrain suitable for settlers were balanced by assertions that the Punjab was not hostile to British interests and was a strong barrier to Islamic aggression; and that the British were so mismanaging the precincts already acquired that it was pointless to seize more. Annexation was not destiny but stupidity which undermined princely alliances and misdirected too much effort and expenditure.

The army, in any case, was supposedly able to handle any foes. The press, in the 1840s, continued to show sepoys as sturdy warriors in contrast to their superiors. who followed, to their detriment, an English lifestyle. Commentators disagreed, however, about the troops' psychological fitness, viewing the men as either pampered Brahmins always on

the brink of mutiny or overworked, underpaid lower castes
scorned by Englishmen.

Sepoys' ideas about the overlords hardly squared with
journalists' that Britain had a moral responsibility to uplift
the Indians and thus spawn a glorious monument to itself and
to Christianity. Indeed, treatment of the enlisted was only
one item on a long list of malfeasance. Serials indicted the
British, masters by force, for betraying a trust by advancing
themselves without elevating the population. More and more,
observers castigated the Double Government for employing inept
men in a world where disaffection spread quickly; abolishing
traditions of long standing; committing extortion by means of
the Company's salt and opium monopolies; furnishing insufficient medical care, education, justice, and public works;
condoning slavery, crime, caste prejudice, and idolatry; pro-
hibiting most people from participating in government; incur-
ring bills in nonessential conflicts in a country with a poor
treasury: in sum, pushing citizens' forebearance to the limit.
Even if the intention of individuals was remedial and John
Company was better in personnel than John Bull or in administration than the Moghuls, the ultimate verdict of most
papers in the 1840s was that the British had to alter their
ways in order to stay in India.

This conclusion seemed amply verified by the mutiny of
1857. Yet, before that event, stories in the 1850s again
featured India as the East India Company charter came up for
another renewal and Parliament replaced Directorial appointment with competitive testing. As earlier, there was little
unanimity about the Company. Pro-Company articles cataloged
its good deeds, as the ban on suttee and the creation of an
infrastructure. Its outlays might have been larger, scribes
speculated, but for the price of British expansion to which
it had objected. Company servants, with practical experience,
were surely above a bureaucracy chosen by examinations. But
the Haileybury men were not to prevail. Their history of
rudeness to Indians and the Company's of repugnance to inno-
vation combined to antagonize many. While Parliament extended
the charter, the controversy surrounding that action and the
commencement of the civil service indicated to some that the
days of the Company were numbered.

Reading the papers about 1855, nevertheless, there was
little hint of imminent disaster. If anything, there was a
kind of tranquility with time to talk of India's ancient
civilization, its Young Bengals, its diverse populace, and

their even more diverse customs and characteristics. There
was also time to reexamine Central Asia, as Persia moved
toward Herat.

A few columnists still wanted Afghanistan, not only as
an obstacle to Russia but also as the redemption for a dis-
grace which, they presumed, inspired animosity in Sind and
the Punjab. A few others recommended the conquest of Herat
or, reiterating an earlier plan, the deployment of British
officers in the Afghan and Persian armies. Most authors
welcomed cooperation with Dost Mohammed and conciliation of
Persia. They repeated that nature protected India. To coerce
Persia might drive it into Russia's arms; and to swallow it
would rouse French and Russian jealousies too much.

Insofar as there was less anxiety about the borders,
there was more confidence that India's domestic problems could
be solved. True, some essays specifically suspected Russia's
intentions or generally referred to providence and preserva-
tion as justifications to aggrandize; but, the Czar was dis-
tracted in Crimea and the accumulation of principalities was,
to most, unwarranted and undesired. England would do well,
instead, to ameliorate the world of those within its jurisdiction.

The press frequently saluted the British regime as
righteous, surviving because its subjects preferred it. But
this theory of an "empire of opinion" did not go uncontested.
Indians, many reminded, had hardly selected the British and
probably despised them. The sovereigns might prevent anarchy but neither their decorum nor their operation reflected
Christianity. They must benefit the Indians to deserve India.

As the key to existence was, for most natives, the land,
taxes had to be adjusted and resources developed. The soil
was capable of yielding the desired cotton and tea if ryots,
a cheap, docile, and abundant labor force, had agricultural
tools and training and honest creditors. With police to
thwart thieves and a railroad to reach markets quickly, sales
would burgeon. Capitalist rivalry would weaken caste dis-
tinctions and volume harvests would permit purchase of more
British goods. No matter that Britain had previously ruined
local cotton and silk manufacturing, diverted revenues to
finance campaigns, or compelled toilers to cultivate the
poppy, all of which abetted the terrible famines. Now India
would thrive.

Before this prediction could be fulfilled, the episode designated as mutiny erupted. If the mutiny did little else, it certainly intruded India into the minds of British readers. Most periodicals, not published daily, were unable to headline crises. Rather, authors dissected the causes and consequences of the revolt. Few doubted that it was no revolution, grateful that caste and religion hindered any sense of nationalism, but there concurrence ceased.

Journalists attributed the origins of the rebellion to either British misgovernment or native malevolence. As to the first, the Double Government had reputedly exasperated the people with exorbitant taxes, too fast or too slow social adjustments, too many missionaries and too few judges. Worst of all, the British had annexed at whim, often displacing princely functionaries and soldiers, defying residents' antipathy, and squandering money. Because Oudh, the most recent acquisition, was home to many sepoys whose families lost preferments at annexation, its takeover was pinpointed as the catalyst for insurgency.

Those who objected to this analysis countered that there had been no widespread insubordination among troops or people, except in Oudh. Therefore, the fault had to lie not with the British but with the Indians. The sepoys had mistaken the latest cartridge as an impediment to their salvation. Another and angrier version told of a rampage by soldiers long coddled. Yet a third rendition spoke of the men as instruments of either a Muslim conspiracy to regain authority or a princely management of the free press to achieve the same result.

The last seemed unlikely as many writers thanked the rajahs for their aid or at least their neutrality. The irregulars and the Sikhs were also specially praised. Magazines singled out the telegraphy as critical in saving British rule and venerated the mutiny's heroes as symbols of their country's right to the subcontinent.

Even as the mutiny endured, serials propounded programs for India's future. Searching for a scapegoat, commentators called for the abolition of the Company and the appointment of a minister and council. Parliament must become better acquainted with India, disavow expansion, undertake public works, and educate the people for some role in government, though without real power, else Britain would soon lose India in a genuine revolution.

For those who yearned to punish the natives, the execution of soldiers was not enough. Collaborators should be fined and their possessions confiscated. Everyone should be disarmed. Freedom of the press should be revoked. To insure against a new outbreak, fewer Brahmins should be enlisted; more forts and railroads should be built; and colonization should be encouraged, notwithstanding the overpopulation, in order to ease the debt from the mutiny with new capital and to form an English bastion. To such observers, annexation was not an evil. The Punjab, Oudh, and Sind, among others, had advanced after their imperial incorporation. But the policy was impolitic. If the princes remained insecure, they might rally against Britain the next time.

The furor about the mutiny quieted in the journals of the 1860s but recollections lingered, sometimes quite poignantly in the pieces by those who had lived through it. The estimates about causality did not alter much but, understandably, those about effects were amended as time passed. The Company was finally buried, acknowledged as an outmoded institution though with some good employees. The new administrators, irrespective of high salaries, were apparently no better. Said to suffer more from the climate and a sense of exile than had their predecessors, the competition men were also very reserved towards the natives. This distance was supposedly born of scholarly backgrounds which had imbued an awareness of obligation but none of humanity. Some narratives inferred that bureaucrats, and other English, might be efficient in running India but not very decent to its citizenry. Likewise, more than one British author thought that, after the mutiny, Anglo-Indian papers published only the bad qualities of Indians, conveying a real disdain for them as persons.

Periodicals also derided the new ministry as a sinecure equal to any Directorship and equally unresponsive to Indian affairs. Hence, reviewers reprimanded the Indian Office for having the same faults as the East India Company. The government, some noted, regarded India as a material enterprise, not a moral trust. The years after 1857 brought many new laws but few real achievements. Public works were an exception as canals were dug, roads repaired, and railways extended, accelerating trade and, incidentally, the formation of a national consciousness. But many essays were dissatisfied with the slow pace of legal and economic reforms. Even with recent irrigation and transportation, low wages and profits meant that peasants were still susceptible to famine. Opium returns were flexible, depending on Chinese buyers, but were ordinarily more

remunerative than those of cotton, whose market was far more
volatile. Indigo was steady but a major dispute in Bengal
between planters and ryots about contract terms shook production, and some of the press, in the early 1860s. Assamese
tea purportedly could be more gainful if men would work in
the province instead of leaving for jobs overseas. All these
products reportedly prevented the planting of cereals for
consumption. Without more English initiative, investment,
and instruction, the papers assumed that substantial progress
was unlikely.

Not surprising was the distraction with internal security. The fright about Russia, so prevalent before, had
virtually evaporated. If the record showed that Auckland
had engaged in an unjust war, Kabul was now courting London by
resurrecting the Russian menace. While some observers exhorted
the government not to sign any treaty of mutual limitation with
the Czar, but to extend its sphere to Persia, stories about the
frontiers were not numerous. More engrossing was the theme of
Indians against the Raj.

Most authors admitted that a native army was indispensable to secure India. British soldiers allegedly ailed from
the water, improper sanitation, alcoholism, and an ennervation
bred by the heat. If Brahmins were dangerous, then other
castes, Eurasians, and irregulars, most loyal during the mutiny, should be hired. Forts would counteract any urban plots
and the inclusion in administration of the gentry, who were
said to like office, might shield Britain from any mass unrest. Above all, the princes were pivotal to counterpoise
insurrection. Hence, when the opportunity to claim Mysore
arose, serials discouraged it as a betrayal of the guarantees
of 1858.

Because the mutiny was, for many, a test of England's
title to India, surviving the episode with power intact seemed
to confirm that title. London should not abandon the subcontinent: India was more than ever an emblem of British imperialism. British supremacy would bestow stability and prosperity yet; and, some prayed, Christianity. If subjection
accompanied these advantages, so be it. India had always been
conquered, although never by such paternalists. With British
ideas and money, India could catapult its sovereign to Eastern
domination, this too justifiable. Only the head of an elite
deserved such a position and the periodicals were ever more
certain that the British were special. Command of the East
would also, the more cynical mentioned, exclude rivals.

Detractors further indicated that the British had been no
better than the Moghuls, often worse; and that if the Anglo-
Saxons were as honest as they professed, they would prepare
India for independence. But, by the late 1860s, memories of
the mutiny began to fade. Life in Calcutta and the Mofussil
went on, mirrored by a press content that things would be so
for a very long time.

d. Indian Ocean

   The Indian Ocean dependencies discussed in nineteenth-
century periodicals were Ceylon, Mauritius, and Burma. None
received extensive coverage but Ceylon was the most commonly
featured of the three.

<u>Ceylon</u>

   The few articles about Ceylon in the 1830s centered on
the economy, a typical topic for the next three decades.
Writers tended to promote the island's commercial assets,
among them, a good climate, fertile soil, and cheap labor.
With more colonists and public works, Ceylon, reporters
guessed, would flourish. If there were misgivings about the
government control of cinnamon and pearls, there were also
congratulations that the British coming had secured property
rights. Once natives were placed in token offices, replacing
allegedly incompetent East India Company men, appreciation of
British suzerainty would be forthcoming.

   By the 1840s, opinions about Ceylon and its people were
more sophisticated. Narratives distinguished among ethnic
groups and their habits. By these years also, ideas about the
economy were more complex. The long-established cinnamon
trade was described as declining, thanks in part to British
failure to develop adequate drainage. But Britons, civilian
and military, were apparently buying land on which to grow
coffee. Further, some magazines hoped that the government
would encourage the cultivation of rice, a major source of
food. The chief concern was the workers. Because planters
could not afford to import Indians, journalists advised owners
to treat local tillers well, notwithstanding their reputation
for laziness.

   When an uprising occurred in 1846, essayists analyzed
its origins, citing settlers' insolvencies, an unpopular
governor, and inhabitants' preference for Dutch rule. The
last was particularly distressing to those who had trusted

that the majority had accepted British authority. The entire
episode was bothersome to those who had commended Ceylon's
commerce, environment, and strategic location as rationales
for its retention.

Interest in the rebellion continued in the columns of
the 1850s. Reporters appended high taxes to the list of
causes; and endorsed Parliament's criticism of the use of
martial law and flogging to deal with insurgents. Serials
also noted that revenue was down and famine was back so the
British dominion was harder to justify. But proponents declared that the rulers' systems of justice and finance had
improved life and that the island would be necessary for
trade should India be lost. With coffee an increasingly important product, imperialists scarcely noticed that rice was
inadequate because the British had not constructed irrigation
tanks or repaired old ones, remnants of a once dynamic civilization. Indeed, over the years, scribes more and more disapproved of residents, because of their religions, customs, or
traits. Without the education and conversion of natives,
observers were less optimistic of progress in a place consistently depicted as extraordinarily beautiful.

The delight with geography and the dejection about the
locals' behavior persisted into the 1860s. But, by then, a
more serious matter had developed. After the mutiny in India,
contributors considered Ceylon to be vital for regional defense. They fretted that soldiers, heretofore badly housed
and supplied with foul water, were falling to disease instead
of preparing to meet attacks. Barracks and rations had to be
healthier. Railroads had to be constructed more rapidly and
grievances, eliminated. To curb potential unrest, the success
with coffee had to be repeated with other products. Since the
British dominated the bureaucracy and the bar, planters would
find the investment climate as profitable as the atmospheric
one was pleasant. With tax reforms, irrigation projects, and
Chinese workers, Ceylon would thrive. Moreover, this outcome
would likely safeguard a British presence in the area in-
definitely.

Mauritius

In contrast to Ceylon, which was not much in the papers
of the 1830s, Mauritius made headlines in that decade. The
issue was emancipation and the arguments were similar to those
penned about the West Indies. Most journalists condemned
London for undermining property rights, even with indemnity.

Articles denounced Sir John Jeremie whose activity as Public
Prosecutor they interpreted as hostile to proprietors' interests. When masters, unable to reconcile themselves to
their lost status, rioted, magazines were sympathetic to their
plight, if not to their method of expressing it. Explaining
that the demonstrators had been roused by the humiliated rev-
olutionary Gallic emigrès who ran the local press, Englishmen
suggested that the anxiety of the owners not be underestimated.
There were enough problems assimilating this former French
possession into the British Empire without provoking the
French by subverting their wealth and position. Parliament,
commentators counseled, should spend less time worrying about
slaves and more about the dislocations which their unshackling
would beget.

This subject extended into the 1840s but with a different
emphasis. Although there was mention that freedom guaranteed
the gratitude of the freed, most reviews concentrated on the
economy. Advocates of slavery insisted that British policy
had bankrupted the island. The liberated had become unre-
pentant idlers in spite of any inducements offered them to
return to the fields. Consequently, planters had to hire, at
great expense, Indians to care for the cane. But a new labor
force alone would not rejuvenate the estates: owners must have
self-government. Opponents saw the demand for an assembly
otherwise. They categorized it as a technique to reimpose
bondage whereby proprietors would pass such strict anti-
vagrancy statutes as to drive former slaves back to the fields.
Mauritius, these writers contended, had enough laborers but
conditions of employment were so oppressive that people refused
to resume drudgery. Critics accused overseers of filling
blacks with liquor until they were so intoxicated that they
signed long-term contracts with dubious provisions and of
importing Indians in order to create competition to keep wages
low. Badly treated, physically and psychologically, the newcomers were also victims who reputedly did not significantly
raise sugar output.

Many publications echoed, in the 1850s, this evaluation
of the Indian so they were ready to plead for Chinese immigrants. By this point, statements about Mauritius were less
shrill. Gazettes implied that the French ambiance was more
charming than chilling and the bid for representation was more
efficient. In the few paragraphs printed about the island in
the 1860s, circumstances appeared to be changing. Authors
credited the expansion of sugar manufacture for a general
financial improvement and saluted the Indians for their thrifty

and energetic role in this renaissance. But the press still
disparaged the emancipated, adding insolence to the earlier
charge of indolence. If the freed contributed at all to the
island's renewal, serials thought that it was only due to the
whip. The air of confidence that they exuded about the future
of Mauritius certainly did not include its largest citizenry.

Burma

The notes on Burma in nineteenth-century journals dealt
with two themes: market opportunities and frontier security.
In the 1830s and 1840s, the first predominated. Promising
such resources as minerals, teak, rice, salt, and sugar,
Burma, scribes speculated, could rapidly become lucrative
with more English capitalists and Chinese toilers. Although
most papers regarded the Burmese people as no menace, some
writers believed that the Burmese kings posed a threat to
British interests in the region. This danger, based on notions
about the monarch's demeanor and the monarchy's disintegration,
might require enlarging the British sphere gained earlier.

Outlining the merits of such a scheme in the 1850s and
1860s, sponsors assured readers that the proposal would turn
swamps into fecund farms whose crops would be exchanged for
British manufactures. Likewise, the conquerors would save the
population from autocracy by means of an annexation which
would certainly be more honorable than that of Sind, already
accomplished. Besides, the Burmese dynasty had for too long
insulted its neighbors. Only military defeat would curb its
hauteur and permit its vanquishers to fulfill their destiny
in Asia.

Those unenthusiastic about having more of Burma were
convinced that the remainder of the country was a jungle not
worth the money or the manpower to capture and to hold; and
that, by the 1850s, the East India Company was too busy with
other recent acquisitions to administer more territory. By
the 1860s, irrespective of the concern about India's safety,
editors allotted little space to words about a Burmese adventure or, indeed, to words about Burma.

e. Far East

British imperial interests in the Far East comprised,
for nineteenth-century journalists, relations with China,
especially with respect to the acquisition of Hong Kong; the
dependencies of the Malay Peninsula; and influence in Borneo.

China

The chief issue between Britain and China discussed in periodicals in the 1830s and 1840s was the sale of opium. At first, columnists did not take seriously the Chinese ban on importation. They classified the prohibition as a temporary reaction to the termination of the East India Company's monopoly of the China trade. Most affirmed that Peking, notorious for its isolationism, was more anxious about the arrival of a mob of merchants than about the effects of the drug on its citizens. Additionally, some serials were sure that the mandarins secretly encouraged smuggling. Still, if the British could not sell opium, they could barter other legitimate goods for the tea that they craved. Under no circumstamces was war warranted. A conflict would interrupt, if not destroy, the tea market and aggression, to compel the purchase of what many considered an immoral product, would detract from Britain's reputation in the East. Instead, London should obtain either a concession at Chusan, which was close to the tea and silk districts and was purportedly without the kind of local restrictions found in Canton; or offshore islands as bases from which to supervise tea shipments. How to achieve these results was unclear but increasingly immaterial. For, by the 1840s, with the outbreak of fighting, the use of force became more acceptable to the press.

In the wake of the confiscation of a large amount of opium in 1839, Britain had gone to war. Articles quickly divided about the merits of the struggle. Patrons argued that it was necessary for several reasons. Britain had to sell opium, else its silver would have to pay for tea. Cessation of opium cultivation would disrupt the Indian economy to no purpose: if the Chinese did not get the drug from British suppliers, they would get it from others. Also, if the Chinese could not restrain widespread demand, they should legalize the transfer of narcotics. Finally, Britain must teach the Chinese to be less arrogant; otherwise, it would lose its honor as well as its opium revenue. Besides, a British victory would rescue the inhabitants from a tyrannical government and might discourage Russia from moving into the country. These last two goals would only become reality if China joined the empire, an outcome even the most ardent warmongers disavowed. Rather, they sought the opening of more ports to British wares which, they presumed, the Chinese millions awaited; and the construction of inland forts to protect those items in transit. Advocates further pushed Parliament to seek reparations from the Chinese in order to compensate the smugglers for their losses in 1839.

Opponents of this proposal countered that indemnification would appear as an official ratification of subjects' illegal activities. Parliament, stories declared, had already tolerated blatant contraband by Englishmen knowing it to be a direct violation of an order by the authorities in China. Given this situation, the confrontation was unjustified and, in spite of success in the field, requesting reparations was obviously improper. To do so would certainly confirm the suspicion in Chinese minds that Britain's true purpose was to have power. To writers of this ilk, the Treaty of Nanking merely indicated British contempt for the sovereignty of China.

Even the war's supporters were none too pleased by its outcome. While they welcomed the access to the five ports and the monies for the captured opium, they were disappointed that Hong Kong, not Chusan or Formosa, was now in the empire. They judged Hong Kong, in contrast to the others, to be worthless for commerce; Formosa to be more suitable for investments; and Chusan to be ideal for defense against French ambitions in the area. Although some postulated that its good harbor might make Hong Kong an important garrison, most considered its climate unhealthy for troops. In the 1840s, the island offered little to suggest its future prosperity.

If the struggle had mixed results to reporters, it did enlarge their readers' awareness of China. As a consequence of the war, for the next decades, essays multiplied about the place and its residents.

In the 1850s, paragraphs about China proliferated because of the so-called Taiping Rebellion. Initially, publications sympathized with rebels who were understood to favor Christianity and foreign trade. But, as chaos ensued, magazines began to fear that it would endanger British commerce. Meantime, talk of new hostilities erupted. Although opium was still significant to many, they did not regard it as the main issue for renewed strife. By mid-century, old theories about the returns from the drug's sale were more than balanced by realizations of liabilities therein. The Chinese, concerned specifically about the drain of silver and generally about British aspirations, might, commentators warned, retaliate by canceling the 1842 privileges or even all tea transactions. After all, observers noted, Britain wanted tea more than China wanted opium. Further, if there was any anticipation of

Christianizing the people, helping them to remain drug de-
pendent was hardly suitable conduct.

When, in 1858, the Chinese captured the ARROW in an
attempt to reduce piracy, the vessel, with an expired British
registry, was soon the center of another controversy. Some
scribes saw the incident as the perfect chance to exhibit
British might and to renegotiate the arrangements of 1842.
Asserting that the Chinese had not respected the terms of
Nanking, reviewers hinted that a second conflict, and a second
treaty, might confer greater benefits on the British. Hong
Kong, if somewhat improved by British rule, was, to these
interpreters, crowded and dirty, with too many criminals and
too few goods. Alternatively, winning Chusan would better
serve both trade and defense.

What these analysts did not realize, but others did, was
that Hong Kong was a refuge for the pirates and smugglers
about whom the Chinese complained. If the British resumed the
battle, they would do so without any righteousness for they had
breached more of the 1842 agreement than had China; and they
had maligned that government to its subjects and the world.
If Britain wished to demonstrate its preeminence, it should
set a different example for the Chinese. Combat would only
prove that the British aim was to exploit China. Triumph in
arms would not lead to wider markets but might provoke an
encounter with a Russia outraged by Albion's extravagant
expansionism.

By the 1860s, after a new treaty had guaranteed the
ports but had not licensed inland fortresses, the papers were
more apprehensive about security. Allegedly, Russia and
France were both on the verge of penetrating the interior.
The only solution, for some columnists, was for the British to
establish a Chinese protectorate. Else, they could never ef-
fectively bar competition. However reluctant to undertake
this action, London should recognize it as an obligation as
well as an advantage. For, theoretically, British jurisdiction would extend the progressivism which British merchants
had introduced.

Foes of this scheme were satisfied with the prior con-
cessions. Through trade alone, China would, they predicted,
undergo material and social transformation. Unless the Chinese developed a cotton industry serious enough to threaten
Britain's or restricted emigration so as to deprive British
possessions of workers, there was no reason to extend Britain's

domain. Besides, the new treaty had transferred Kowloon to
the empire. This territory would, magazines hoped, widen the
business of Hong Kong. There, the press now affirmed, the
shops of both the Chinese and the British were flourishing
and the harbor, so long ignored as a mercantile asset, was
bustling. By contrast, writers no longer viewed Hong Kong as
a valuable military outpost. Instead, in a kind of role re-
versal, they postulated that assignment for Singapore.

Singapore and the Malay States

Early in the era, 1832-1867, the principal motif of
articles about Singapore was its excellence as an emporium.
Consistently named as the architect of this status was Sir
Stamford Raffles. Journalists credited Raffles with intrud-
ing on Dutch domination by designating Singapore as a free
port. Only in the 1840s did they voice anything about the
impact that the Treaty of Nanking was having on Singapore.
But, as Hong Kong seemed to erode Singapore's sales, a subtle
shift occurred in news of the latter city. Gradually, more
words were inked about its harbor which, though not much for-
tified, was by the 1860s being advertised as an excellent
location for a naval base.

Another emphasis in periodicals was the mixed population
of Singapore. In the 1840s, analysis centered on the Chinese
who engaged in many enterprises. To do manual labor, as road-
work, there were convicts from India and Hong Kong. But to
entice a measurable number of British, reporters expected that
there would have to be more comforts on shore and less plunder
on the sea.

Piracy was even worse in the Malay States than in
Singapore. Yet, authors tried to inspire a British takeover,
avowing that the natives would welcome such a move. In return
for bringing order, the British, imperialists supposed, would
be rewarded by a long coast and such products of the interior
as spices, minerals, and tin. Coastal harbors were good spots
from which the navy could thwart marauders of the India-China
trade and inhibit Dutch ambitions. Indigenous resources could
be tapped by employing the Chinese whom the Dutch had reputedly induced to come in order to depress the Malays. Likewise,
with British forts, British colonists would congregate to
cultivate the soil and to purchase imperial goods. Accounts
of Borneo best manifested the media's excitement about the
future of this region.

Borneo

Starting in the 1840s, essayists paid greater attention
to Borneo because of the exploits of Sir James Brooke. Brooke
had gained command of the northern part of the island which he
ruled as a sort of satrapy. Typically, the press applauded
his performance as he opened markets and assisted natives.
Nonetheless, his suppression of pirates met sharp, if short
rebuke for being unusually cruel. Overall, Brooke was something of a hero to journalists, a paradigm for other imperialists.

Brooke's deeds also prompted magazines to record the
riches of Borneo, either actual as coal, timber, and minerals
or awaited, as cotton. Observers surmised, as they had about
other places, that Borneo would blossom with British capitalists and Chinese workers. Migrants would journey there if
Parliament would eliminate searobbers by reaching from its
foothold in Labuan to annex the whole island and perhaps
others. New dependencies would preserve the Hong Kong-
Singapore route and furnish the means to contain the Dutch.
Even without these profits, Britain had an obligation to help
the populace economically and religiously.

Opinions about the people of Borneo varied but contributors agreed that large-scale colonization would be detrimental. Rather, a few missionaries should convert the residents and a few more investors should direct finances. The
inhabitants were intelligent: the Dyaks had only to be dis-
suaded from headhunting, the Malays from buccaneering, and the
Chinese from plotting in their secret societies.

By the 1860s, the desire of gazettes to have Borneo was
as evident as was evidence of London's vacillation. Yet, if
most of the island was not to be within the empire, the Brooke
estate at least would long link Borneo and Britain.

f. Pacific Ocean

The Pacific, in nineteenth-century periodicals, meant
at first only Australia. Gradually, however, they published
much about New Zealand and some about Norfolk and Pitcairn
Islands and Fiji.

Australia

In the 1830s, the most popular topic was the continent's

potential for British emigrants. Not surprisingly, most journalists, dazzled by its space but ignorant of much of its
topography, stressed Australia's promise of good pasturage,
farmlands, fishing, and minerals. This promotion became very
fervent after the rebellion in Canada when, some papers speculated, people bound for North America could be persuaded to
try a more tranquil Australia. Only a few writers noticed
that Canada was much closer, in terms of distance and trade,
to Britain than was the region of the Southern Cross.

The expense of traveling to Australia was only one item
on a list of limitations to immigration. Others mentioned
were the presence of natives, the policy of transportation,
and the disposition of land.

While narratives commonly depicted the aborigines as
primitive, there unanimity stopped. Some serials thought that
the locals were harmless, the prey of the bushranger who pro-
voked them to violence against any European. Therefore, to
ensure the peace of future settlers, the British had to safeguard native rights. Alternatively, other articles declared
that the indigenous were so backward as to impede progess and
thus should be removed.

If the Australians might be one kind of menace to colonists, convicts were another. Some essays regarded transportation as bad for both prisoners and free, a sentence which
did not redeem felons but did lower the morals of young settlements and might discourage settlement altogether. Conversely, many people held that it was practical, furnishing
cheaply those public works necessary for a colony to grow,
giving the guilty the opportunity for a new life, and ridding
Britain, physically and financially, of criminals.

The issue that led to the most discussion about Australia
was the disposition of land. Although observers assumed that
the native did not own the soil, they divided about whether
wastelands should be managed by the government. The most notorious technique was that of South Australia. Reporters concluded that the high sale price there was either a major in-
novation which would move labor, surplus and poor in Britain,
to utility and wealth in the colony; or a catastrophic error
which would transform workers into serfs and escalate the costs
of farming.

By the 1840s, the decade in which Australia really became visible, general news had to share pages with regional

tidings. One of the wider matters which persisted was the treatment of locals. Papers continued to urge the government to befriend the natives by isolating them from convicts, liquor, and disease; and by teaching them. If this advice sounded altruistic, it was consistent with the louder demand for missionaries to restrain colonial oppression.

This concern may have been anticipatory. As writers reiterated Australia's need of a labor force, they suggested that London send pauper children and prostitutes. No one seriously worried about the decorum of such persons but columnists strongly condemned the behavior of former felons. Bushrangers apparently terrorized the outback while shepherds harassed aborigines.

Notwithstanding these problems, periodicals flaunted Australia. They painstakingly detailed exploration and usually extolled the climate and resources. Testimony that the continent was worthwhile came from anxieties about its defense, especially against the United States and France, and its self-government. While many authors judged Australia as unready for responsible rule, they were certain that it was going in that direction, a direction, they wanted to be sure, which would not culminate in independence.

Of the separate colonies, each received some, though not always complimentary attention in the 1840s. Paragraphs castigated the South Australia land project but celebrated the colony's new-found copper. They monitored Van Diemen's Land (later Tasmania), busy coping with the convicts whose industry it required since it purportedly had little capital with which to build an infrastructure. Western Australia got bad reviews which, its supporters believed, discouraged immigrants. New South Wales still dominated the colonial wool market, although there was evidence that the quality did not merit the price of shipping to England. Port Phillip, soon to be separated from New South Wales as Victoria, seemed enmeshed in such evils as land speculation, unemployment, and droughts. Finally, there was talk about the Coburg Pennisula being developed if Chinese workers were available.

At mid-century, Australia no longer had to be advertised. While magazines still sought immigrants, the search was more selective. Scribes distained the poor and criminals but attempted to recruit respectable women, to marry bush husbands, and members of the middle classes, to set the correct social tone. If more Irish were flocking after the famine, so

too were the Chinese, soon to be the victims of prejudice.
What brought the Chinese and countless others was gold; what
brought the cry for better manners was the lifestyle of the
diggers who, in the eyes of critics, drank to excess and
spent money foolishly. What also irked authors was how many
settlers were abandoning their farms for the gold camps. Nonetheless, prosperity was the watchword in the 1850s, a prosperity which came from sheep as well as from gold. Only a few
contributors found Australia's limited water supply, bushrangers, and land allocation disquieting. To journalists who
did, most troublesome was the squatter whose acreage appeared
to foreclose the continent's earlier guarantee of enough space
for everyone. The natives, never a real danger, were hardly
a concern. If some humanitarian ideas of the 1840s endured,
as that the English killed Australians by means of rum, disease, and guns, widespread solicitude for aborigines' welfare
did not exist.

Among the regions, Victoria, previously portrayed as
unappealing, was now painted as a model, with farms, pastures,
and gold to enrich it; with self-government to reduce it as
a burden for Britain; and without convicts to pollute it.
Also granted self-government in this decade was New South
Wales, whose keystone, Sydney, periodicals hailed as a significant imperial city. South Australia, thriving thanks to copper, wool, and farms, essayists again censured for its land
sale program as they did Western Australia for its dependence
on transportation, now viewed as more an economic than a moral
nuisance. Queensland, heretofore neglected, was the hope for
more tropical produce.

Accounts in the 1860s chronicled some very successful
colonies in Australia. New South Wales was allegedly booming,
energized by either its convict roots or its resolution to
overcome them. Van Diemen's Land, while not so wealthy, had
some of the same exhuberance. Queensland was probably perfect
for cotton but high wages and reliance on Chinese labor were
likely drawbacks. Victoria, with less gold but other goods,
seemed bothered only by how to break up its large squatter
tracts. If any area looked bleak in the gazettes, it was
Western Australia. Without gold, good soil, or capital, the
territory was not attracting settlers. Hence, it accepted
convicts who, magazines charged, took to alcoholism and crime
as responses to mistreatment.

Apart from this precinct, the future of Australia, in
the press, seemed marvelous. In the perennial stories about

exploration, writers revealed their faith that expeditions
would discover new sources of wealth even greater than the
gold which had reshaped the whole economy. True, gold had
raised diggers above their station and had presented new
chances for robbery by the bushrangers. True also, the natives were reputedly as primitive as when the British first
disembarked. Absent aid, some posited, the locals were better
restricted to special enclaves, as they had been in Van
Diemen's Land, than become extinct in the wake of the colonists.
But, on the whole, essays affirmed that substantial improvements had been accomplished in the years between 1832 and 1867.
All regions had some public works, newspapers, access to railroads, and educational and legal systems similar to ones at
home. If columnists regretted the Australian imprudence about
defense, they delighted in the continent's genuinely British
societies. If only the colonies would federate, and thus stop
any rivalry, they would become a major state, one which would
add even more luster to the British crown than they all did
separately. So, Australia, by 1867, was, in the minds of
journalists, about to come of age.

New Zealand

The amount of news about New Zealand fluctuated in the
time between 1832 and 1867. Yet, from the beginning, there
was one preponderant theme in articles about the islands.
This subject was native-colonist relations, particularly with
respect to the control of land. In the 1830s, as later, opinions about the Maoris were mixed. On the one hand, writers
regarded the natives as superior to many groups whom the British had encountered in the course of their imperialism; on the
other, the Polynesians had a history of cannibalism and had
not benefited from contacts with whalers and runaway convicts.
But the British, reviewers theorized at first, could counteract these bad examples. Moreover, New Zealand would, as other
colonies, relieve Britain of its excess population; be an
Anglo-Saxon stronghold in the Pacific; and barter timber, flax,
and whale-oil for home goods.

The only drawback was the title to land. In the 1830s,
no one questioned that the natives owned the terrain. Less
obvious was how it should be acquired from them. Some believed that the missionaries were insulating the Maoris from
land sharks; others, that the missionaries were the sharks;
and still others, that private companies would cheat the natives. Only the British government, it seemed, could supervise transfers without prejudice.

Title rights were, by the 1840s, a major source of controversy. As commentators became convinced that New Zealand
was valuable for British trade and power, they urged people
to venture to the islands. With sufficient British there,
London could counteract French moves in the Pacific, enlarge
the sales of whale-oil and timber, and develop a market in
wool. But, as more persons went overseas, many in companies,
the papers filled with details about the interrelationship
between land transfers and native rights. Some essays echoed
earlier ideas about the role of ministers, especially those
of the Church Missionary Society; and about the responsibility
of the home government to shield the Maoris, not only from
land jobbers but also from those who would corrupt with guns
and liquor instead of displaying other British habits. The
progress that newcomers were supposed to carry was being lost
in the struggle for deeds.

Those who favored the colonists justified their possession on two bases: that the Maori claim to ownership was in-
valid with respect to unoccupied areas; or that, even if valid, Britain had a right to unused territories if they were
vital for its surplus and if they were settled systematically.
Opponents, with equal vigor, held that the Maoris' notions of
proprietorship differed from those of the British; that the
natives never grasped the concepts of permanent transfer or
wastelands; and that, therefore, Parliament had an obligation
to honor the Maori interpretation. Whatever else might be
unclear, the heightening of tensions was not. Reports of
armed conflict began to penetrate the gazettes. Champions of
the natives asserted that they raided settlements because
these enclaves violated some ancient taboo. Other contributors responded that the newcomers, forbidden to retaliate,
were vulnerable to attack by the locals.

Matters seemed more serious in the 1850s. While journalists went on predicting New Zealand's future as a trading
partner, they also acknowledged that economic growth depended
on workers. With a good climate and low taxes, the islands
could lure more immigrants if only native-colonist interaction was happier. One reviewer theorized that the Maoris
could be won over with money. Wanting British goods, they
might be employed to construct public works. Their pay would
permit them to purchase imports and its continuation would
keep them submissive. A few other writers counseled settlers
to intermarry with a people characterized as advanced and
Christianized. Still others induced from the circumstances
that time was not on the side of the Maoris: and, if so, as

they died off, their world would inevitably pass to the British. However, most serials described ongoing strife. They reprinted old indictments of missionaries and appended glosses, as that ministers had manipulated Maoris against colonists. Prior safeguards seemed ineffective. The government's decision, in the Treaty of Waitangi (1840), to ratify land sales only between itself and the natives had constantly irritated immigrants; and its installation of a local assembly had restricted the Maoris from that direct access to the British bureaucracy which they had previously enjoyed. As antagonism grew, some scribes asked for troops to protect the colonists, a far different request from the petitions of the 1830s.

The 1860s were years of war, war which confirmed that neither land rights had been established nor native-settler disputes resolved. The first struggle, which some papers labeled a revolt, was said to have numerous causes. Magazines blamed missionaries for keeping the two sides apart; London for its arbitrary treatment of the locals, first as independents, then, with Waitangi, as subjects; colonists for inciting confrontation because they knew that they had British backing; and the Maoris for overreacting to the loss of their lands.

In this strife with the land league, the British, according to the press, spent too much and gained too little. Although the settlers had enhanced the value of land, they should not count on support for their resort to force when other ways to acquire territory existed. These included the previously postulated ideas of racial amalgam and of patience as the Maoris decreased; and the new notion of purchasing only on the South Island, where the natives were apparently ready to sell. Generally, at this point, the periodicals still accepted the land tenure of the Maoris.

This acquiescence ended when the movement known as Pai Marire began. Essayists defined the new faith as a rejection of Christianity, hence proof that Britain had failed to civilize the New Zealanders. Certain that the Maoris had no understanding of their obligations as British subjects, papers represented Pai Marire as a confirmation of tribal loyalty and a repudiation of an alien culture which conveyed neither wealth nor status. Once commentators decided that the fighting was as much a clash of societies as of owners, anatagonism to the Maoris increased. That they had to be taught a lesson and that they could not assert dubious tribal rights to usurp land bargains were popular slogans. The future of the country, accounts said, rested with the settlers. They, not the

Colonial Office, must control native policy. Surely they would give the chiefs some access to power but land had to remain British property. These views were quite dissimilar from the 1830's declarations that the Maoris were the rightful proprietors whose lives could only be enriched by the British. Yet, the opinions expressed in the 1860s demonstrated the same concerns as thirty years before, evidence that New Zealand's horizon was, for the moment, clouded.

Norfolk and Pitcairn Islands

News of Norfolk Island commenced in the 1840s. Portrayed as very beautiful, with a fine climate and fertile soil, the island was nevertheless considered a hellish place because of its felonry. Authors assumed that this population was susceptible neither to the lash nor to religion as means of reform. Only the methods of Alexander Maconochie allegedly improved the guilty.

By mid-century, the discipline of Maconochie seemed to be having an effect. Reporters visualized prisoners, incorrigible on arrival, as busy farmers whose regeneration was likely. Indeed, the redeemed were reputed to be going to Van Diemen's Land to work as servants.

The identification of Norfolk Island as a criminal bastion ceased in the 1850s. In that decade, the Pitcairn Islanders, descendants of the H.M.S. BOUNTY crew, petitioned to relocate because they had outgrown the resources of their own island. Papers remarked that the transfer would be advantageous for both economic and psychological well-being.

In the 1860s, the Pitcairners, pictured as decent and industrious, dominated stories about Norfolk although reference to Maconochie's impact on convicts was occasionally made. By this time, the intimation that the Pitcairners suffered because of their exclusivity before their transplantation broadened into an avowal that they had bad blood. Irrespective of any inbreeding, they appeared healthy in Norfolk, in contrast to any earlier sojourn in Tahiti. In Norfolk, they traded with New Zealand and New South Wales and purportedly applied the same simple laws which they had enacted in Pitcairn. To the press, the Pitcairners were happy innocents.

Fiji

If journalists imagined the Pitcairners as innocuous,

they envisioned the Fijians as fierce and brutal. The first words about the Fijians filtered into magazines in the 1840s when a few pages recounted the islanders' cannibalism and bellicosity.

Within ten years, this supposed savagery was less emphasized as the islands became more important in British minds. Writers noted that Fiji could supply cotton and sugar or could serve as a base to protect an Antipodes-British Columbia postal route and against French aggression in the Pacific. Hence, periodicals, averring that Fiji would be an imperial asset and that the Fijians had progressed thanks to missionaries, usually approved the Fijian desire for closer ties with the British.

A debate about the addition of Fiji to the empire livened accounts about the islands in the 1860s. Imperialists highlighted the chain's location and harbors for defense; and its climate, conducive to the now desperately sought cotton. Stories in favor of acquisition carefully rebutted arguments for its rejection. First, even if not directly en route between British North America and Australia, the islands would be the only coaling stations in the area. Second, the natives would plant cotton if they received reasonable wages. Third, problems of land transfer akin to those in New Zealand would not arise if the British paid Fijians fairly for titles. Conversely, opponents of annexation contended that the Fijians would be more self-reliant without British intervention and would be easier to convert without British multitudes ashore. While the destiny of Fiji was to be in the empire, that fate was not altogether apparent in the papers of the 1860s.

g. British North America

British North America was a complex subject for journalists to investigate in the nineteenth century. The region was a curious mixture of the familiar and the unknown, of settlements long established and tracts infrequently traversed. Thus, coverage varied in scope and detail as travelers, soldiers, explorers, and a host of others published their observations; and some, who never visited, did likewise.

Items that preoccupied writers in the 1830s were trade, immigration, and defense. With respect to the first, the effects of tariffs, particularly that on timber, made news. Ideas diverged about the timber levy: some were sure that it would create jobs and clear forests; others were equally certain that it would inspire the rash speculation which ordinarily led to bankruptcy. Even if tariffs were arguable, periodicals usually agreed that British North America was a good market for British goods, a market which would expand once the rail-road opened the west to the surplus population at home.

This conviction that North America could house many was hardly limited to its western reaches. In fact, most of those districts were closed thanks to the monopoly of the Hudson's Bay Company, whose men reputedly endured bad weather, terrible solitude, and hostile natives to barter for fewer and fewer furs. Rather, in the 1830s, reviewers focused on the east. They praised Newfoundland's fishing, Prince Edward Island's harbors, Nova Scotia's coal reserves, New Brunswick's timber, and the Canadas' cheap land and high wages. All of these places wanted hard workers who could conquer the often rugged terrain and more often harsh climate. At this time, contrib-utors said little about the natives who might be displaced except that the British government ought to ensure their rights. But the press did not explain how to reconcile these rights with the mass colonization being promoted.

If native title was not recognized as a hazard to set-tlement, the Canada rebellion was. Authors also identified the revolt as the initial stage in the loss of all British possessions on the continent. Columns, at great length, pre-sented contradictory causes. The most common were the actions of London and the activities of the French.

Analysts indicted the British government for its con-stant and uninformed interference in local affairs, conduct which had also allegedly irritated settlers in New Brunswick, Nova Scotia, Prince Edward Island, and Newfoundland. Further, writers censured the British for designating colonial offices as sinecures without reference to the ability of appointees. If Parliament did not grant some measure of self-government to its colonists, publications warned, it would soon have no colonies. Also criticized, obviously in a spirit of parti-sanship, were Sir Francis Head, for being too domineering, and the Whigs, for being too conciliatory.

By contrast, other essays announced that the uprising was a plot by the French. Typically these theorists absolved the HABITANTS but charged their leaders with conspiracy, demagogues determined to control Lower Canada who had taken advantage of Britain's division of the province and pledge of full civil rights.

If there was much wrangling among gazettes about the reasons for the insurrection, there was much more about its aftermath. Serials conceded rebel amnesty as a means to the future peace but under what jurisdiction rebels would live was less absolute. Depending on party affiliation, narrators classified Lord Durham as savior of or traitor to the empire. Some were positive that reuniting the Canadas was the first step in federating the eastern provinces, thereby forming a permanent foothold for Britain in North America. There was even conjecture that the components of a new entity have seats in Parliament to confirm ties to England. Other papers were unequivocal that Durham's plan would perpetuate French domination of Canada which would culminate in struggles between Gallic and British residents. In the ensuing chaos, Canada, scribes prophesied, would have no immigrants but would be easy prey for the United States.

The obsession with the United States as predator was the third major theme of periodicals in the 1830s. When they mentioned defense, it was always in a Yankee context. Cautions might be specific, as that the States had financed French resisters in Canada or would manipulate the Maine boundary question into a political and strategic victory; or general, as that Brother Jonathan was perennially poised to invade. Only rarely did someone realize that war could hurt the nation's commerce and might disrupt the south's slavery. Even less often did anyone postulate that British North America might not be worth defending, that its sales and settlers did not balance the price to administer and protect. So voices of independence were minimal. British North America was simply too big to surrender without forfeiting prestige, as most reviewers comprehended.

Yet anxiety about losing the country deepened in the 1840s. The United States remained the enemy, not only on the Maine frontier but also in Oregon. Imperialists were more fervent about the latter boundary, partly because they thought that Britain had gotten the worst of the bargain in the east and partly because they discerned the worth of the west, with its opportunities for Pacific markets and millions of inhabitants. Moreover, readers were lectured, Britain should prevail based on the law of discovery and the morality of its treatment of the natives. Whatever the outcome in Oregon, commentators imagined that British pioneers were ready and willing to fend off Yankee aggression. To strengthen this resolve, railroads had to be built and the colonies joined. Confederation, with local government and imperial members in

Parliament, would, allies presumed, not only institute a
strong nation alongside the United States but also bind that
nation closer to London.

Anything that brought better interaction was warranted
in the 1840s as disputes of earlier days persisted in bedevil-
ing British-North American relations. Tariffs, deprecated
because they compelled colonists to purchase British manufactures, were denounced anew when they were cancelled. Writers attributed widespread economic decline primarily to free
trade and secondarily to the diminution of immigrants, who
spelled capital and labor.

Perhaps magazines themselves inhibited immigration as
they carried news of ongoing instability in Canada. For example, they replayed the rebellion when Parliament took up the
question of whether to indemnify some rebels. With hindsight,
essayists recapitulated such origins as US incitement, British tyranny, and French separatism; cataloged new ones, as
Methodist provocation, Upper Canadian oligarchy, and HABITANT
unpreparedness for participatory rule; and examined one more
time, Durham's significance for the empire. To counteract
the unsavory vision of Canada which they had helped to popu-
larize, journalists enumerated the territory's many blessings.
It had responsible government, an active trade, and excellent
credit. In other words, Canada was ideal for the thrifty and
self-motivated to be successful. Additionally, the dependency
did not have hostile natives. In fact, the tribes were models
of dignity compared to the European who had debauched them by
means of disease, liquor, and guns. Even as the British took
their lands, the natives scarcely protested so they were all
but forgotten. Those pages printed about them described their
virtues and vices, looks and lifestyles, in words which implied that soon all tribes would be extinct.

Most articles, discounting native title to realty, supposed that Canada would always be Britain's. This hypothesis,
however, conflicted with that of some Canadians. The price
of monarchy and the constant fear of war had motivated some
local pleas for annexation to the United States but most British periodicals would have none of it.

As extensive as were the accounts of Canada, other regions slowly shared the limelight, not always for the better.
Observers peculiarly disapproved of the east in the 1840s.
They criticized Newfoundland's terrible weather, poor soil,
and misrule; Prince Edward Island's absentee owners who

ignored its possibilities for cultivation; and New Brunswick's
renters who ruined the land. Conversely, narrators extolled
Red River's game and Vancouver Island's fishing. Hudson's
Bay Company came under fire for its exclusion of colonists,
a policy said to result in exploitation of the natives for
the sake of higher returns to shareholders. Going west was
not to be just a Yankee pastime if the magazines had their
way.

By the so-called high Victorian years, the discovery of
gold in British Columbia further sparked zeal for the west.
The ore, together with the area's timber and salmon, would
surely reward newcomers. Contributors also lauded anew
Vancouver Island whose harbors were excellent for trade and
defense. And the fishing along the Pacific coast seemed to
compensate for the losses to the United States of fisheries in
the east.

As for the older eastern districts, articles about
Canada still predominated. The colony had apparently recovered
well from the upheavals of the 1830s for now essays portrayed
it as prosperous, with a stable government and good educational system. Although reporters occasionally chastised
HABITANTS for their adherence to customs which were purportedly
unprofitable, any tensions between French and British settlers
appeared to have dissipated. Likewise, columnists congratulated all Canadians for their loyalty to the Crown. Whether
that loyalty was sufficient to guard against incursions from
the United States was another matter. Some writers, reiterating the fear of Yankee belligerency, were convinced that the
booming economy to the south would motivate the Canadians to
apply for statehood; others had faith that any invasion could
and would be resisted.

The possibility that Canada might one day be a state was
part of a larger discussion about its value to the empire.
While a few averred that Canada was a burden, in taxes and for
security, most deemed it an asset. Papers ordinarily heralded
its resources and space for British emigrants and, more impor-
tantly, its function as the linchpin of British North America.
Losing it could precipitate the loss of the continent and, at
least one author supposed, of the West Indies as well. Simply
put, much of Britain's power and prestige derived from Canada.

Some serials realized, nevertheless, that staying in
Canada and all of British North America must be cost effective.
Increasingly, therefore, reviewers appealed for confederation

even though they thought that the Colonial Office was opposed
to such a scheme. This league, with internal self-government
and representatives at Westminster, would save money for rate-
payers on both sides of the Atlantic. But, to succeed, a pre-
requisite was a transcontinental railroad. The line would not
only link the colonies intellectually and economically but also
invite settlement of the west and secure the Pacific routes.

In the 1860s, as before, trade, defense, and immigration
were topics which always found their way into the news about
British North America. This decade was, in fact, a time of
widespread coverage. Demands for a transcontinental railroad
grew in direct proportion to authors' fears of French and Russian activity in the Pacific. Indeed, gazettes hailed the
railroad as far better than Suez to safeguard the Eastern holdings. Curiously, while the press projected other hypothetical
foes, it discoursed less about the United States, busy with
its Civil War and the aftershocks.

Not only did the Yankee specter turn up more sporadically
in periodical pages, but the War between the States was credited with influencing immigration to British North America.
And what the war did not do, propagandists tried to achieve.
Prince Edward Island, so plagued by problems with its land
grant absentees that troops had to be summoned in 1865, was
advertised for its climate and soil; Nova Scotia, for its
flourishing farms; New Brunswick, for its jobs; and the Red
River tracts, for their minerals. Nonetheless, to most
scribes, British Columbia was the new Eden. Enriched by gold,
furs, and woods, its future was surely to control the Pacific
if only, some sighed, as many British would go there as had
Chinese. Because the lands of the Hudson's Bay Company promised much wealth, some writers protested renewal of its charter. If Members extended the Company's license, they would
foreclose millions of acres to extensive colonization and
doom countless natives to ongoing abuse. Surprisingly, Canada,
previously the darling of journalists, was not so in the 1860s.
Supposed to be in debt from its 1830's rebellion and its 1850's
public works, censured for its recent tariffs, Canada did not
look very desirable for people wanting to advance financially.
Some Britons even affirmed that, should Canada ever fall to
the Yankees, few from the mother country would pay to get it
back. Not all viewers were so unfriendly. Many reminded
readers that Canada was the historic center of allegiance
against the United States, had taken thousands of immigrants
over the years, and had a lively trade with Britain. Further-
more, Canada had both sophisticated cities and substantial

farmlands to tempt colonists.

By now, both in Canada and in much of British North America, colonial life was no longer a struggle for survival in the backwoods. However, as towns sprouted across the landscape, the number of natives declined. Pushed from their homes, demoralized and diseased, the tribes were commonly identified as martyrs to the cause of British imperialism. Although essayists intermittently prescribed intermarriage with and conversion of the indigenous, implicit in many stories was the sense that an era had passed. Thus, many columnists spoke of native customs as oddities to be noticed instead of a heritage to be nurtured.

If the railroad was to unite British North America in one fashion, federation was to do so, and sooner, in another. The passage of the British North America Act generated considerable news. Articles no longer underlined the merits of association: these were assumed. Rather, papers wondered about the future relationship between the federation and Britain. If it was obvious that old colonial concepts and methods would not apply, what would replace them was less so. Perhaps, some speculated, the North Americans might enter appropriate British ministries or, perhaps, the young state could join with Britain in voluntary association as an equal. However the connections between the confederation and London evolved, or dissolved, the process would take time. In magazines of 1867, therefore, 1 July of that year marked the commencement of the Dominion of Canada, not the termination of the British Empire in North America.

h. Caribbean and South America

The Caribbean and South America were not terms which nineteenth-century journalists used. They wrote principally about the West Indies, collectively and individually, and collaterally about Central America and the Falkland Islands.

West Indies

To the press, the West Indies meant the islands of the Caribbean and the Bahamas, Bermuda, and British Guiana. Study of these dependencies was both generic and specific.

The West Indies were popular in the 1830s. Early in the decade, serials debated the emancipation of slaves. Not unexpectedly, contributors who disfavored it depicted slaves as

healthy and happy, citing those in Barbados and British Guiana
as evidence. Several scribes said that bondage gave Africans
stability and discipline and Europeans suitable laborers.
Opponents, also conventionally, painted a grim picture of
habitual mistreatment terminating in premature death and eter-
nal damnation. For, as papers, particularly those with a religious affliation, complained, masters kept missionaries away.
Other gazettes endorsed this policy because, they noted, the
ministers' message gave them too much influence, as the Baptists reputedly exercised in Jamaica.

As it became clear that freedom was forthcoming, the
discussion became one of timing. Postponement, foes of emancipation affirmed, was essential for many reasons. First,
slaves must be prepared for their new status. Imagined to be
long accustomed to paternalism and inherently lazy while living
in a lush climate, they would never again work unless they
learned the artificial wants which motivated industry. Without
instruction, economic catastrophe would ensue, destroying the
productivity of the smaller islands and damaging that of the
larger. Only poor soil, as in the Bahamas, might compel black
energy but reporters considered that chain to have little commercial value. Also, immediate liberty would deprive planters
of property and might deprive Britain of strategic naval bases
if the rioting, anticipated at emancipation, exploded into
rebellion.

The arrangements ending slavery somewhat assuaged advocates of delay for, at least temporarily, apprenticeship would
guarantee hands; and compensation, cancel debts. But these
new orders caused as much argument in the magazines as had the
issue of manumission itself.

For the remainder of the 1830s, therefore, the aftermath
of emancipation made headlines. Compensation, champions declared, was lawful. It paid owners for their slaves who had
been acquired and maintained at great expense and with the
sanction of the government. Alternatively, others responded,
the money was unnecessary, inappropriate, and immoral. The
indemnity was not mandated because proprietors would save funds
previously spent on support; not suitable because their financial problems were their own fault; and not right because,
whatever the statutes, humans were by nature free. Of these
statements, that of mismanagement was the most prevalent and
would remain so. Columnists accused planters of being absentees who cared only about profits, which their powerful
lobby at Westminster preserved. Their unconcern had encouraged

overseers to harm people and to ravage the soil. Insolvent before emancipation, many estates survived only because of the sugar tariff.

Even more in dispute than compensation was the operation of apprenticeship. Its enemies equated it to slavery, especially in Jamaica. The assembly and courts of that island were, narrators told readers, notorious for oppression of the apprentice, institutions which upheld old wrongs and denied new rights. By contrast, emancipationists claimed, in places where the system had not been adopted, as Antigua and Bermuda, life had improved for former slaves. If owners feared that blacks would not toil in the fields, the press reminded planters that it was they who had associated fieldwork with degradation. But friends of apprenticeship did worry, even more after Parliament canceled it earlier than had been originally planned. With this development came the first requests for replacements, notably Indians. The free could then be shipped back to Africa or employed as local troops in an atmosphere thought fatal for Europeans.

In the 1840s, the theme in the periodicals was the imminent ruin of most of the region. Authors did name exceptions: St. Kitts and Antigua were allegedly prospering; Barbados had shops, hotels, roads, and a thrifty peasantry; Bermuda, even with convicts, was content, a comfortable mood for a defense station; and the only trouble in the Bahamas seemed to be a conflict between Anglican and Baptist missionaries.

In general, however, the thesis of articles was the decline of the plantations, once again attributed in part to the planters. Without ties to the West Indies, owners had failed to comprehend the need to change, emotionally and economically, to save their holdings. As old charges were leveled, they were met by new exculpations. For example, having had time to evaluate compensation, some essayists concluded that it was insufficient, that more capital was indispensable to sustain sugar. Others reported that the British had the skill, experience, and money to operate but lacked laborers. Blacks were unwilling to work except for exorbitant wages. Apprenticeship had obviously been too short to train them to be subservient after freedom. Hence, as one author proposed and others inferred, the government should enact serfdom. Otherwise, without cultivators, the estates would have to be abandoned.

The search for substitutes led to yet another major
controversy in the gazettes. The quarrel focused on whether
to bring people from overseas to handle the cane. Sponsors
pledged good earnings and government supervision of conditions;
and predicted cheaper sugar as newcomers, competing with the
manumitted, would keep remuneration low. The latter outcome
would benefit British buyers and drive slave-grown sugar from
the market. Dreaming of moral results to complement the monetary ones, writers widely promoted immigration. Most wanted
to have Indians or Chinese, imagined to be energetic. Other
commentators recommended West Africans, who would absorb British civilization in the islands and disseminate it upon their
return home. Some also suggested convicts and blacks from
British North America, whose leaving would make room for more
British settlers.

    This case did not persuade adversaries. Instead, they
regarded the project as akin to bondage. Men would not be
kidnapped or bought but they would be enticed by lies and the
consequences would be the same. If immigrants did not die
from abuse en route or in the fields, they would suffer psychologically, so distant from family and culture. To postulate
that the transaction would ameliorate them or their contacts
when they went back was a sham. Their arrival, moreover, could
lead to other evils. For instance, if only males came, the
resulting disproportion of the sexes in most islands would
impair local virtue.

    More serious was the concern that immigrants would drive
blacks from jobs for not all of the liberated had fled the
plantations. The introduction of rivals, if understood as a
technique to perpetuate servitude, might induce the remaining
ex-slaves to go, or worse. Locals in Dominica, peaceful after
emancipation, had rioted when they decided that the census was
a device to resume slavery. The landing of numerous foreigners
could breed much wider discontent. To return to the fields,
nonetheless, employees had to receive fair salaries. All the
talk about indolence was, to many writers, really talk about
the failure to hire blacks cheaply. If proprietors spent
money on mechanization rather than immigration, they could do
with fewer hands and pay them more. But, these analysts realized, new employers were simply old masters. They missed the
authority which they had once exercised. Even when enough
labor apparently was available, as in Jamaica and Trinidad,
whites maneuvered to keep ex-slaves subordinated. Thus, articles proclaimed, the emancipated had to be shielded from
brutality if they recultivated the estates, protection perhaps

impossible while their former owners controlled the bench and bar.

Before the press could make a final assessment about immigration, another crisis arose. Parliament's cancellation of the sugar tariff destroyed the artificial price upon which the planters depended. Some reviews were convinced that the decision would move Britons to buy cheaper slave-grown sugar, so these narratives forecast that the West Indies would decay even more rapidly unless the islands became more competitive. The continuing use of expensive and outmoded processes, together with the designation of substantial capital as profit, would have to stop.

Unhappily, as the papers reflected, the 1850s were not a time of rejuvenation. Except for the proposition that London should federate the islands, essays were neither positive nor innovative. They reiterated the now familiar opinions about the planter, indicting him for malfeasance or nonfeasance, or acquitting him as a victim of Exeter Hall philanthropists or Manchester liberals.

Journalists were less divided about two other matters, the condition of Jamaica and the character of former slaves. The island, considered the centerpiece of the British Caribbean domain, seemed to be in deep trouble. Blacks were demoralized; Chinese and Indians, ineffective; overseers, unfit; and proprietors, still missing. What plantation policies had not devastated, free trade had.

As many contributors were sure about Jamaica's deterioration, others were almost as absolute about the nature of ex-slaves. Compared to the freemen of the United States, the West Indians were, in many British minds, immoral, idle, and, worst of all, impudent. The only ways to teach them deference were to recruit them for the army or to whip them in the fields.

Since blacks were unlikely to react to the lash with greater endeavor, the pressure for replacements grew more urgent. Indians might not be so energetic but Trinidad and British Guiana apparently sought them. Stories characterized estate holders in both locales as more sensible than they had once been and promised renewed affluence with foreign toilers. In addition to Indians, Africans, some accounts theorized, might do if Parliament and the public could be persuaded that servitude was not being reintroduced. The Chinese, diligent

workers, were perchance corrupt. Slaves from the United
States might be the best choice. Given liberty, they would
hardly bargain about wages but purchasing them might be expensive.

Attention to the West Indies was, in the 1860s, somewhat greater, if not more optimistic. Serials published yet
again the popular concepts about economic disintegration.
Columnists convicted the British, by now customarily, for
cruelty to slaves, apprentices, and immigrants alike; determination to retain blacks in financial, educational, legal,
and emotional servility; ineptitude with money yet greedy for
it; and apathy about the resources of the islands.

To refute these criticisms, other accounts resorted to
the equally hackneyed ideas of previous decades, chief of
which was the need for cultivators. Some Chinese had come
and Indians were disembarking in larger numbers but not fast
enough to meet the demand. St. Vincent seemed to want them;
St. Lucia and Grenada seemed to want more. In Trinidad, the
press alleged that the readiness to renew contracts was proof
of Indians' well-being and associated them with the island's
prosperity. Even if they took jobs from the black, who was
purportedly turning to vice and crime, many papers continued
their pleas for more aliens. Meantime, until there were sufficient outsiders, West Indians must resume tillage. Except
for Barbados, where fertile land was scarce, blacks were not
doing so voluntarily. Therefore, some reviewers proposed
compulsion. For instance, commanders could order black troops
to care for the cane, notwithstanding that men might enlist
just to avoid such exertion. From this experience, advocates
declared, the men would learn the self-control that their
parents had derived from slavery. Besides, as an occasional
Briton remarked, members of the younger generation were as
cheerful laboring under a hot sun as had been their forebears.
Even if there were laws against compulsion, supporters believed
that such rules did not apply to the West Indies. Only a few
journalists pointed out that blacks, with some assistance,
could succeed as artisans and small farmers.

Irrespective of the papers' preoccupation with management and workers, authors did not say much about trade in the
1860s. There were hopes that sugar could be sold in West
Africa in exchange for food and that sugar sales would pick
up when the Civil War in the United States ended. There were
also whispers that a public works program or military colonization could restore prosperity. But the possibilities for

recovery were few.   Many people instead foresaw disaster.

The events which confirmed, to several commentators, this
fate for the West Indies occurred in Jamaica.   The island
typified for all sides the difficulties of the region and the
roles of the major protagonists therein.   Planters had a long
history of being inept.   Financially, they had applied compensation to discharge old mortgages and had incurred new debts
to import Indians and Africans rather than modernized sugar
processing.   Politically, they had manipulated the local
assembly to insure their own interests and to deny justice to
others.   The media thought that blacks were also at fault.
They supposedly had disdained religion because of its costs
and constraints, grown more slothful, and experimented with
crime.   Parliament was blamed too, for having passed free
trade without regard for its impact.

When riots flared in 1865, few reviewers were astonished.
In some articles, the disturbances were the product of longstanding grievances, as heavy taxes, no rights, and poverty.
In other essays, the agitation was the result of recent bad
harvests.   And in still other paragraphs, the affair was the
offspring of a conspiracy to overthrow the regime, a plot
ascribed to the Baptists but one that was hard to prove.

As there were varied explanations of causality, so there
were of responses to the happenings.   Most magazines concurred
that Governor Edward Eyre had overreacted, especially by continuing martial law after there was no real danger and by
authorizing the wholesale burning of houses.   His allies
claimed that both acts were necessary to save Jamaica for the
empire.   Additionally, Eyre's defenders were convinced that
blacks had no appreciation of British legal procedures, as
trial by jury, and kept nothing but plunder in abodes that were
little more than shacks.   While Eyre's policies were question-
able, the shock of the riots was not.   Recovery, the press was
certain, would not be rapid in Jamaica which unfortunately was,
as before, the symbol of the state of the West Indies.

Central America

In the 1830s, Britons infrequently noticed this region.
When they did, it was to describe the landscape of British
Honduras or to bemoan the earlier Scottish failure to colonize
Panama.   Gradually, interest swelled, in proportion to the
increase of Britain's Pacific holdings, in either a railroad
or a canal somewhere across Central America.

By the next decade, the interest had become livelier, partly because the United States seemed to covet the area. To shield its own power and profits, Britain, reporters urged, should build a canal. Panama's climate, physical features, and few workers allegedly made it unfeasible but Nicaragua might be ideal, not that London wanted to expand beyond British Honduras. That dependency, while rich in mahogany, was not thriving according to columnists. They portrayed owners as uneasy about high taxes, free trade, and liberated blacks; and angry because they had little sway in the local assembly, said to be run by the governor. Given potential trouble there, Britain should not, narrators counseled, seek more possessions in the vicinity, only security for its trade routes.

Anxiety about Yankee imperialism heightened in the 1850s. Writers identified the source of tension as the Clayton-Bulwer Treaty. This pact, they averred, allowed the United States to challenge without cause British suzerainty in Honduras and the Moskito protectorate. This challenge must be answered else the States would next preempt the current timber trade, thereafter monopolize other sales, and eventually command the ocean link to the irreparable harm of the Pacific colonies belonging to Britain.

In light of this concern, it is rather odd that someone propounded cooperation with the United States in a joint canal venture. The press much preferred multinational sponsorship of a neutral waterway or, understandably, sole British supervision. By mid-century, observers less favored Nicaragua, in print because its handicaps were similar to Panama's; by inference, because they suspected Washington's influence in Managua.

Apprehension about the United States persisted into the 1860s when there was also worry about Mexico, at least while it was a French client. If mahogany exports and an interoceanic connection would never be safe without British troops, Honduras, some recognized, had few roads and much malaria. For the moment, then, gazettes did not target it as a military priority; and Central America in the 1860s did not appear to be any kind of priority for any author.

Falkland Islands

Stories about the Falklands in the 1830s spoke of the islands as well-situated for a stopover between Britain and the Antipodes and for a convict settlement. However, scribes did not anticipate much commerce since the only local products were fish, peat, and potatoes.

By the 1840s, estimates of the Falklands rose in correlation to cares about the defense of the Australian route. There were some words about colonization for the islands reputedly had a pleasant climate and good pasturage but the government was not encouraging migration.

As years passed, the South American route did not become as significant as writers initially dreamed. Hence, the Falklands all but vanished, if momentarily, from the news.

i. Africa

The African dependencies did not receive equal attention in nineteenth-century serials. Journalists more often discussed the British possessions in the south rather than the older ones along the west coast, these only sporadically mentioned. By contrast, there was an increasing output of material about the explorations of East and Southeast Africa, thanks largely to the activities of such men as John Speke and David Livingstone. Reviews often outlined the conditions of a journey or reactions to it without noticing any imperial implication. Reporters occasionally hinted about trade, defense, and the like but, before 1867, they seldom articulated ideas about British control of, or even influence in these territories.

South Africa

Throughout the period, 1832-1867, articles about South Africa concentrated on the interrelationships among the Dutch and British colonists, the British government, and the natives. In the 1830s, authors were sympathetic to the locals. The media looked upon blacks not as wholly virtuous but nevertheless as victims. Essays alleged that the tribes had been mistreated by the settlers and the authorities. Contributors censured the Boers for enslaving Hottentots and stealing the cattle of people known as Kaffirs; and the British for taking the best acreage and dealing with the owners as if they were depraved. The papers charged that London tolerated behavior which was already causing war between Europeans and Africans. To avoid further conflicts, periodicals advised the government to seize the entire region. In that case, some cynics suggested, the British should kill the natives as fast as possible which would be cheap and humane. Otherwise, there were

warnings that oppression could last only until the tribes had
many guns. Writers who were less pessimistic hoped that the
Africans would be converted but others conjectured that missionaries, with their notions of equality, would inflame their
disciples. Perhaps the most sensible policy, some Britons
hypothesized, would be to abandon the area, an idea which
most commentators dismissed as either impractical or unprofitable. Withdrawal would not end the strife and might exacer-
bate it. Besides, the district reputedly had great potential,
the Cape with its farmlands and Natal as a gateway to an ivory
trade with the Zulus.

By the 1840s, assessment of South Africa was mixed. The
press commonly lauded Natal for its soil, climate, and coal
but deplored its lack of labor and capital as newcomers, sen-
sitive to continuing discord, avoided it. Magazines also extolled the Cape's value for trade, defense, and space for
immigrants. While British residents there opposed Parliament's
plan to ship a convict population, they welcomed other workers.
Propagandists asserted that colonists would find high wages,
Britain would be relieved of its rebellious poor, and more
British could push the natives from the fertile terrain which
they still possessed. The endorsement of tribal displacement
marked a shift of attitude among journalists, a change that
soon extended beyond notes on the Cape to most coverage of
South Africa.

As strife went on, papers became more hostile to natives.
Narrators denounced Africans as cattle thieves who reveled in
plunder or were roused by misguided philanthropists. Since
Britain had established its right to the territory with divine
benediction, the locals must be punished by losing their ani-
mals and their homes. They would construe anything less severe
as weakness and would resume their raids. Prior efforts at
conciliation had merely left the settlers at risk. The government should adopt the Boer methods of border patrols and re-
taliation. Moreover, some reporters castigated London for
allowing the Boers to migrate: failure to respond to their
grievances had seriously reduced the defense force.

Only a few gazettes thought that the confiscation of
stock by natives was a reaction to that of land by the
Europeans. If true, the arrival of a multitude would aggravate
the situation and culminate in more violence. Instead of
fighting native wars, Britain should try to civilize the natives. Observing that many Hottentots had converted to Christianity, some authors believed that other Africans would

likewise: as Christians, they would be effective guards
against forays by their brothers or the Boers.

During the 1850s, the pages on South Africa multiplied
but their focus remained native-colonist-government interaction. Where before reviewers had indicted the Briton and
the African, now they complained most about London. The government, they agreed, had been inadequate but there consensus
ceased. Some paragraphs stated that Parliament had been
supercilious to the Boers, chastising them for their conduct
when that of the British was little better. Then, when the
treks began, Members had labeled the Boers rebels, further
alienating them. Other essayists insisted that the Boers had
systematically exterminated the indigenous population and
undermined British sovereignty so they deserved no compassion.

Publications also blamed the home government for mis-
handling the natives. Journals friendly to the settlers professed that they had been caught between rulers' indifference
to their welfare and neighbors' savagery. Because some columnists assumed that the African would never assimilate
Western culture, they counseled that the natives be treated
with severity. Particularly, they should be expelled from
British jurisdiction. This decision would also give colonists
access to the resources of British Kaffraria and might remove
the locals from the sway of ministers teaching ideas of racial
equality and realty rights.

Alternatively, other interpreters condemned the government for its leniency toward the immigrant. They reproached
Britain for shielding citizens who expropriated from and
murdered the previously peaceful inhabitants. These scribes
deemed the breakup of Kaffraria as unjust to the natives and
hazardous to the settlers who would then be closer to more
dangerous tribes. As any likelihood of subduing the natives
disappeared, with that would go all schemes for large-scale
colonization. For, with ongoing war, stories cautioned, South
Africa would never attract the immigrants who were essential
for its development.

The interest in newcomers paralleled that in specific
colonies. In the 1850s, reporters emphasized the Cape's role
in the eastern defense network and its wine and tobacco. But,
writers grumbled, the district had too many Dutch for a British community. Articles voiced the same annoyance about Natal,
increasingly important as a source of cotton. They also began
to study the Orange River settlement. Pictured as fertile,

with a hospitable climate and without hostile natives, the
place was imagined to be perfect for agriculture and pasturage. Additionally, a few noticed that the Transvaal, in Boer
hands, had excellent soil. Perhaps the Cape, Natal, and the
Orange River could be federated with an invitation to the
Transvaal to join. When the Colonial Office, in 1854, gave
local autonomy to the Orange River, imperialists classified
the grant as yet another betrayal of the British position in
South Africa.

As the so-called Kaffir Wars finished in the late 1850s,
magazines began to analyze the effects of the strife. Usually,
commentators categorized the struggles as ones of self-defense
for Britain after which the Africans still held much worthwhile land. Allegedly the Cape suffered a loss of prestige
and money but recovered by the 1860s. Natal, in that decade,
without enough toilers and capital for its cotton and sugar
production, was growing more slowly. To expand commerce
generally, papers recommended the employment of tribesmen to
construct public works. This seeming testimony that race relations were improving was contradicted by the news that Natal
was pondering some future limitation of African voting rights,
given the large number of natives there. Nonetheless, the
best evidence that, for the moment, peace had come to South
Africa was the fact that the Colenso controversy made headlines in the 1860s. This episcopal dispute, however heated,
was a welcome if temporary respite from words of war.

Sierra Leone

Sierra Leone was preponderant in articles about West
Africa. In the 1830s, the climate was a popular topic. Essayists cited the weather as fatal for all Europeans, if they continued to dress and eat as they did at home, and as demoraliz-
ing for the military. In the ennui bred by the temperature,
soldiers gambled or drank to excess. If narrators concurred
about the atmosphere, they did not about the economy. Some
were sure that Sierra Leone would never prosper because it had
no staple crop whereas others declared that palm-oil, vanilla,
and coffee sales could be lucrative if better managed.

The concern about trade extended into the 1840s. Although Sierra Leone was by then buying cotton goods, liquor,
and tools from the British, contributors saw that it had
neither the skill nor the funds to raise tropical produce
for exchange. Without these requisites, Sierra Leone would
not flourish so some advised London to encourage blacks to

work in the West Indies whose civilization they could share
upon their return. This project was not intended for former
slaves who were being rehabilitated very slowly. Because
they had difficulty learning new crafts but lived in Freetown,
at least one author suggested that the government allot them
jobs. Meantime, both the Church Missionary Society and the
Muslims were reportedly active in proselytizing the liberated.

During the 1850s, life for those removed from slave
ships seemed to be better. Even though blacks off a slaver
were ordinarily quite ill, they recovered rapidly, the press
thought, thanks to good food, clothes, and housing. Missionary teachers also instructed Africans so that, by the 1860s,
they had become, in some British eyes, a respectable middle
class.

The major problems detailed in the 1850s had to do with
the Europeans. The climate was an ongoing nuisance but authors
broadcast a new and more serious matter. They chided British
bureaucrats for failure to build public works and imposition
of excessive taxes. To ameliorate the condition of Sierra
Leone, one journalistic solution was to unite it with Liberia,
whose administration was presumed to be sound, whose residents
had a common heritage of slavery, and whose coast would en-
hance Sierra Leone's commercial activity. Further, the union
would relieve Britain of the costs of ruling but would, sponsors guessed, leave intact its trade advantages. Whatever
the merits of this proposition, neither it nor Sierra Leone
was judged newsworthy in the 1860s.

Gold Coast

The few pages about the Gold Coast in the 1830s and
1840s spoke of its products and its natives. While writers
appreciated the area's gold, ivory, and palm-oil, they wondered
about the effects of interaction between Africans and Europeans. Some accounts affirmed that the British brought justice
and energy; others, that Britons corrupted the indigenous.

In the 1850s, as periodicals postulated incorrectly that
Britain would enlarge its sphere inward, they outlined its
future responsibilities. Albion, articles admonished, should
not merely make money but should build roads, guarantee peace
through law, and promote Christianity.

London many have listened to this guidance since, by
the 1860s, analysts perceived natives as better intellectually

and morally, noting particularly their attainments of skills
and their services as magistrates. They would, some observers
promised, soon be trained to grow cotton. Likewise, the effect of quinine on the troops seemed to confirm that the environment need not be deadly for Englishmen who would direct
such an endeavor. In the paragraphs of the 1860s, the future
looked bright for the Gold Coast.

Niger River

From the 1830s through the 1860s, reviewers had high
hopes for this region, even when its atmosphere appeared harm-
ful to the British. Gazettes recorded at length expeditions
up river and assured readers that residents were waiting to
barter palm-oil and kola nuts, among other things, for British
guns and liquor. Some authors advocated the creation of a
British dependency along the river for moral and political as
well as financial reasons. From such a foothold, patrons
theorized, the British could halt the slave trade, move into
the interior, and bar other countries from the vicinity.

In the 1840s, columnists occasionally singled out the
nearby island of Fernando Po as a possible colony. They
praised its harbor and soil which might be profitable for cotton, coffee, and sugar, even if disease decimated colonists.
In the 1850s, when the first chance to take Lagos came, supporters reproved London for ignoring its duty because of the
cost. Ironically, in the 1860s, when Lagos became part of the
empire, opponents announced that it was unnecessary for either
markets or converts.

Gambia

Stories about Gambia were scarce until the 1850s. Then
they concentrated on listing the traits of the natives and
their improvement since British supremacy. Trade was supposedly limited by a bad climate, tribal taxes, and much thieving.
When the locals allegedly thwarted its few markets, Britain,
c. 1855-1862, resorted to force to retain them, a tactic which
contributors applauded as imperative to curb African provoca-
tions. In spite of this episode, pages of the 1860s expressed
some optimism that the Gambians could cultivate cotton. Should
they have to be enslaved to achieve this goal, they would at
least not be uprooted. However, even without cotton, Gambia
might be a bulwark against French imperialism in West Africa,
which would make it an asset for the British.

St. Helena

Magazines published few sentences about St. Helena in the 1830s and 1840s. Essays stressed, logically for a defense outpost, the troops' ability to stall aggression aimed at the Eastern possessions. While there was satisfaction, in the 1830s, that the East India Company was spending a substantial sum to garrison soldiers, there was also chagrin that their numbers were too small to be effective. Therefore, to do the routine work vital to the upkeep of a fort, the press asked for Chinese and Indians, sure to be lured by high wages.

By the 1840s, the capability to meet an enemy challenge seemed adequate. If there were troubles, they arose from boredom, both of the military and of rescued slaves lodged there temporaily. Presumably this condition contributed to the dearth of narratives about St. Helena.

That this isolated island made even a little news is itself proof of the media's romance with the empire. Curiosity commingled with concern and certainty produced, for four decades, a deluge of documents in which historians can now delight.

SECTION I

Check-list of London Magazines Dealing with
the British Empire, 1832-1867

THE ABORIGINES' FRIEND[*]

1. 1855-1858
2. Published for the Aborigines' Protection Society
3. and Colonial Intelligencer
4. Supersedes and superseded by THE COLONIAL
   INTELLIGENCER
6. British and Foreign Aborigines' Protection Society
7. Annually; quarterly; semi-annually
9. British Library

ALEXANDER'S EAST INDIA MAGAZINE

1. 1831-1842 (checked from 1832)
2. R. Alexander
3. and Colonial and Commercial Journal; and Colonial
   Magazine; and Colonial Magazine with Which Is
   Incorporated THE MEERUT UNIVERSAL MAGAZINE
6. A Society of Gentlemen from India
7. Monthly
8. 2s.6d.
9. British Library

---

* This section is coded as follows:
   1. Dates of run
   2. Publisher
   3. Subtitle
   4. Supersession
   5. Editor
   6. Sponsor (e.g., a society)
   7. Time of publication
   8. Price
   9. Location inspected (with remarks about missing
      volumes, numbers, and pages)

THE ANTI-SLAVERY REPORTER[1]

    1. 1825-1836 (checked from 1832)
    2. Printed for the Society
    4. Superseded by THE BRITISH EMANCIPATOR (classified as a newspaper by the British Library) and THE BRITISH AND FOREIGN ANTI-SLAVERY REPORTER
    6. London Society for the Aboilition of Slavery Throughout the British Dominions
    7. Monthly
    9. British Library: missing #7 (only number printed between 1833 and 1836)

THE ANTI-SLAVERY REPORTER[2]

    1. 1846-1909 (checked 1846-1867)
    2. Peter Jones Bolton
    4. Supersedes THE BRITISH AND FOREIGN ANTI-SLAVERY REPORTER
    6. British and Foreign Anti-Slavery Society
    7. Monthly
    8. 5d.
    9. Newark Public Library

THE ASIATIC AND COLONIAL QUARTERLY JOURNAL

    1. 1846-1850
    2. James Madden
    7. Quarterly
    9. British Library: missing VI, #11 (June, 1849)

THE ASIATIC JOURNAL

    1. 1816-1845 (checked 1832-1845)
    2. Parbury, Allen and Co.
    3. and Monthly Register for British and Foreign India, China, and Australasia; and Monthly Miscellany; and Monthly Review
    4. Superseded by THE COLONIAL AND ASIATIC REVIEW
    7. Monthly
    9. British Library

AUSTRALASIAN GOLD FIELDS

    1. 6 March 1852
    2. G.J. Yonge
    3. Monthly Circular of Intelligence for Emigrants, Who Propose To Become Connected, in Mining Pursuits, with the Melbourne Gold and General Mining Association

6. The Melbourne Gold and General Mining Association
7. Monthly
8. 1d./2d. stamped
9. British Library

THE AUSTRALIAN AND NEW ZEALAND MONTHLY MAGAZINE

1. 1842
2. Smith, Elder, and Co.
3. for New South Wales, Van Diemen's Land, Western
   Australia, Port Phillip, South Australia, and
   New Zealand
5. Henry Capper
7. Monthly
8. 2s.
9. British Library

THE BRITISH AND FOREIGN ANTI-SLAVERY REPORTER

1. 1840-1845
2. Lancelot Wild
3. under the Sanction of the British and Foreign Anti-
   Slavery Society
4. Supersedes THE ANTI-SLAVERY REPORTER[1] and THE
   BRITISH EMANCIPATOR (classified as a newspaper by
   the British Library); superseded by THE ANTI-
   SLAVERY REPORTER[2]
6. British and Foreign Anti-Slavery Society
7. Bimonthly
8. 3d.; 4d.
9. British Library: missing #16, #17 (1841); #18, #19
   (1844)

THE BRITISH FRIEND OF INDIA MAGAZINE

1. 1842-1846
2. Smith, Elder, and Co.; Sherwood, Gilbert, and Piper
3. and Indian Review; and General Colonial Review
7. Monthly
8. 1s.
9. British Library: very imperfect VII (1845)

THE CANADIAN, BRITISH AMERICAN, AND WEST INDIAN MAGAZINE

1. 1839
2. C. Mitchell
7. Monthly
9. British Library

THE CANADIAN PORTFOLIO

    1. 1838
    2. Charles Fox
    3. Conducted by John Arthur Roebuck and Other Friends
       of Canada
    7. Weekly
    8. 6d.
    9. British Library

CAPTAIN PIDDING'S CHINESE OLIO AND TEA TALK

    1. 1844-1845
    2. George Berger
    7. Weekly
    8. 2d./3d. stamped
    9. British Library

THE CHINESE AND JAPANESE REPOSITORY

    1. 1863-1865
    2. W.H. Allen and Co.
    3. of Facts and Events in Science, History, and Art
       Relating to Eastern Asia
    5. Rev. James Summers
    7. Monthly
    9. British Library

COLBURN'S UNITED SERVICE MAGAZINE

    1. 1843-1890 (checked through 1867)
    2. Henry Colburn
    4. Supersedes THE UNITED SERVICE MAGAZINE
    7. Monthly
    9. New York Public Library

THE COLONIAL AND ASIATIC REVIEW

    1. 1852-1853
    2. John Mortimer
    4. Supersedes THE ASIATIC JOURNAL and THE COLONIAL
       MAGAZINE AND EAST INDIA REVIEW (merger)
    7. Monthly
    8. 2s.6d.
    9. British Library

THE COLONIAL INTELLIGENCER

    1. 1847-1854; 1859-1909 (checked through 1867)
    2. Published for the Society

3. or Aborigines' Friend; and Aborigines' Friend
4. Supersedes and superseded by THE ABORIGINES' FRIEND
6. British and Foreign Aborigines' Protection Society
7. Monthly
8. 2d.
9. British Library: missing IV (1851-1854)

THE COLONIAL MAGAZINE

1. 1840-1842
2. Fisher, Son, and Co.
3. and Commercial-Maritime Journal
4. Superseded by FISHER'S COLONIAL MAGAZINE
5. Robert Montgomery Martin, Esq.
7. Monthly
9. British Library

THE COLONIAL MAGAZINE AND EAST INDIA REVIEW

1. 1849-1851
2. John Mortimer
3. and Foreign Miscellany
4. Supersedes SIMMONDS'S COLONIAL MAGAZINE; superseded
     by THE COLONIAL AND ASIATIC REVIEW
5. William H.G. Kingston, Esq.
7. Monthly
9. British Library

THE COLONIST

1. 1848
2. Trelawney Wm. Saunders
5. William H.G. Kingston, Esq.
6. Society for the Promotion of Colonization
7. Monthly
8. 3d. or 21s. per 100
9. British Library

THE EMIGRANT'S GUIDE TO THE GOLD FIELDS

1. August, 1853
2. Piper Brothers and Co.
3. Containing, Among Other Information, the Fullest
     Details as to Their Past and Present Position,
     Their Future Prospects, Etc.
7. Monthly
9. British Library

THE EMIGRANT'S PENNY MAGAZINE

    1. 1850-1851
    2. T. Saunders (Plymouth: J.B. Rowe)
    7. Monthly
    8. 1d.
    9. British Library

THE ENGLISH MAIL

    1. 15 February 1866
    2. Robert Russell Baron
    3. for India, Australia, China, and the Colonies
    7. Monthly
    8. 1s.
    9. British Library

FISHER'S COLONIAL MAGAZINE

    1. 1842-1845
    2. Fisher, Son, and Co.
    3. and Commercial-Maritime Journal; and Journal of
        Trade, Commerce, and Banking
    4. Supersedes THE COLONIAL MAGAZINE
    7. Monthly
    9. British Library

THE FOREIGN AND COLONIAL QUARTERLY REVIEW

    1. 1843-1844
    2. Whittaker and Co.
    4. Superseded by THE NEW QUARTERLY REVIEW
    7. Quarterly
    9. British Library

THE FRIEND OF AFRICA

    1. 1841-1843
    2. John William Parker
    4. Superseded by THE FRIEND OF THE AFRICAN
    6. The Committee of the Society for the Extinction of
        the Slave Trade and the Civilization of Africa
    7. Bimonthly; monthly
    8. 2d./3d. stamped
    9. New York Public Library

THE FRIEND OF THE AFRICAN

    1. 1843-1846
    2. John W. Parker

4. Supersedes THE FRIEND OF AFRICA
7. Monthly
8. 3d./4d. stamped
9. British Library

THE JOURNAL OF CIVILIZATION

1. 1841
2. John Snow
3. Christian Missionary Civilization: Its Necessity,
    Progress, and Blessings (volume title)
6. Society for the Advancement of Civilization
7. Weekly
8. 3d.
9. British Library

JOURNAL OF THE EAST INDIA ASSOCIATION

1. 1867-1909 (checked 1867)
2. William Clowes and Sons
6. East India Association
7. Semi-annually
8. 3s.
9. British Library

THE JOURNAL OF THE ROYAL ASIATIC SOCIETY

1. 1834-1867
2. John W. Parker
3. of Great Britain and Ireland
6. Royal Asiatic Society of Great Britain and Ireland
7. Quarterly
9. British Library

THE NEW QUARTERLY REVIEW

1. 1844-1846
2. John W. Parker
3. or, Home, Foreign, and Colonial Journal
4. Supersedes THE FOREIGN AND COLONIAL QUARTERLY REVIEW
7. Quarterly
8. 6s.
9. British Library

OVER THE SEA

1. 1 January 1867
2. W. Macintosh
3. A Record of Emigrant and Colonial Life

7. Monthly
8. 1d.
9. British Library

SIDNEY'S EMIGRANT'S JOURNAL

1. 1848-1849; new series 1849-1850
2. W.S. Orr and Co.
3. and Traveller's Magazine
5. Samuel and John Sidney; new series Samuel Sidney
7. Weekly; new series monthly
8. 2d./3d. stamped; new series 6d.
9. British Library

SIMMONDS'S COLONIAL MAGAZINE

1. 1844-1848
2. Foreign and Colonial Office
3. and Foreign Miscellany
4. Superseded by THE COLONIAL MAGAZINE AND EAST INDIA
   REVIEW
5. P.L. Simmonds, Esq.
7. Monthly
9. British Library

THE UNITED SERVICE JOURNAL

1. 1829-1841 (checked from 1832)
2. Henry Colburn and Richard Bentley
3. and Naval and Military Magazine
4. Superseded by THE UNITED SERVICE MAGAZINE
7. Monthly
9. New York Public Library

THE UNITED SERVICE MAGAZINE

1. 1842-1843
2. Henry Colburn and Richard Bentley
3. and Naval and Military Journal
4. Supersedes THE UNITED SERVICE JOURNAL; superseded
   by COLBURN'S UNITED SERVICE MAGAZINE
7. Monthly
9. New York Public Library

SECTION II

Check-list of Articles on the Empire in
British Periodicals, 1832-1867

AINSWORTH'S MAGAZINE

1   Medwin, Capt. [Thomas]. "A Bengal Yarn," II (1842), 57-
     63 (officer life).

2   Leslie, Frank [Carter, Henry]. "Recollections of an
     Execution in China," III (1843), 130-33 (opium smuggler).

3   Ainsworth, W. Francis. "The 'Holy Island' of the Mediter-
     ranean," III (1843), 335-43 (Malta).

4   Ainsworth, W. Francis. "The Euphrates Expedition," V
     (1844), 222-25.

5   "PEREGRINE PULTENEY; OR, LIFE IN INDIA," V (1844), 364-68.

6   "Indian Guide-Book," V (1844), 373-74.

7   [Ainsworth, W. Francis]. "The Political Mission to the
     East," VI (1844), 183-87 (Euphrates expedition).

8   "THE SETTLERS IN CANADA," VI (1844), 374-76.

8a   "NEW SOUTH WALES," VI (1844), 413-16.

9   [Ainsworth, W. Francis]. "The Victims of Bokhara," VII
     (1845), 142-44 (see #11; Central Asia).

10   " 'The Dynasty of the Lions': the Panj-ab, Lahore, and
     Kashmir," VII (1845), 345-52.

11   [Ainsworth, W. Francis]. "The Victims of Diplomacy," VII
     (1845), 396-400 (see #9; Central Asia).

12   "The Cobourg Peninsula and Port Essington," IX (1846),
     249-50.

13   Ward, Mrs. [Harriet]. "A South African Pic-nic," X (1846),
     172-75.

13a Ainsworth, W. Francis, Esq. "The Expedition in Difficul-
     ties," XII (1847), 46-57 (Euphrates with notes on India).

14   [Ainsworth, W.H.]. "The Islands and Shores of the Pacif-
      ic," XII (1847), 149-56 (naval stations).

15   Ainsworth, W. Francis, Esq. "Progress of Australian Dis-
      covery," XII (1847), 343-48.

16   "Every-Day Life in the Wilds of North America," XIII
      (1848), 477-82 (Hudson's Bay Company territory).

17   "The Bermudas," XV (1849), 10-13.

18   "Van Diemen's Land," XV (1849), 535-36.

19   Powlett, Frederick, Esq. "Port Phillip," XVIII (1850),
      171-72.

20   Cornu, Madame [Albine Hortense]. "Wellington and the
      Mahrattas," XXII (1852), 524-26 (India).

21   "FOREST LIFE IN CEYLON," XXV (1854), 121-27.

22   Reeves, Arthur Robinson, Esq., A.B. "Physiology of an
      Australian Emigrant Ship," XXV (1854), 306-17.

ALL THE YEAR ROUND

23   "Bungaree, King of the Blacks," I (1859), 77-83 (Austral-
      ia).

24   "An Empire Saved," I (1859), 109-12 (India).

25   "European Mutiny in India," I (1859), 324-25.

26   "A Piece of Blood-Money," I (1859), 394-96 (Australian
      convict life).

27   "Economy in Sheepskin," II (1859-60), 132-35 (Australia).

28   "War Paint and Medicine Bags," II (1859-60), 421-25 (Brit-
      ish North America).

29   "Beyond Good Hope," III (1860), 7-11 (Natal).

30   "Taking Pirate Junks," III (1860), 178-80 (China).

31   "Chinese Ways of Warfare," III (1860), 205-06.

32   "How the World Smokes," III (1860), 247-51 (opium use).

33   "The Paper Walls of China," III (1860), 319-24 (behavior).

34   "The Coolie Trade in China," III (1860), 365.

35   "Chinese Fighting Men," III (1860), 502-04.

36   "Chinamen Afloat," IV (1860-61), 116-20.

37   "The Man for China," IV (1860-61), 221-23 (impact of war).

38   "Flaws in China," IV (1860-61), 414-19 (Taipings).

39   "The Englishman in Bengal," IV (1860-61), 468-70.

40   "Episcopacy in the Rough," IV (1860-61), 470-74 (British
      Columbia).

41   "The Jamaica Revivals," IV (1860-61), 521-24.

42   "Under the Golden Feet," V (1861), 102-07 (Burma).

43   "A Two-Year Old Colony," V (1861), 294-97 (Queensland).

44   "India and Cotton," V (1861), 375-79.

45   "A Fair on the Ganges," V (1861), 523-26.

46   "Footprints Here and There: Australian Milk and Water,"
      VI (1861-62), 13-17 (natives).

47   "Cotton Cultivation in Bengal," VI (1861-62), 91-92.

48   "New Zealand," VI (1861-62), 130-32.

49   "Nil Darpan," VI (1861-62), 158-64 (Bengal indigo).

50   "Cotton-Fields," VI (1861-62), 256-60 (India).

51   "Famine in India," VI (1861-62), 519-23.

52   "Aboard an Emigrant Ship," VII (1862), 111-15.

53   "From the Black Rocks, on Friday," VII (1862), 232-40
      (New Zealand).

54   "The Great Shoe Question," VII (1862), 381-84 (Young
      Bengal).

55   "PUNCH in India," VII (1862), 462-69.

56   "Up and down in the Great Sun Garden," VII (1862), 511-
      14 (Borneo).

57   "State and Prospects of Cotton," VIII (1862-63), 322-30
      (India).

58   "Housekeeping in India," VIII (1862-63), 491-97.

59   "Indian Servants," IX (1863), 416-20.

60   "The Story of Governor Wall," IX (1863), 443-44 (India).

61   "PUNCH in Australia," IX (1863), 610-16.

62   "Something to be Done in India," X (1863-64), 103-07
      (army life).

63   "A Maori Court-Martial," X (1863-64), 162-64 (New Zealand).

64   "Yesterday and To-Day in India," X (1863-64), 184-90.

65   "Competition Wallahs," X (1863-64), 203-05 (Indian civil
      service).

66   "Settled among the Maoris," X (1863-64), 309-12 (New
      Zealand).

67   "The Latest News of the BOUNTY," X (1863-64), 330-32
      (Norfolk Island).

68   "Military Mismanagement," X (1863-64), 349-52 (India).

69   "The Bengal Police," X (1863-64), 371-72.

70   "For Labrador, Sir?" X (1863-64), 379-81.

71   "Trifles from Ceylon," X (1863-64), 402-06 (see #79).

72   "China Ornaments," X (1863-64), 419-21 (Shanghai).

73   "England over the Water," X (1863-64), 461-63 (Australia).

74   [Blanchard, Sidney Laman]. "Indian Railways," X (1863-64),
      564-68; XI (1864), 31-34.

75   " 'Making Tea' in India," XI (1864), 56-60.

76   "Fighting in West Africa," XI (1864), 131-36.

77   "The Rupee to the Rescue," XI (1864), 174-79 (India).

78   "A Gold Digger's Notes," XI (1864), 181-86 (Australia).

79   "More Trifles from Ceylon," XI (1864), 198-202, 249-53,
      293-99, 400-02, 418-21 (see #71).

80   "Farmers in Muslin," XI (1864), 272-74 (India).

81   "Going to Law in Ceylon," XII (1864-65), 80-84.

82   "Backwoods Life in Canada," XII (1864-65), 190-92.

83   "Openings in Ceylon," XII (1864-65), 342-48.

84   "Something Like a Conjuror," XIII (1865), 57-60 (India).

85   "The Bundleman on the Plains," XIII (1865), 371-73
      (Australia).

86   "Up and down Canton," XIV (1865-66), 15-19.

87   "Our Colonies," XIV (1865-66), 150-53.

88   "Wild-Boar Hunting in India," XIV (1865-66), 330-32.

89   "Cholera in India," XIV (1865-66), 423-27.

90   "New China," XIV (1865-66), 471-74 (Australia).

91   "Under Fire," XV (1866), 125-27 (Indian mutiny).

92   "Black is Not QUITE White," XV (1866), 173-77 (Jamaica).

93   "Horse-Racing in India," XV (1866), 247-51.

94   "The Salmon Harvest," XV (1866), 270-73 (British Colum-
      bia).

95   "Life Sown Broadcast," XV (1866), 355-56 (Australian
      fauna with notes on natives).

96   "With Opium to Hong-Kong," XV (1866), 537-40.

97   "Cuagnawagha," XV (1866), 543-48 (Canadian native vil-
      lage).

98   "Horses for Indian Service," XVI (1866), 282-83.

99   "On the Wallaby," XVII (1866-67), 157-59 (Australian
      digger).

100   "With Jean Baptiste," XVIII (1867), 232-37 (Canadian
      HABITANTS).

THE ANTHROPOLOGICAL REVIEW

101   Fraser, A.A., Esq., F.A.S.L. "Seeman on the Inhabitants
      of the Fiji Islands," I (1863), 355-65.

102   Reddie, James, Esq., F.A.S.L. "Slavery," II (1864), 280-
      93.

103   "Mythological Legendary Tales of South Africa and of
      the Esquimaux in Greenland," III (1865), 138-45.

104   Wyman, Jeffries, M.D. "Observations on the Skeleton of
      a Hottentot," III (1865), 330-35 (South Africa).

105   "Explorations in South West Africa," IV (1866), 243-52.

106   "The Sect of Maharajas," IV (1866), 252-59 (India).

107   "The Khonds of Orissa," IV (1866), 360-66 (India).

108   D., C.W. "Flower and Murie on the Dissection of a Bush-
      woman," V (1867), 319-24 (South Africa).

THE ARGOSY

109   An Australian Settler. "My Chinese Neighbour," II
      (1866), 161-68.

110   An Old Indian. "Famine Stricken," II (1866), 469-77
      (India).

BELGRAVIA

111   Blanchard, Sidney L. "Hill Scandals," I (1866-67), 166-
      74 (Indian colonial life).

BENTLEY'S MISCELLANY

112   Yuh Fung, Chin-San, and Lew-Yew-Tsae. "China - the Real
       State of the Case," VII (1840), 479-83 (opium trade).

113   Addison, H.R. "Hours in Hindostan," X (1841), 121-25,
       242-50; XIII (1843), 36-40, 101-04, 263-67, 382-83,
       459-75.

114   "Warren Hastings," X (1841), 627-30 (India).

115   Kennedy, R. Hartley, M.D. "The Suttee: the Narrative of
       an Eye-Witness," XIII (1843), 241-56 (India).

116   One of the Female Prisoners. "The English Captives at
       Cabul: a Personal Narrative," XIV (1843), 1-10, 140-
       62; XV (1844), 19-30, 187-97.

117   Ross, John Wilson. "The Runaway Negro: a Narrative of
       the Island of St. Vincent," XV (1844), 58-67.

118   "Indian Luxuries," XV (1844), 469-70.

119   Addison, H.R. "The Native Sentinel," XV (1844), 621-22
       (India).

120   "The Marquess Wellesley, K.G.," XIX (1846), 170-71
       (India).

121   Taylor, Dr. W.C. "The Seat of War: the Sikhs and the
       Punjab," XIX (1846), 358-69.

122   Costello, Louisa Stuart. "Lahore," XIX (1846), 449-54.

123   Kean, C. "Adventures in New Zealand in 1845," XX (1846),
       314-20.

124   Schomburgh, Sir Robert. "Steam-Boat Voyage to Barbados,"
       XXII (1847), 30-41.

125   Schomburgh, Sir Robert. "Pictures of Barbados," XXII
       (1847), 286-92.

126   B., J. "Sketch of Personal Adventures during a Trip
       Overland from Sydney to Port Phillip," XXII (1847),
       343-53.

127   Duncan, John. "Some Account of the Last Expedition to
       the Niger," XXII (1847), 412-16, 469-80.

128   Schomburgh, Sir Robert. "Rambles in Search of the
       Picturesque in Barbados," XXII (1847), 443-49.

129   Taylor, W.C., LL.D. "Lord Hardinge and the Recent Victo-
       ries in India," XXIII (1848), 1-8 (Punjab).

130 McQuhae, Peter, Captain of Her Majesty's Ship DAEDALUS.
"Visit to His Highness Rajah Brooke, at Sarawak,"
XXIII (1848), 65-72.

131 "China and the Chinese," XXIV (1848), 287-94.

132 Ward, Mrs. [Harriet]. "The Emigrant Party; or, Our Last
Treck [sic] in Southern Africa," XXIV (1848), 472-76.

133 St. John, James Augustus. "Position of Sir James Brooke
in the Indian Archipelago," XXV (1849), 71-83.

134 Ward, Mrs. [Harriet]. "The Happy Valley; or, the Emigrant's Home," XXV (1849), 289-97 (South Africa).

135 St. John, James Augustus. "Sir James Brooke and the
Pirates," XXV (1849), 347-57 (Borneo).

136 Huntley, Capt. Sir H.V., R.N. "A Visit to Royalty in
the Gambia," XXV (1849), 589-95.

137 "Recollections of Canada: the Scenery of the Ottawa,"
XXVI (1849), 489-97.

138 Huyghue, S.D. "A Winter's Journey," XXVI (1849), 630-37
(British North American surveyor).

139 Huyghue, S.D. "My First Winter in the Woods of Canada,"
XXVII (1850), 152-60.

140 St. John, James Augustus. "Defence of Sir James Brooke's
Policy," XXVII (1850), 286-97 (Borneo).

141 Wheatley, G.W. "Some Account of the Late Lieut. Waghorn,
R.N., the Originator of the Overland Route," XXVII
(1850), 349-57 (India).

142 An Oriental Traveller. "Women in the East," XXVII (1850),
379-84 (India).

143 Crowquill, Alfred. "Our Pen and Ink Gallery: Major Herbert Edwardes," XXVII (1850), 400-03 (Punjab).

144 Huyghue, S.D. "Forest Incidents: Recollections of Canada," XXVII (1850), 472-77.

145 "A Dignity Ball in the Seychelles," XXVIII (1850), 55-
63.

146 Cole, John Jones. "A Sketch of the Siege of Mooltan,"
XXVIII (1850), *449-*60 (Punjab).

147 "The Pilgrim in India," XXVIII (1850), 520-22.

148 "Ceylon and the Singhalese," XXIX (1851), 224-32.

149   "The Valley of Bunnoo and the Siege of Mooltan," XXIX
       (1851), 233-47 (Punjab).

150   "Lord Gough's Late Victories in India," XXIX (1851),
       335-36 (Punjab).

151   "My Volunteer Troop in Kafirland," XXIX (1851), 355-60
       (South Africa).

152   "The Kaffirs, and Kaffir Wars," XXIX (1851), 408-15
       (South Africa).

153   "Latest Account of New Zealand," XXIX (1851), 443-45.

154   "Recollections of a Settler at the Cape of Good Hope,"
       XXIX (1851), 549-60.

155   "The 'Phenomenon' of the Cape of Good Hope," XXIX (1851),
       607-16.

156   "Historical Sketches of the Cape of Good Hope," XXX
       (1851), 184-94.

157   Cole, Alfred W. "The Cape and the Kafirs; or, Notes of
       Five Years' Residence in South Africa," XXX (1851),
       241-54, 378-410, 457-74, 587-602; XXXI (1852), 33-51.

158   "Calcutta," XXX (1851), 361-68.

159   "My First Visit 'to the Rock'," XXX (1851), 411-18
       (Gibraltar).

160   "Our Indian Empire under Lord Auckland and Lord Ellen-
       borough," XXX (1851), 628-39.

161   "Sir Charles Napier and the Unhappy Valley," XXXI
       (1852), 82-88 (Sind).

162   "Society in India," XXXI (1852), 242-49.

163   "Mr. Squier and Nicaragua," XXXI (1852), 442-52.

164   "Modern India," XXXI (1852), 465-73.

165   "Jack Sepoy," XXXII (1852), 77-88 (India).

166   "Canadian Sketches," XXXII (1852), 300-09, 381-89.

167   "Writers and Cadets," XXXII (1852), 328-36 (India).

168   "Lord Hardinge," XXXII (1852), 452-60 (Punjab).

169   "How We Talked about the Burmese War," XXXII (1852),
       461-70.

170   A Native. "Leaves from the Sketch-Book of an Australian
       Squatter," XXXIII (1853), 403-14.

171   "Sir Walter Gilbert and the Indian Army," XXXIII (1853), 627-32.

172   "India; and Its Administration," XXXIV (1853), 157-64.

173   Reach, Angus B. "Chaka - King of the Zulus," XXXIV (1853), 292-99 (South Africa).

174   Mundy, G.C. "My First Adventure in Australia: a Tale of Twenty Years Ago," XXXIV (1853), 489-505, 607-20.

175   [Mackenzie, Capt. Colin]. "Recollections of a Journey to Jellalabad," XXXVI (1854), 379-90.

176   "An Asiatic Campaign," XXXVI (1855), 423-40 (Central Asia).

177   "The Annexation of Nagpore," XXXVIII (1855), 31-35.

178   "Central America," XXXIX (1856), 260-69.

179   "Expedition to the Niger," XL (1856), 129-40.

180   "The Euphrates Valley Railway and Indo-European Telegraph," XL (1856), 262-76.

181   "The Persian War," XLI (1857), 152-61.

182   Ravenstein, E.G., Corresp. F.G.S. Frankfort. "The Russians on the Amur," XLI (1857), 551-63 (China).

183   "China and the Chinese," XLII (1857), 48-58.

184   "Our Indian Empire," XLII (1857), 258-65.

185   "The English in India," XLII (1857), 331-46.

186   F., F. "Seven Years of an Indian Officer's Life," XLII (1857), 379-86, 530-34, 581-87.

187   "The East India Company," XLII (1857), 415-24.

188   F., F. "The Grand Mosque and Imperial Palace of Delhi," XLII (1857), 546-50.

189   F., F. "An Old Indian Officer on the Causes of the Indian Revolt," XLII (1857), 600-02.

190   "The Calcutta Petition," XLII (1857), 621-30 (Indian mutiny).

191   B., J.W. "The Bheel Tribe of Candeish," XLIII (1858), 29-31 (India).

192   "The Causes of the Indian Mutiny," XLIII (1853), 60-68.

193   Tremenheere, Henry, Esq. "How is India to be Governed?" XLIII (1858), 111-23.

194 "Oude and the Defence of Lucknow," XLIII (1858), 414-24.

195 A Madras Officer. "Indian Reminiscences," XLIII (1858), 475-80 (Indian mutiny).

196 "From Delhi to Cawnpore," XLIII (1858), 642-50.

197 Stapley, Martin. "A Few Words about South Australia," XLIV (1858), 89-94.

198 M., V.D. "Up among the Pandies; or, Personal Adventures and Experiences of a Ferringhee, Being Sketches in India, Taken on the Spot," XLIV (1858), 448-54; XLV (1859), 33-39, 204-10, 281-88, 421-27, 530-39, 611-19.

199 "Journal of a Week's Shooting in the Eastern Province of Ceylon, in January 1857," XLIV (1858), 551-63.

200 "From Sydney to England VIA Panama," XLV (1859), 80-94.

201 "Notes on the Ionian Islands - Corfu," XLV (1859), 493-503.

202 "Lord Elgin's Mission," XLVII (1860), 136-43 (China).

203 "Cephalonia: Notes on the Ionian Islands," XLVII (1860), 173-78.

204 "The French Embassy in China," XLVII (1860), 483-91.

205 "Progress of New Zealand," XLVIII (1860), 360-61.

206 "The Indigo Planter in Bengal," L (1861), 171-77.

207 "History of the First Battalion of Royal Marines in China, from 1857 to 1859," LI (1862), 398-405.

208 DuCane, Capt. E.F., R.E. "The Convict System in the Colonies," LI (1862), 513-27.

209 Andrews, Alexander. "The Diet and Dainties of Australian Aborigines," LI (1862), 544-49.

210 "A Winter Voyage up the St. Lawrence," LII (1862), 282-89.

211 "Colonel Goddard's March across India," LII (1862), 378-85, 516-23 (Indian mutiny).

212 S., F. "A Trip from Belgaum to the Falls of Gokah," LIII (1863), 206-07 (India).

213 "A Reminiscence of Ceylon: the Lower Badulla Road," LIII (1863), 542-50.

214 "Canada in 1865: Physical, Political, and Social," LVIII (1865), 111-12.

215 C., L.H. "A Visit to the Ruins of Beejapore," LX (1866), 381-87 (India).

216 Beaver, Barrington. "A Rough Tramp over the Rocky Mountains and Canoe Voyage down the Fraser to Cariboo," LX (1866), 476-84, 622-31 (British Columbia).

217 G., T.W. "An Up-Country Fair in Behar, India," LX (1866), 514-21.

218 Knighton, William, Esq. "The Isthmus of Suez Canal," LXII (1867), 275-80.

219 "Dufton's ABYSSINIA," LXII (1867), 487-98 (notes on East Africa and India).

220 "An Indian Railway," LXII (1867), 499-506.

BENTLEY'S QUARTERLY REVIEW

221 [Mozley, J.B.]. "Indian Conversations," I (1859), 183-226.

BLACKWOOD'S EDINBURGH MAGAZINE

222 M'Queen, James, Esq. "Geography of Africa - QUARTERLY REVIEW," XXXI (1832), 201-16 (notes on Niger River).

223 [Alison, Archibald]. "The West India Question," XXXI (1832), 412-23.

224 [Alison, Archibald]. "The Great West India Meeting," XXXI (1832), 807-19.

225 [DeQuincey, Thomas]. "M'Gregor's British America," XXXI (1832), 907-27.

226 [Scott, Michael]. "Plan for the Gradual Abolition of Negro Slavery," XXXII (1832), 87-90 (West Indies).

227 [Wilson, John]. "Upper Canada. By a Backwoodsman," XXXII (1832), 238-62.

228 An Inhabitant of the Island. "A Short Statement of the Causes That Have Produced the Late Disturbances in the Colony of Mauritius," XXIII (1833), 199-205.

229 [Alison, Archibald]. "The East India Question," XXXIII (1833), 776-803.

230 Macqueen, James. "British Tropical Colonies," XXXIV (1834), 231-57, 611-40 (West Indies).

231 [Mallalieu, Alfred]. "The Canada Question," XXXVII (1835), 909-27.

231a   [Wilson, John]. "The Hindu Drama," XXXIV (1834), 715-
        38; XXXV (1835), 122-50 (notes on Indian history).

231b   [Alison, Archibald]. "The First Session of the Reformed
        Parliament - West Indies - East Indies - Domestic
        and Foreign Policy of Ministers," XXXIV (1834), 776-
        804 (notes on India and West Indies).

232   [Bell, James Stanislaus]. "India," XXXVIII (1835), 803-
        08.

232a   [Alison, Archibald]. "What Is Our External Policy and
        Condition?" XXXIX (1836), 780-92 (notes on the
        empire).

232b   [Hamilton, Thomas]. "Despatches of the Duke of
        Wellington," XLI (1837), 1-20, 200-17, 445-62, 706-14
        (India).

233   [Croly, George]. "Sierra Leone," XLI (1837), 693-700.

234   [Forsyth, William]. "The British Colonization of New
        Zealand," XLII (1837), 784-95.

235   [Croly, George]. "A Sketch of the Canadas," XLIII
        (1838), 214-27.

236   [Mallalieu, Alfred]. "Ministerial Policy in the Cana-
        das," XLIII (1838), 228-47.

237   [Wylie, Macleod]. "Canada and Ireland," XLIII (1838),
        385-95.

238   [Alison, Archibald]. "The Reciprocity and Colonial
        Systems," XLIV (1838), 317-34 (trade).

239   "Colonial Misgovernment," XLIV (1838), 624-37.

240   [Croly, George and Wilson, John]. "New South Wales,"
        XLIV (1838), 690-716.

241   [Alison, Archibald]. "Affairs in the East," XLIV (1838),
        769-78 (India).

242   [Holme, Frederick]. "Persia, Afghanistan, and India,"
        XLV (1839), 93-105.

243   [Croly, George]. "Mitchell's Second and Third Expedi-
        tions," XLV (1839), 113-29 (Australia).

244   [Alison, Archibald]. "Colonial Government and the
        Jamaica Question," XLVI (1839), 75-90.

245   [Wilkes, John]. "Turkey, Egypt, and the Affairs of the
        East," XLVI (1839), 100-15.

246 [Alison, Archibald]. "Colonial Neglect and Foreign Propitiation," XLVI (1839), 752-66.

247 [Alison, Archibald]. "The Afghanistan Expedition," XLVII (1840), 241-52.

248 [Mallalieu, Alfred]. "War with China, and the Opium Question," XLVII (1840), 368-84.

249 [Holme, Frederick]. "Khiva, Central Asia, and Cabul," XLVII (1840), 512-26.

250 [DeQuincey, Thomas]. "The Opium and the China Question," XLVII (1840), 717-38.

251 [DeQuincey, Thomas]. "Postscript on the China and the Opium Question," XLVII (1840), 847-53.

252 [Smith, William Henry]. "The Boundary Question," XLVIII (1840), 331-37 (British North America).

252a [DeQuincey, Thomas]. "Foreign Politics," XLVIII (1840), 546-62 (notes on Central Asia).

253 [Croly, George]. "Africa," XLIX (1841), 109-13 (West).

254 [Holme, Frederick]. "The Secret Societies of Asia - the Assassins and the Thugs," XLIX (1841), 229-44 (India).

255 [DeQuincey, Thomas]. "The Dourraunee Empire," XLIX (1841), 281-302 (Afghanistan).

256 [Croly, George]. "Warren Hastings," XLIX (1841), 423-37, 638-56 (India).

257 [Holme, Frederick]. "Results of Our Affghan Conquests," L (1841), 161-74.

258 [Croly, George]. "The Canadas," L (1841), 642-57.

259 [DeQuincey, Thomas]. "Canton Expedition and Convention," L (1841), 677-88.

260 [Phillimore, J.G.]. "Lewis ON THE GOVERNMENT OF DEPENDENCIES," LI (1842), 213-33.

261 [Croly, George]. "Five Years in India," LI (1842), 474-86.

262 [Croly, George]. "Cabul and Affghanistan," LI (1842), 676-90.

263 [Holme, Frederick]. "Affghanistan and India," LII (1842), 100-12.

264 Young, Gilbert. "Why Not Colonize Cabul," LII (1842), 155-58.

265   [Macpherson, William]. "Human Sacrifices in India,"
         LII (1842), 177-83.

266   [Phillimore, J.G.]. "Merivale on Colonies and Coloniza-
         tion," LII (1842), 206-23.

266a   [Croly, George]. "Marquis Wellesley," LII (1842), 606-
         13 (see #282a; notes on India).

267   [McNeill, John]. "Eyre's Cabul," LIII (1843), 239-65.

268   [Holme, Frederick]. "The Evacuation of Affghanistan,"
         LIII (1843), 266-79.

269   [Holme, Frederick]. "Occupation of Aden," LIII (1843),
         484-95.

269a   [Neaves, Charles]. "Lord Ellenborough and the Whigs,"
         LIII (1843), 539-50 (Afghanistan and India).

270   [Mallalieu, Alfred]. "Commercial Policy - Ships,
         Colonies, and Commerce," LIV (1843), 406-14, 637-49.

271   [DeQuincey, Thomas]. "Ceylon," LIV (1843), 622-36.

272   [Walton, William]. "On the Best Means of Establishing
         a Commercial Intercourse between the Atlantic and
         Pacific Oceans," LIV (1843), 658-71 (Central America).

273   Williams, John [Phillips, Samuel]. "News from an
         Exiled Contributor," LV (1844), 184-96 (Port Phillip).

274   [Alison, Archibald]. "Free Trade and Protection," LV
         (1844), 259-68, 385-400 (notes on the empire).

275   [Croly, George]. "Ethiopia," LV (1844), 269-91 (notes
         on Aden).

276   [Holme, Frederick]. "Colonel Davidson's Travels in
         India," LV (1844), 321-33.

277   [Alison, Archibald]. "Imprisonment and Transportation,"
         LV (1844), 533-45.

278   [Holme, Frederick]. "Indian Affairs - Gwalior," LV
         (1844), 579-92.

279   Macqueen, James. "Africa - Slave Trade - Tropical
         Colonies," LV (1844), 731-48 (notes on East Africa,
         Niger River, and trade).

280   [DeQuincey, Thomas]. "Affghanistan," LVI (1844), 133-
         52.

281   [Croly, George]. "The Overland Passage," LVII (1845),
         204-18 (sea and land passage from India to the
         Mediterranean).

282   [Phillips, Samuel]. "Mr. Brooke of Borneo," LIX (1846), 356-66.

282a   [Croly, George]. "The Marquess Wellesley," LIX (1846), 385-407 (see #266a; notes on India).

283   [Gordon, J.T.]. "The Campaign of the Sutlej," LIX (1846), 625-44 (Punjab).

284   [Hardman, Frederick]. "Hochelaga," LX (1846), 464-76 (Canada).

285   [Hardman, Frederick]. "Mohan Lal in Afghanistan," LX (1846), 539-54.

286   [Burge, William]. "Lord Metcalfe's Government of Jamaica," LX (1846), 662-72.

287   [Croly, George]. "North America, Siberia, and Russia," LXI (1847), 653-72.

288   [Croly, George]. "The Navigation of the Antipodes," LXII (1847), 515-33.

289   [Hardman, Frederick]. "Research and Adventure in Australia," LXII (1847), 602-14.

290   [Aytoun, W.E.]. "Our West Indian Colonies," LXIII (1848), 219-38.

291   [Hardman, Frederick]. "Hudson's Bay," LXIII (1848), 369-82.

292   [Croly, George]. "Colonisation," LXIV (1848), 66-76.

293   [Alison, Archibald]. "The Navigation Laws," LXIV (1848), 114-28.

294   [Hardman, Frederick]. "Kaffirland," LXIV (1848), 158-70 (South Africa).

295   [Smith, William Henry]. "Colonisation - Mr. Wakefield's Theory," LXV (1849), 509-28.

296   [Hogan, J.S.]. "Civil Revolution in the Canadas," LXV (1849), 727-41 (see #298 and #300).

297   [Alison, Archibald]. "The Crowning of the Column, and Crushing of the Pedestal," "- postscript on Canada," LXVI (1849), 108-31, 131-32 (colonial policy).

298   [Hogan, J.S.]. "Civil Revolution in the Canadas - a Remedy," LXVI (1849), 471-85 (see #296 and #300).

299   [Alison, Archibald]. "The Transportation Question," LXVI (1849), 519-38.

299a [Alison, Archibald]. "Free Trade at its Zenith," LXVI (1849), 756-78 (notes on Canada and West Indies).

300   [Hogan, J.S.]. "Civil Revolution in the Canadas," LXVII (1850), 249-68 (see #296 and #298).

301   [Alison, Archibald]. "The Ministerial Measures," LXVII (1850), 377-89 (colonial government).

302   [Burton, J.H.]. "The New Zealanders," LXX (1851), 414-30.

303   [Makgill, George]. "Johnston's NOTES ON NORTH AMERICA," LXX (1851), 699-718.

304   [Hardman, Frederick]. "Sketches from the Cape," LXXI (1852), 289-98 (Cape Colony).

305   [Hardman, Frederick]. "Forest Life in Canada West," LXXI (1852), 355-65.

306   [Johnston, J.F.W.]. "Gold: Its Natural and Civil History," LXXI (1852), 517-41.

307   [Hardman, Frederick]. "Five Years in the West Indies," LXXI (1852), 668-84.

308   [Hardman, Frederick]. "Nepaul," LXXII (1852), 86-98.

309   [Patterson, R.H.]. "The Celestials at Home and Abroad," LXXII (1852), 98-113 (Chinese).

310   [Alison, Archibald]. "Gold - Emigration - Foreign Dependencies - Taxation," LXXII (1852), 203-17.

311   [Hardman, Frederick]. "Residence and Rambles in Australia," LXXII (1852), 300-15.

312   [Johnston, J.F.W.]. "The Romance of Mairwara: a Tale of Indian Progress," LXXIII (1853), 207-15.

313   [Warren, Samuel]. "The Paradise in the Pacific," LXXIII (1853), 647-70 (Pitcairn Island).

314   [Hardman, Frederick]. "Six Months with the Malays," LXXIII (1853), 702-17 (East Indies).

315   [Alison, Archibald]. "Gold and Emigration: in Their Effects, Social and Political," LXXIV (1853), 117-28.

316   [Hardman, Frederick]. "The Insurrection in China," LXXIV (1853), 203-19.

317   [Hardman, Frederick]. "A Painter in Persia," LXXV (1854), 1-18 (note on Russian influence).

318 [Patterson, R.H.]. "The Past and Future of China," LXXV (1854), 54-74.

319 [Oliphant, Laurence]. "A Sporting Settler in Ceylon," LXXV (1854), 226-42.

320 [Patterson, R.H.]. "The National Life of China," LXXV (1854), 593-608.

321 [Keene, H.G.]. "Young Bengal," LXXV (1854), 648-57.

322 [Johnson, G.B.]. "The Growth and Prospects of British America," LXXVI (1854), 1-17.

323 [Robertson, T.C.]. "The Gangetic Provinces of British India," LXXVI (1854), 183-205.

324 [Johnson, G.B.]. "The Coming Fortunes of Our Colonies in the Pacific," LXXVI (1854), 268-87.

324a [Smith, William Henry]. "THE LIFE OF LORD METCALFE," LXXVII (1855), 202-20 (Canada, India, and Jamaica).

325 [Oliphant, Laurence]. "Notes on Canada and the North-west States of America," LXXVII (1855), 438-50, 569-82, 701-14; LXXVIII (1855), 39-54, 165-80, 322-38.

326 [Baynes, C.R.]. "The Indian Civil Service," LXXIX (1856), 456-70.

327 [Yule, Henry]. "Letters from the Banks of the Irawadee," LXXIX (1856), 536-61 (Burma).

328 [Patterson, R.H.]. "India under Lord Dalhousie," LXXX (1856), 233-56.

329 [Oliphant, Laurence]. "African Travel," LXXX (1856), 489-502 (Red Sea region with notes on Aden).

330 [Patterson, R.H.]. "Our Indian Empire," LXXX (1856), 636-59.

331 [Patterson, R.H.]. "The War in Asia," LXXXI (1857), 135-52 (Persia).

332 [Wilson, Andrew]. "Life in Central Asia," LXXXI (1857), 612-25.

333 [Aytoun, W.E.]. "American Explorations - China and Japan," LXXXI (1857), 702-18.

334 [Hamley, Charles]. "Life of Sir Charles J. Napier," LXXXII (1847), 94-110, 241-64 (notes on Sind).

335 [Aytoun, W.E.]. "Representation of the Colonies," LXXXII (1857), 110-28 (British North America).

336   [Trevor, George]. "The Bengal Mutiny," LXXXII (1857),
      372-92.

337   [Patterson, R.H.]. "The Syrian Route to the East,"
      LXXXII (1857), 506-18 (Egyptian route and alternates).

338   [Oliphant, Laurence]. "Notes on the Isthmus of Panama,"
      LXXXII (1857), 541-52.

339   [Brownlow, Francis]. "A Few Words about the Khyber,"
      LXXXII (1857), 605-15 (India).

340   [Trevor, George]. "The Company's Raj," LXXXII (1857),
      615-42 (India).

341   [Hamley, Charles]. "Our Indian Empire," LXXXII (1857),
      643-64.

342   [Patterson, R.H.]. "The Religions of India," LXXXII
      (1857), 743-67.

343   [Cave-Browne, John]. "The Poorbeah Mutiny - the Punjab,"
      LXXXIII (1858), 94-101, 239-45, 589-603, 641-66;
      LXXXIV (1858), 24-42.

344   [Brougham, James Peter]. "The First Bengal European
      Fusiliers," LXXXIII (1858), 121-37, 719-33; LXXXIV
      (1858), 73-85.

344a [Burton, Richard F.]. "Zanzibar; and Two Months in East
      Africa," LXXXIII (1858), 200-24, 276-90, 572-89
      (notes on natives).

345   [Kaye, J.W.]. "A Familiar Epistle from Mr. John Company
      to Mr. John Bull," LXXXIII (1858), 245-58 (see #347,
      #348, and #351; India).

346   [Burton, J.H.]. "Our Convicts - Past and Present,"
      LXXXIII (1858), 291-310.

346a [Wilson,Andrew]. "Stories from Ancient Sind," LXXXIII
      (1858), 311-24 (history).

347   [Kaye, J.W.]. "A Few More Words from Mr. John Company
      to Mr. John Bull," LXXXIII (1858), 370-84 (see #345,
      #348, and #351; India).

347a [Oliphant, Margaret]. "The Missionary Explorer,"
      LXXXIII (1858), 385-401 (notes on Southeast Africa
      cotton).

348   [Kaye, J.W.]. "Mr. John Company to Mr. John Bull on the
      Rival India Bills," LXXXIII (1858), 484-97 (see #345,
      #347, and #351; India).

349 [Trevor, George]. "Oude," LXXXIII (1858), 622-40.

350 [Patterson, R.H.]. "The Defeat of the Factions: the Whigs VERSUS Our Indian Empire," LXXXIII (1858), 756-76.

351 [Kaye, J.W.]. "John Company's Farewell to John Bull," LXXXIV (1858), 338-51 (see #345, #347, and #348; India).

352 [Alison, Archibald, Jr.]. "Lord Clyde's Campaign in India," LXXXIV (1858), 480-514.

353 [Patterson, R.H.]. "Lord Canning's Reply to the Ellenborough Dispatch," LXXXIV (1858), 625-34 (India).

354 [Robertson, T.C.]. "The Indian Mutiny and the Land-Settlement," LXXXIV (1858), 701-08.

355 [Hamley, Charles]. "Burmah and the Burmese," LXXXV (1859), 31-48.

356 [Kaye, J.W.]. "The Royal Proclamation to India," LXXXV (1859), 113-26.

357 [Patterson, R.H.]. "The Castes and Creeds of India," LXXXV (1859), 308-34.

358 [White, James]. "Christianity in India," LXXXV (1859), 462-80.

358a Speke, J.H. "Captain J.H. Speke's Discovery of the Victoria Nyanza Lake, the Supposed Source of the Nile," LXXXVI (1859), 391-419 (notes on natives).

359 [Osborn, Sherard]. "On Allied Operations in China," LXXXVI (1859), 627-32.

360 [Kaye, J.W.]. "The Future of India and Her Army," LXXXVI (1859), 633-46.

361 [Osborn, Sherard]. "The Fight on the Peiho," LXXXVI (1859), 647-67 (China).

362 [Hamley, Wymond]. "A Visit to the Columbia River, and a Cruise round Vancouver's Island," LXXXVII (1860), 215-25.

363 [White, James]. "Lord Elgin's Mission to China and Japan," LXXXVII (1860), 255-77.

364 [Osborn, Sherard]. "Our Position with China," LXXXVII (1860), 430-40.

365 [Kaye, J.W.]. "What We Have Done for the Princes of India," LXXXVII (1860), 497-510.

366   [Osborn, Sherard]. "War and Progress in China," LXXXVII
       (1860), 525-42.

366a   Speke, J.H. "Captain Speke's Adventures in Somali
       Land," LXXXVII (1860), 561-80, 674-93; LXXXVIII
       (1860), 22-36 (notes on Aden).

367   [Ballard, J.A.]. "The Pursuit of Tantia Topee,"
       LXXXVIII (1860), 172-94 (India).

368   [Kaye, J.W.]. "The Transition-State of Our Indian
       Empire," LXXXVIII (1860), 241-52.

369   [Trevor, George]. "The Administration of India,"
       LXXXVIII (1860), 542-64.

370   [Ballard, J.A.]. "Our Only Danger in India," LXXXVIII
       (1860), 688-97.

371   [Ballard, J.A.]. "English Embassies to China," LXXXIX
       (1861), 42-64.

372   [Kaye, J.W.]. "The Indian Civil Service - Its Rise and
       Fall," LXXXIX (1861), 115-30, 261-76.

373   [Greathed, W.W.H.]. "The China War of 1860," LXXXIX
       (1861), 373-84.

374   [Kaye, J.W.]. "The Punjab in 1857," LXXXIX (1861), 501-
       16.

375   [Kaye, J.W.]. "The Demise of the Indian Army," XC
       (1861), 100-14.

376   [Ballard, J.A.]. "The Persian War of 1856-57," XC
       (1861), 343-63.

377   [Bourke, Robert]. "Canada - Our Frozen Frontier," XCI
       (1862), 102-17.

378   [Gleig, G.R.]. "The Defence of Canada," XCI (1862),
       228-58.

379   [Wilson, Andrew]. "Six Weeks in a Tower," XCI (1862),
       715-37 (China).

380   [Keene, H.G.]. "The Land Revenue of India," XCII (1862),
       598-606.

381   [Patterson, R.H.]. "British North America," XCII (1862),
       696-713.

382   [Osborn, Sherard]. "Progress in China," XCIII (1863),
       44-60, 133-48.

383   [Patterson, R.H.]. "Indian Prosperity," XCIV (1863),
       198-216.

384   [Patterson, R.H.]. "Gold and Social Politics," XCIV
        (1863), 499-520.

384a   [Burton, J.H.]. "Captain Speke's JOURNAL," XCV (1864),
        1-24 (East Africa with notes on natives).

385   [Clerk, Claude]. "Herat and Afghanistan," XCV (1864),
        462-74.

386   Bono-Johnny [Fraser, Alexander Charles]. "A Groan over
        Corfu," XCV (1864), 583-96.

387   [Patterson, R.H.]. "The Great Indian Question," XCV
        (1864), 597-614.

388   [Patterson, R.H.]. "Our Trade," XCVI (1864), 492-513
        (notes on the empire).

388a   [Oliphant, Laurence]. "Nile Basins and Nile Explorers,"
        XCVII (1865), 100-17 (notes on natives).

389   [Patterson, R.H.]. "The Rate of Interest," XCVII (1865),
        589-609, 706-21; XCVIII (1866), 73-90 (effect on
        India).

390   [Chesney, C.C.]. "Thirty Years' Policy in New Zealand,"
        XCVII (1865), 739-53.

391   [Mackay, Charles]. "The Negro and Negrophilists," XCIX
        (1866), 581-97 (notes on Jamaica).

392   [Mackay, Charles]. "British America," C (1866), 156-69.

393   Cheadle, W.B. "The Great Woods in Winter," C (1866),
        360-66 (Canada).

394   [Gleig, G.R.]. "The Legacy of the Late Government," C
        (1866), 393-408 (notes on India).

395   [Wilson, Andrew]. "Celestial Rule and Rebellion," C
        (1866), 604-22 (China).

396   [Wilson, Andrew]. "Foreign Interference with the Tai-
        pings," C (1866), 683-97 (China).

397   [Gleig, G.R.]. "The Army," CI (1867), 133-47, 261-80
        (colonial defense).

398   [Wilson, Andrew]. "Colonel Gordon's Chinese Force," CI
        (1867), 165-91.

399   [Chesney, George T.]. "Sir Charles Wood's Administra-
        tion of Indian Affairs," CII (1867), 686-702.

THE BRITISH AND FOREIGN REVIEW

400   [McNeill, John and Urquhart, David]. "Russia, Persia, and India: THE DESIGNS OF RUSSIA," I (1835), 253-98.

401   [Fraser, James Baillie]. "TRAVELS IN BOKHARA," I (1835), 459-91 (Central Asia).

402   "Hindostan," II (1836), 186-209.

403   [Fraser, J.B.]. "Persia," II (1836), 425-63; III (1836), 335-61.

404   [Chapman, H.S.]. "Duties on Timber: the Colonies," II (1836), 623-53 (Canadas).

405   "Colony of the Cape of Good Hope," IV (1837), 341-67.

406   [Reeve, Henry]. "Penal Colonies: Australia," V (1837), 89-133.

407   "Government of India: DESPATCHES OF THE MARQUESS WELLESLEY," VI (1837), 160-209.

408   [Chesney, F.R.]. "Steam Navigation on the Euphrates: Colonel Chesney's Expedition," VI (1837), 235-68.

409   [Welford, R.G.]. "British Colonization," VI (1837), 472-505.

410   [Young, G.A.]. "Lower Canada," VII (1838), 193-224.

411   [Chorley, H.F.]. "Mrs. Jameson's WINTER STUDIES AND SUMMER RAMBLES," VIII (1839), 134-53 (Canada).

412   [Taylor, Meadows]. "The Native Princes of India and the East India Company," VIII (1839), 154-245.

413   [Young, G.A.]. "The Canadas," VIII (1839), 286-329.

414   "War beyond the Indus: the Treaty of Lahore," VIII (1839), 609-37 (Afghanistan).

415   "CONFESSIONS OF A THUG," IX (1839), 534-54 (India).

416   [Bisset, Andrew]. "Our Relations with China: the Opium Question," X (1840), 341-98.

417   [Welford, R.G.]. "Progress and Prospects of the Self-Supporting Emigration System," X (1840), 493-540.

418   [Taylor, Meadows]. "Administration of India," XI (1840-41), 151-210.

419   "The Appellate Courts of the British Empire," XII (1841), 287-302.

420   "Ceylon," XII (1841), 385-96.

421 "The Disasters in Affghanistan: Lieutenant Eyre's Narrative," XIV (1842-43), 384-410.

422 [Taylor, Meadows]. "State of Thuggee in India," XV (1843), 246-92.

423 "The Ameers of Sinde," XVI (1843-44), 198-262.

424 [Ward, John]. "The Oregon Territory," XVI (1843-44), 560-86.

425 [Banfield, Thomas Charles]. "The French Slave Colonies: the Sugar Question," XVII (1844), 559-605.

426 "Lord Ellenborough's Government of India," XVII (1844), 646-67.

427 [Taylor, Meadows]. "Education in India," XVIII (1844), 146-78.

THE BRITISH QUARTERLY REVIEW

428 "Australia: Angas and Haydon," V (1847), 29-49.

429 "Hindu Medical Missions," VI (1847), 356-74.

430 "Borneo," VII (1848), 49-73.

431 "Cotton-Growing: American and Indian," IX (1849), 354-84.

432 "England and Her Colonial Empire," X (1849), 463-502.

433 "Sierra Leone - Colonial Government," XI (1850), 38-61.

434 "Physical Features of South Africa," XII (1850), 338-60.

435 "States of Central America," XIII (1851), 173-89.

436 "Dixon's MAIRWARA - Indian Civilization," XIII (1851), 525-40.

437 "Missions in South Africa," XIV (1851), 106-13.

438 "Afghanistan and the Punjab," XV (1852), 220-40.

439 "Australia and Its Wealth," XVI (1852), 238-66.

440 "China - Its Civilization and Religion," XVI (1852), 396-418.

441 "India and Its Government," XVII (1853), 481-534.

442 "The Revolution in China," XVIII (1853), 309-54 (Taipings).

443 "The Insurgent Power in China," XXII (1855), 110-44 (Taipings).

444   "Russian Aggression and British Statesmanship," XXII
       (1855), 201-43 (Central Asia).

445   "The Cape of Good Hope and British Caffraria," XXIV
       (1856), 381-421.

446   "The Chinese Question and the New Parliament," XXV
       (1857), 510-26.

447   "The Chinese - Their Rebellions and Civilization," XXVI
       (1857), 46-74.

448   "African Discoveries," XXVI (1857), 382-415 (notes on
       cotton and Niger River).

449   "The Cotton Dearth," XXVI (1857), 416-48 (India).

450   "The Government of India and the Mutinies," XXVI (1857),
       476-504.

451   "Dr. Livingstone's African Researches," XXVII (1858),
       105-32 (Southeast Africa).

452   "Projected Communications with the East," XXVII (1858),
       133-51 (Euphrates and Suez).

453   "India as It Is - India as It May Be," XXVII (1858),
       202-44.

454   "Commerce with India: Past and Present," XXVII (1858),
       510-35.

455   "India and the House of Commons," XXVIII (1858), 199-
       226.

456   "The Punjab and Its Administration," XXIX (1859), 433-
       63.

457   "Tennent's Account of Ceylon," XXX (1859), 339-60.

458   "Financial Resources of India," XXX (1859), 465-81.

459   "McLeod's EASTERN AFRICA," XXXI (1860), 328-51 (Mauri-
       tius and South and Southeast Africa).

460   "China and Japan," XXXI (1860), 466-91.

461   "Prison Ethics," XXXII (1860), 42-70 (notes on trans-
       portation).

462   "The West Indies - Past and Present," XXXII (1860), 98-
       122.

463   "Havelock," XXXII (1860), 122-42 (India).

464   "Church Questions in Australia," XXXII (1860), 169-79.

465 "Atkinson's TRAVELS - Amoor, India, and China," XXXII
(1860), 304-40.

466 "Chinese Characteristics," XXXIII (1861), 150-81.

467 "Canada," XXXIII (1861), 374-91.

468 "Our Commerce with China," XXXIII (1861), 468-85.

469 "The West Indies," XXXV (1862), 416-28.

470 "Gibraltar and Spain," XXXVI (1862), 321-38.

471 "Indigo, Rent, and Ryots," XXXVII (1863), 245-76 (Bengal).

472 "Self-Government in India," XXXVIII (1863), 421-48.

473 "Travels in the Himalayas," XXXIX (1864), 120-44 (India
and Sikkim).

474 "The Sepoy War, and What Led to It," XLI (1865), 1-37
(India).

475 "Lessons from the Cotton Famine," XLI (1865), 358-80.

476 "Facts from Savage Life," XLI (1865), 380-411 (natives
in the empire).

477 "THE ECONOMY OF CAPITAL - Foreign Trade," XLI (1865),
442-76 (gold).

478 "The Outbreak in Jamaica," XLIV (1866), 452-74.

CHAMBERS'S (EDINBURGH) JOURNAL

479 "New South Wales," I (1832-33), 15.

480 "Emigration — New Brunswick," I (1832-33), 93-94.

481 "British Colonies," I (1832-33), 108.

482 "Emigration - Upper Canada," I (1832-33), 109.

483 "Our East India Possessions," I (1832-33), 116.

484 "Value of Property in the British Empire," I (1832-33),
128.

485 "Emigration," I (1832-33), 149-50.

486 "Rise of the East India Company," I (1832-33), 181-82.

487 "The Ionian Islands," I (1832-33), 189-90.

488 "Living in Jamaica," II (1833-34), 44.

489 "Discoveries in Africa," II (1833-34), 171-72 (Niger
River).

490   "Remarkable Travels in Uncivilized Countries: Carver, in North America," II (1833-34), 189-90, 222.

491   "Ramble in Southern Africa," II (1833-34), 335-36.

492   "Swan River Settlement," II (1833-34), 350-51 (Western Australia).

493   "Manners of West India Slaves," II (1833-34), 387-88.

494   "A Word to Intending Emigrants," III (1834-35), 63-64.

495   "Biographical Sketches: Rammohun Roy," III (1834-35), 213-14 (India).

496   "A Settler in Canada," III (1834-35), 215-16.

497   "The Canadian Press," III (1834-35), 254-55.

498   R., Mr. "Who Should Go to Canada?" IV (1835-36), 21-22.

499   R., Mr. "Particulars regarding Canada," IV (1835-36), 118-19.

500   "The Thugs," IV (1835-36), 333-34 (India).

501   "Cave Temples in the East," V (1836-37), 13-14 (India).

502   "The Religion of the Hindoos," V (1836-37), 102-03.

503   "Sketches of the Gold Coast," V (1836-37), 115-17.

504   "Sketches of India - Calcutta," V (1836-37), 242-43.

505   "The Forming of Colonies," V (1836-37), 268-69.

506   "The Princess Sumroo," V (1836-37), 293-94 (Oudh).

507   "The Fur Trade," VI (1837-38), 6-7 (Hudson's Bay Company).

508   "The Darien Expedition," VI (1837-38), 26-27 (Central America).

509   "Emigration on a Large Scale," VI (1837-38), 90-91.

510   "Music at Sydney," VI (1837-38), 117.

511   "Visit from a Canadian Settler," VI (1837-38), 252-53.

512   "A Fair in India," VI (1837-38), 284-85.

513   "Last Embassy to China," VI (1837-38), 311-12.

514   "Colonisation of New Zealand," VI (1837-38), 311-12 (see #543).

515   "Logan's NOTES ON A JOURNEY IN CANADA," VII (1838-39), 5-6.

516 "Wild Sports of the East: Buffalo Hunting," VII (1838-39), 20-21 (India).

517 "Macomo, the Caffre Chief," VII (1838-39), 22-23 (South Africa).

518 "Commerce of the Indian Archipelago," VII (1838-39), 34-35 (East Indies).

519 "Wild Sports of the East: Tiger Hunting," VII (1838-39), 47 (India).

520 "Emigration to New South Wales: Account of the Country," VII (1838-39), 124-25; ": Capabilities for Settlement," 132-33; ": Convict System - Free Settlers," 142-43.

521 "New South Wales: Experiences of a Settler," VII (1838-39), 149-51; ": Advice to Settlers," 182-83.

522 "Emigration to South Australia," VII (1838-39), 229.

523 "Picture of Sydney," VII (1838-39), 244-45.

524 "Mitchell's Exploratory Expeditions in Australia," VII (1838-39), 292-93.

525 Authoress of "Backwoods of Canada" [Traill, Catherine Parr Strickland]. "The Mill of the Rapids: a Canadian Sketch," VII (1838-39), 323-24.

526 Authoress of "Backwoods of Canada" [Traill, Catherine Parr Strickland]. "Canadian Lumberers," VII (1838-39), 380-81.

527 "Transportation - as a Punishment," VIII (1839-40), 6-7.

528 "Education in India," VIII (1839-40), 38-39.

529 "Travels in the Burman Empire," VIII (1839-40), 287-88.

530 "Junction of the Atlantic and Pacific Oceans," VIII (1839-40), 315-16 (Central America).

531 "Recollections of Calcutta by an Officer," VIII (1839-40), 352.

532 "Excursion across Van Diemen's Land," VIII (1839-40), 371-72.

533 "Mr. [C.A.] Bruce's Report on Assam Tea," IX (1840-41), 2-3.

534 "The Camp and Court of Runjeet Sing," IX (1840-41), 91-92 (Punjab).

535   "South-Australian Emigration: Further Communications
       from Emigrants," IX (1840-41), 100-01.

536   "Forbes's Ceylon," IX (1840-41), 150-51.

537   "Malta, by a Traveller," IX (1840-41), 228-29.

538   "Maconochie on the Convict System in Australia," IX
       (1840-41), 250-51.

539   "Recent Proceedings in and respecting New Zealand,"
       IX (1840-41), 269-71.

540   "The West Indies since the Abolition of Slavery: Jamaica
       - the Emancipation," IX (1840-41), 292-93; "Jamaica
       - the Consequences of Emancipation," 299-300.

541   "Kennedy's NARRATIVE [of the Campaign of the Army of
       the Indus in Sind and Kaubool in 1838-39]," IX (1840-
       41), 342-43.

542   "Guerney's Visit to the West Indies," IX (1840-41), 365-
       66, 390-91.

543   "Colonisation of New Zealand - Further Proceedings,"
       IX (1840-41), 398-99 (see #514).

544   Traill, Mrs. [Catherine Parr Strickland]. "Heroism in
       the Bush," IX (1840-41), 405-06 (Canada).

545   "Notices respecting New Colonies," X (1841-42), 22-23.

546   "Occasional Notes: Emigration," X (1841-42), 117.

547   "Opium-Smoking," X (1841-42), 133 (India).

548   "Condition of a Cluster of Highland Emigrants in New
       South Wales," X (1841-42), 204-05.

549   "The Condition of American Indians," X (1841-42), 220-
       21.

550   "Recent Progress of South Australia," X (1841-42), 325-
       26.

551   "THE CANADAS IN 1841," X (1841-42), 332-33, 350-51.

552   "Mr. Petrie on New Zealand," X (1841-42), 357-58.

553   "Governor Grey's Australian Expeditions," X (1841-42),
       395-96, 406-07.

554   "The Canadian Lumberer," X (1841-42), 399-400.

555   "Catlin's Work on the North American Indians," XI (1842-
       43), 19-20, 39-40.

556   "Madras," XI (1842-43), 60-61.

557   "Mr. [R.G.] Jameson on New Zealand and Australia," XI
      (1842-43), 93-94 (Australia).

558   A Lady. "Notes on a Residence in the Bush," XI (1842-
      43), 173-75, 179-80, 188-89 (Australia).

559   "Burnes on Cabool," XI (1842-43), 178-79.

560   "A Sketch of Pekin," XI (1842-43), 214-15.

561   "Moffat on South Africa," XI (1842-43), 270-71.

562   "Vigne's Work on Upper India," XI (1842-43), 284-85.

563   "NEWFOUNDLAND IN 1842," XI (1842-43), 299-300.

564   "Proposed Fourth Colony in New Zealand," XI (1842-43), 303.

565   "Masson on Afghanistan," XI (1842-43), 316.

566   "Present State of Things in New Zealand," XI (1842-43),
      359-60.

567   "The Boors [sic] or Dutch Farmers of South Africa," XI
      (1842-43), 404-05.

568   "Overland Routes to India," XI (1842-43), 413-14.

569   "An Ambassador Resident in China," XII (1843), 30.

570   "Young's Residence on the Mosquito Shore," XII (1843),
      36-37 (Central America).

571   "Lord Selkirk's Settlement in Prince Edward Island,"
      XII (1843), 42-43.

572   "Oregon," XII (1843), 61-62.

573   "Why Sugar Is So Dear," XII (1843), 142-43 (West Indies).

574   "The Affghan Captives," XII (1843), 157-58.

575   "The Colonisation Circular," XII (1843), 183.

576   "Jottings on the Colonies," XII (1843), 246-47.

577   "The Late Expedition to the Niger," XII (1843), 258-60.

578   "Disasters of the Niger Expedition," XII (1843), 270-71.

579   "Discoveries on the North Coast of America," XII (1843),
      277-78, 282-83 (Hudson's Bay Company territory).

580   "Adventures and Field Sports in Ceylon," XII (1843),
      290-91.

581   "Proposed Canal across the Isthmus of Suez," I N.S.
      (1844), 94-95.

582   "Sinde and Its Ameers," I N.S. (1844), 123-25.

583   "MEMOIRS OF A GRIFFIN," I N.S. (1844), 170-73 (India).

584   "Journeyings in America by a Young Adventurer," I N.S.
        (1844), 262-65, 302-04, 327-30, 386-89, 410-13 (notes
        on British North America).

585   "Facts about the Chinese," I N.S. (1844), 339-42, 355-
        58, 376-79.

586   Bellew, Capt. "Recollections of Sport in India," II N.S.
        (1844), 96-101, 299-302.

587   "The Mauritius," II N.S. (1844), 219-23.

588   "The Literature of the Chinese," II N.S. (1844), 250-53,
        280-82, 290-93.

589   "NEW SOUTH WALES," II N.S. (1844), 307-10.

590   A Late Resident. "Short Notes on the West Indies,"
        III N.S. (1845), 3-6, 20-23, 44-46, 78-79, 122-24.

591   "The Indian Mail," III N.S. (1845), 46-47.

592   "West India Mail," III N.S. (1845), 265-67.

593   "Glimpses of New Zealand," IV N.S. (1845), 53-56.

594   "Traits of the New Zealanders," IV N.S. (1845), 85-87.

595   "What To Do with Transported Criminals," IV N.S. (1845),
        170-72.

596   B., J. "An Unexpected Visit to Flinders' Island in Bass's
        Straits," IV N.S. (1845), 187-89 (Australia).

597   "New Zealand as a Colony," IV N.S. (1845), 268-70.

598   "A Word on Emigration," IV N.S. (1845), 397-99.

599   "The Punjab," V N.S. (1846), 165-67.

600   "Mr. Brooke in Borneo," V N.S. (1846), 180-82, 200-03.

601   "Castes," V N.S. (1846), 361-63 (India).

602   Ritchie, Leitch. "Progress of Intemperance in India,"
        VI N.S. (1846), 124-25.

603   "Travelling at the Cape of Good Hope," VI N.S. (1846),
        238-39.

604   "A Visit to the Cape," VI N.S. (1846), 246-48 (Cape
        Colony).

605   "THE EMIGRANT," VI N.S. (1846), 246-48 (Canada).

606   "The English in India," VII N.S. (1847), 118-21.

607   "The NEMESIS and the Chinese War," VII N.S. (1847), 155-
       58.

608   "Fortune's Wanderings in China," VII N.S. (1847), 299-
       301.

609   "The British Colonial Trade," VII N.S. (1847), 349-51.

610   "The Interior of Australia," VIII N.S. (1847), 14-16.

611   "The Working Man in Australia," VIII N.S. (1847), 44-46.

612   "Our Indian Connection in Past Times," VIII N.S. (1847),
       81-84.

613   "Plain Answers to Plain Questions about Emigration,"
       VIII N.S. (1847), 120-21.

614   "The Scotch Colony of Otago," VIII N.S. (1847), 185-87
       (New Zealand).

615   "THE BUSHMAN," IX N.S. (1848), 11-13 (Australia).

616   "The Anglo-Indian Press," IX N.S. (1848), 31-32.

617   "Incidents of Winter Life in Quebec," IX N.S. (1848),
       49-52

618   "Want of Labourers in Australia," IX N.S. (1848), 61-63.

619   "The West India Voyager," IX N.S. (1848), 115-18, 135-
       38.

620   "Indian Expertness," IX N.S. (1848), 157-58.

621   "The Indian Archipelago," IX N.S. (1848), 204-06 (East
       Indies).

622   "The English in Borneo," IX N.S. (1848), 265-67.

623   "The Discoveries in Australia," IX N.S. (1848), 277-79.

624   "Indian Recreations," IX N.S. (1848), 303-04.

625   "Five Days in the Wilderness of New Brunswick," IX N.S.
       (1848), 364-66.

626   "Colony of South Australia," IX N.S. (1848), 395-98.

627   "The Sugar Question," X N.S. (1848), 3-5 (West Indies).

628   "St. Andrew's Society of Adelaide," X N.S. (1848), 45-
       47.

629   "Byrne on South Australia," X N.S. (1848), 74-76.

630   "A Ride in South Africa," X N.S. (1848), 156-58.

631   "The Bengalee Doctor," X N.S. (1848), 171-73.

632   "Ashore in Calcutta," X N.S. (1848), 228-30.

633   "The Hudson's Bay Company," X N.S. (1848), 242-45.

634   "Information for Intending Emigrants," X N.S. (1848), 284-86.

635   "The Otago Settlement," X N.S. (1848), 299-300 (New Zealand).

636   "Emigrant Voices from New Zealand," X N.S. (1848), 353-58.

637   "High School of Hobart Town," X N.S. (1848), 430-31.

638   "Central Australia," XI N.S. (1849), 13-15.

639   "Gipsy Sorceries in the Deccan," XI N.S. (1849), 33-34.

640   "Indian Bhang," XI N.S. (1849), 62-63.

641   "A Visit to the Western Ghauts," XI N.S. (1849), 105-07 (India).

642   "Incidents of Canadian Travel," XI N.S. (1849), 233-36.

643   "A Glance at the Sikhs," XI N.S. (1849), 280-82 (Punjab).

644   "Life in New South Wales," XI N.S. (1849), 331-32.

645   "Sierra Leone," XI N.S. (1849), 343-45.

646   "THE MAORI MESSENGER," XII N.S. (1849), 111 (New Zealand).

647   "A New Emigration Field," XII N.S. (1849), 249-51 (Natal).

648   "Indian Police Revelations," XII N.S. (1849), 325-28.

649   "The Pitcairn Islanders in 1849," XIII N.S. (1850), 10-12.

650   "Notes on Immigration: Canterbury Settlement," XIV N.S. (1850), 61-63 (New Zealand).

651   "A Hunter's Life in South Africa," XIV N.S. (1850), 72-76.

652   "Celestial Intelligence," XIV N.S. (1850), 169-72 (see #747; China).

653   "A Voice from Australia Felix," XIV N.S. (1850), 236-39.

654   R., L. "The Gang-Robbers of India," XIV N.S. (1850), 321-24, 344-46.

655 "Malta and Gibraltar," XV N.S. (1851), 43-46.

656 "Panama to Chagres," XV N.S. (1851), 248-51.

657 "Johnston's Tour in America," XV N.S. (1851), 279-82.

658 "Indian Handicrafts," XV N.S. (1851), 342-45.

659 "The Bushrangers," XVI N.S. (1851), 134-38, 285-88
     (Australia).

660 "The Hindoo Funeral," XVI N.S. (1851), 157-58.

661 "Short Cuts to America," XVI N.S. (1851), 203-05 (ways
     to speed travel).

662 "Up the Gambia," XVI N.S. (1851), 273-76.

663 "The Bathurst Diggings," XVI N.S. (1851), 291-94 (New
     South Wales).

664 "A Word on Canada," XVI N.S. (1851), 402-05.

665 "Beggars in the Far East," XVII N.S. (1852), 29-30
     (India).

666 "Notes from Australia," XVII N.S. (1852), 62-63.

667 "Up the Indus," XVII N.S. (1852), 81-82.

668 "Genius for Emigration," XVII N.S. (1852), 107-10
     (Australia).

669 "The Great Afghan Blunder," XVII N.S. (1852), 118-21.

670 "A Word to Genteel Emigrants," XVII N.S. (1852), 143-44.

671 "A Voice from the Diggings," XVII N.S. (1852), 201-03
     (Australia).

672 "The Ayah," XVII N.S. (1852), 249-50 (India).

673 "The Gold-Fever in Australia," XVII N.S. (1852), 282-84.

674 "The Tea-Countries of China," XVII N.S. (1852), 395-97.

675 "The Youngest British Colony," XVIII N.S. (1852), 50-
     52 (Orange River).

676 "The New Convict Establishment in Western Australia,"
     XVIII N.S. (1852), 106-08.

677 "A Day's Pleasuring in India," XVIII N.S. (1852), 171-
     73.

678 "Magic in India," XVIII N.S. (1852), 217-19.

679 "Steam round the Cape," XVIII N.S. (1852), 387-88 (Cape
     Colony).

680   "Dacca Muslin," XVIII N.S. (1852), 393-95.

681   "Ideas about the Diggings," XIX N.S. (1853), 39-42
       (Australia).

682   "The Right Kind of Emigrants," XIX N.S. (1853), 77-78.

683   "Climate and Health in Australia," XIX N.S. (1853), 89-
       92.

684   "Gold-Digging Companies," XIX N.S. (1853), 101.

685   "Sea Route across the Isthmus of Darien," XIX N.S.
       (1853), 183-85 (Central America).

686   A Colonist. "A Voice on Emigration to Australia," XIX N.S.
       (1853), 210-12.

687   "A Word on Canada," XIX N.S. (1853), 253-55.

688   "Notes on the Caffres: by a Neighbour of Theirs," XIX N.S.
       (1853), 329-31 (South Africa).

689   "African Kings at Home," XIX N.S. (1853), 379-82
       (Gambia).

690   "The Modern Parsees," XIX N.S. (1853), 396-99 (India).

691   "Arts and Manufacturing of India," XX N.S. (1853), 45-
       47.

692   "Caffraria," XX N.S. (1853), 59-62 (South Africa).

693   "Major Strickland's TWENTY-SEVEN YEARS IN CANADA," XX N.S.
       (1853), 123-25.

694   "The Rebellion in China," XX N.S. (1853), 163-66
       (Taipings).

695   "Ghosts and Sorceresses in India," XX N.S. (1853), 185-
       87.

696   "Blanks of the Australian Lottery," XX N.S. (1853), 205-
       06 (gold).

697   "Caroline Chisholm: Her Last Seven Years' Work," XX N.S.
       (1853), 241-44 (Australian immigrants).

698   "Notes on Victoria Colony," XX N.S. (1853), 381-83.

699   Chambers, William. "Things as They Are in America,"
       I 3S. (1854), 81-86, 98-103, 131-35, 161-65, 180-85,
       211-15, 234-38, 241-44, 283-86, 300-03, 337-42, 355-
       59, 390-94; II 3S. (1854), 6-11, ET SEQ. (all United
       States).

700 "An Indian Trip," I 3S. (1854), 121-22 (travel by palanquin).

701 "Jottings from the Cape," II 3S. (1854), 76-77 (Cape Colony).

702 "The American Glencoe," II 3S. (1854), 342-45 (Nova Scotia).

703 "Indian Life in Cantonment," II 3S. (1854), 413-16.

704 "India at Home," III 3S. (1855), 117-19 (British government).

705 "A Concert in Sydney: from the Diary of a Wandering Fiddler," IV 3S. (1855), 104-06.

706 "Life at an Indian Court," IV 3S. (1855), 386-89 (Oudh).

707 Hauser, Mishka. "The Roving Fiddler," V 3S. (1856), 14-16 (Victoria).

708 "The Detective in India," V 3S. (1856), 49-52.

709 "THE FUR-HUNTERS OF THE FAR WEST," V 3S. (1856), 338-42 (Hudson's Bay Company).

710 "An Indian Pageant," V 3S. (1856), 385-89 (Oudh).

711 "THE RED RIVER SETTLEMENT," VI 3S. (1856), 53-56 (Hudson's Bay Company territory).

712 "Emigration to America Made Easy," VII 3S. (1857), 95-96.

713 "Progress of Tasmania," VII 3S. (1857), 239-40.

714 "Past and Present of India," VII 3S. (1857), 355-58.

715 "A Glimpse of Sarawak," VII 3S. (1857), 390-93.

716 "The People at Sarawak," VIII 3S. (1857), 93-96.

717 "Social Progress at the Antipodes," VIII 3S. (1857), 152-55, 173-75 (New Zealand).

718 "The Dyaks: by a Personal Acquaintance of Theirs," VIII 3S. (1857), 201-04 (Borneo).

719 "Indian Servants," VIII 3S. (1857), 229-31.

720 "The Indian Revolt," VIII 3S. (1857), 270-71.

721 "A Steerage Passenger's View of Sydney," VIII 3S. (1857), 271-72.

722 "Hindoo Emigrants," VIII 3S. (1857), 389-91.

723   "Babooism," IX 3S. (1858), 45-48 (India).

724   "The Zemindar," IX 3S. (1858), 65-67 (India).

725   "The Ryot," IX 3S. (1858), 132-34 (India).

726   "The Wild White Man," IX 3S. (1858), 177-80 (Australian convict).

727   "Young Bengal," IX 3S. (1858), 199-201.

728   "Nana Sahib," IX 3S. (1858), 223-24 (India).

729   "The Ancient Reservoirs of Aden," X 3S. (1858), 126-28.

730   "Schooling in India," X 3S. (1858), 131-34.

731   "The New Gold-Diggings," X 3S. (1858), 182-85, 197-98 (British Columbia).

732   "By Dak," X 3S. (1858), 236-39 (travel with comments about India).

733   "Travelling in Natal," XI 3S. (1859), 121-24.

734   "A Day with the Goorkhas," XI 3S. (1859), 170-72 (Nepal).

735   "A Settler's Holiday," XI 3S. (1859), 283-86 (South Africa).

736   "A Fit of the Gold-Fever," XI 3S. (1859), 289-92 (New South Wales).

737   "The Goorkhas at Lucknow," XI 3S. (1859), 347-49 (Indian mutiny).

738   "Perils of the Bush," XI 3S. (1859), 359-63 (South Africa).

739   "Port Natal," XI 3S. (1859), 381-83.

740   "Memories of Melbourne," XII 3S. (1859), 145-48.

741   "A Legend of Port Phillip," XII 3S. (1859), 193-97.

742   "Sydney and Its Suburbs," XII 3S. (1859), 296-99, 318-20.

743   "Emerson Tennent's CEYLON," XII 3S. (1859), 395-97.

744   "Russell's DIARY IN INDIA," XIII 3S. (1860), 88-91.

745   "The Maniac Crusoe," XIII 3S. (1860), 166-69 (Bermuda convict).

746   "Adopted in Andaman," XIII 3S. (1860), 177-79 (Indian convicts).

747   "More Celestial Intelligence," XIII 3S. (1860), 237-40 (see #652; China).

748   "Hudson's Bay and Its Furs," XIII 3S. (1860), 293-96.

749   "A Last Picture from the Gallery of the Indian Revolt,"
       XIII 3S. (1860), 302-04.

750   "A Colonial Adventure," XIII 3S. (1860), 332-34 (Nova
       Scotia).

751   "Indian Domestics," XIII 3S. (1860), 366-68 (colonial
       life).

752   "A Paradise of Fools," XIV 3S. (1860), 85-88 (drug use
       in the empire).

753   "Emigrants Afloat," XIV 3S. (1860), 190-92.

754   "Lucknow Kavanagh, V.C." XIV 3S. (1860), 251-54 (Indian
       mutiny).

755   "The Gold-Fields with the Gilt Off," XIV 3S. (1860),
       343-46 (Australia).

756   "Chinese Commerce," XV 3S. (1861), 4-8.

757   "Imprisoned in Burmah," XV 3S. (1861), 105-09.

758   "Indian Grass Widowers," XV 3S. (1861), 145-47 (colonial
       men).

759   "Cotton Countries," XV 3S. (1861), 172-75.

760   "Central Australia," XV 3S. (1861), 242-45.

761   "An Incident of Backwoods' Travel," XV 3S. (1861), 316-
       20 (British North America).

762   "Two Days at Canton," XV 3S. (1861), 350-52.

763   "Chinese Emigration," XVI 3S. (1861), 9-12.

764   "Indian Society," XVII 3S. (1862), 94-96 (colonial life).

765   "The Australian Exploring Expedition," XVII 3S. (1862),
       108-12.

766   "Captive in China," XVII 3S. (1862), 119-22 (British
       seamen in 1842).

767   "A Glance at the Malays," XVII 3S. (1862), 138-41 (East
       Indies).

768   "The Plagues of India," XVII 3S. (1862), 145-51.

769   "Native Industry in India," XVII 3S. (1862), 333-35.

770   "Home from the Colonies," XVII 3S. (1862), 398-400, 404-
       06; XVIII 3S. (1862), 19-22, 59-62, 103-06, 203-06,
       246-49, 347-50, 390-92, 411-14 (Australia).

771   "Beating about the Bush," XVIII 3S. (1862), 91-95
       (Australia).

772   "An Ice Adventure," XVIII 3S. (1862), 106-08 (British
       North American surveyor).

773   "Life in the Forests of the Far East," XVIII 3S. (1862),
       157-60 (East Indies).

774   "A Migratory Town," XVIII 3S. (1862), 175-76 (India).

775   "Fisheries of the Pacific," XVIII 3S. (1862), 249-52.

776   "Telegraph Communication with China," XVIII 3S. (1862),
       287-88.

777   "Gold in Nova Scotia," XVIII 3S. (1862), 319-20.

778   "The Turpins of the Antipodes," XVIII 3S. (1862), 353-
       55 (Australian ex-convicts).

779   "Canadian Winter Weather," XIX 3S. (1863), 68-72.

780   "A Day in the Queensland Bush," XIX 3S. (1863), 102-05.

781   "Cotton," XIX 3S. (1863), 136-38.

782   "Life on Ascension," XIX 3S. (1863), 205-07.

783   "Sepulture," XIX 3S. (1863), 361-63 (how natives deal
       with dead in different ways).

784   "Failure of Springs in the East," XX 3S. (1863), 1-3
       (irrigation in India and Mauritius).

785   "A Raft Adventure," XX 3S. (1863), 79-80 (British North
       America).

786   "A Savage Archipelago," XX 3S. (1863), 139-42 (Andaman
       Islands, India).

787   "Widowed in the Wilds," XX 3S. (1863), 190-92 (South
       Africa).

788   "The Shawls of Cashmere," XX 3S. (1863), 244-46.

789   "Our Mail-Packet Service, Past and Present," XX 3S.
       (1863), 387-89 (service throughout the empire).

790   "The Suez Canal," I 4S. (1864), 60-62.

791   "The First Agricultural Show of Bengal," I 4S. (1864),
       308-11.

792   "The Present Condition of the Pitcairn Islanders," I 4S.
       (1864), 477-80 (Pitcairn and Norfolk Islands).

793   "Arrival of the Mail in Melbourne," I 4S. (1864), 598-600.

794   "A Backwoods' Express," I 4S. (1864), 657-59 (British
       North America soldier's recollection).

795   "On Bank-Service in Canada," I 4S. (1864), 673-78.

796   "Australian Blacks," I 4S. (1864), 686-88.

797   "The Missionary and the Idol," I 4S. (1864), 721-24
       (New Zealand).

798   "Cockatoo Island," I 4S. (1864), 830-32 (Australia).

799   "The British-American Fisheries," II 4S. (1865), 45-48.

800   "Travelling in New South Wales," II 4S. (1865), 158-60.

801   "A Vanishing Race," II 4S. (1865), 238-40 (British North
       America Eskimos).

802   "In Charge of Treasure," II 4S. (1865), 410-14 (soldiers
       in India).

803   "Borneo and the Dyaks," II 4S. (1865), 551-54.

804   "Second Class to New Zealand and Back," II 4S. (1865),
       765-68, 781-84.

805   "The Soonderbuns of Bengal," III 4S. (1866), 45-48.

806   "Indian Emigration," III 4S. (1866), 394-97.

807   "Life in the Mountains of Jamaica," III 4S. (1866), 520-
       22.

808   "Drawing for Farms in Victoria," IV 4S. (1867), 10-14.

809   "Pictures of India," IV 4S. (1867), 45-48 (ideas).

810   "The P. and O.," IV 4S. (1867), 57-59 (mail service in
       the empire).

811   "Modern Savages," IV 4S. (1867), 117-20 (customs of
       different groups in the empire).

812   "A Gantlet of Fire," IV 4S. (1867), 223-24 (Hudson's
       Bay Company employee recollection).

813   "About Assam," IV 4S. (1867), 468-71.

THE CHRISTIAN REMEMBRANCER

814   C., W.B. "West-Indian Slavery," XIV (1832), 558-59.

815   "Anti-Slavery Delusion," XIV (1832), 603-18.

816   "Chapman's Poems," XV (1833), 651-56 (Barbados).

817   "Bishop Coleridge's Charges, Etc.," XVII (1835), 259-66
       (Barbados).

818   "Thornton's INDIA," XVIII (1836), 129-35.

819   "SIX MONTHS OF A NEWFOUNDLAND MISSIONARY'S JOURNAL,"
      XVIII (1836), 201-09.

820   Wilson, Daniel. "Extracts from Bishop Wilson's Charge:
      Delivered to the Clergy of the Archdeaconry of Bombay,
      December, 1835," XX (1838), 34-39.

821   "Trevelyan's EDUCATION OF THE PEOPLE OF INDIA," XXI
      (1839), 14-21.

822   C., W.B. "News from Australia," XXI (1839), 744-47; XXII
      (1840), 37-39.

823   "THE COLONIAL MAGAZINE, Etc.," XXII (1840), 127-29.

824   R., B.C. "Religious Destitution in New South Wales,"
      XXII (1840), 485-88.

825   "Grey's AUSTRALIA," III N.S. (1842), 35-47.

826   "Consecration of Five New Colonial Bishops," IV N.S.
      (1842), 335-36.

827   "The Khonds of Goomsur and Boad," IV N.S. (1842), 378-
      88 (India).

828   "Southern Africa," IV N.S. (1842), 547-64, 636-60.

829   "Church Missionary Society," V N.S. (1843), 52-70.

830   "China and Its Inhabitants," V N.S. (1843), 311-24.

831   "Affghanistan," V N.S. (1843), 606-39; VI N.S. (1843),
      1-41.

832   "Colonial Emigration - New South Wales," VI N.S. (1843),
      585-614.

833   "Colonial Emigration - New Zealand," VII N.S. (1844),
      393-426.

834   "Missions: Grant's Bampton Lectures," VIII N.S. (1844),
      25-39 (missionary work in and outside of the empire).

835   "The Church in the Colonies - Canada," VIII N.S. (1844),
      149-68.

836   "University of Toronto," VIII N.S. (1844), 372-407.

837   "Baber the Emperor," X N.S. (1845), 133-43 (India).

838   "The Early Colonial Church," XII N.S. (1846), 184-221.

839   "Slave-grown Sugar," XII N.S. (1846), 325-76 (West
      Indies).

840   "Head's EMIGRANT," XIII N.S. (1847), 41-61 (Canada).

841   "The Recent Consecration of Colonial Bishops," XIV N.S.
      (1847), 419-35.

842   "Borneo," XV N.S. (1848), 20-55.

843   "Colonization: the Canterbury Association," XIX N.S.
      (1850), 445-70 (New Zealand).

844   "The Newfoundland Mission," XX N.S. (1850), 488-508.

845   "Canterbury Settlement," XXVI N.S. (1853), 300-02
      (New Zealand).

846   "The Church in India," XXVIII N.S. (1854), 45-78.

847   "The Maori Race," XXXI N.S. (1856), 430-44 (New Zealand).

848   "Imperialism," XXXII N.S. (1856), 265-326 (analysis of
      the idea with emphasis on Napoleon III but notes on
      India).

849   "PARAMESWARA-JNYANA-GOSTHI: Christianity and Hinduism,"
      XXXV N.S. (1858), 81-129.

850   "Livingstone's MISSIONARY TRAVELS," XXXV N.S. (1858),
      130-58 (notes on trade possibilities of the Zambezi
      area).

851   "Personal Details and Incidents of the Indian Mutiny,"
      XXXV N.S. (1858), 362-401.

852   "The Church Missionary Society and the Indian Episco-
      pate," XXXVI N.S. (1858), 64-101.

853   "What is Wanted in the Church's Missions," XXXVII N.S.
      (1859), 60-81.

854   "Church Missions," XXXVIII N.S. (1859), 370-87.

855   "Wants of the Church's Missions," XL N.S. (1860), 63-81.

856   "The Discipline of the Clergy," XLII N.S. (1861), 251-
      76 (notes on New Zealand).

857   "Conference on Missions," XLIV N.S. (1862), 253-72.

858   "Africa and the Church," XLVII N.S. (1864), 261-81
      (notes on all areas).

859   "New Zealand, as It Was and as It Is," XLVII N.S. (1864),
      427-54.

860   "Trinity College, Toronto," XLVIII N.S. (1864), 279-317.

861   "Egerton's TOUR THROUGH SPITI," XLIX N.S. (1865), 357-
      75 (India).

THE CONTEMPORARY REVIEW

862   "Indian Questions," I (1866), 123-41.

863   Fremantle, W.H. "Church Government in the Colonies," I
      (1866), 311-42.

864   Grahamstown, H. [Cotterill, Henry]. "Church Government
      in the Colonies: a Reply," II (1866), 166-76.

865   Smith, Thomas. " 'Khond' Macpherson," II (1866), 212-39
      (activities of Macpherson in India).

866   Capetown, R. [Gray, Robert]. "Letter from the Bishop of
      Capetown," III (1866), 283-92 (Anglican Church policy
      in the colonies).

867   Fagan, Henry Stuart. "Orissa," IV (1867), 73-89 (India).

868   Fremantle, W.H. "Are the Colonial Churches Independent?"
      V (1867), 489-501.

869   Hutton, James. "The Subsidiary System in India," VI
      (1867), 172-85.

THE CORNHILL MAGAZINE

870   [Bowring, John]. "The Chinese and the 'Outer Barbarians',"
      I (1860), 26-43.

871   [Smith, Albert]. "Inside Canton," I (1860), 412-16.

872   [Oliphant, Laurence]. "Campaigning in China," I (1860),
      537-48.

873   [Kaye, J.W.]. "The House That John Built," II (1860),
      113-21 (see #899a; East India Company).

874   [Townsend, Edward]. "Chinese Pirates," II (1860), 432-
      37.

875   [Harwood, J.B.]. "Chinese Officials," III (1861), 25-32.

876   [Kaye, J.W.]. "The Career of an Indian Officer," III
      (1861), 72-89 (James Outram).

877   [Harwood, J.B.]. "Chinese Police," III (1861), 154-65.

878   [Hunt, Thornton]. "The Convict Out in the World," IV
      (1861), 229-50 (notes on transportation).

879   [Harwood, J.B.]. "Negroes Bond and Free," IV (1861),
      340-47 (West Indies).

880   [Horne, R.H.]. "An Election Contest in Australia," V
      (1862), 25-35.

881 [Patterson, Thomas E.]. "The Winter in Canada," V
    (1862), 204-17.

882 [Galton, Francis]. "Recent Discoveries in Australia,"
    V (1862), 354-64.

883 [Russell, William Howard]. "The Climate and the Work,"
    VI (1862), 241-57 (India).

884 [Mathew, Theobald]. "Capture of the Delhi Prizes," VI
    (1862), 528-34 (Indian mutiny).

885 [Keighley, H.P.]. "Indian Cotton and Its Supply," VI
    (1862), 654-62.

886 [Knollys, W.W.]. "Indian Cossacks," VII (1863), 42-55
    (irregular cavalry).

887 O., J. [Higgins, M.J.]. "The Story of the Mhow Court-
    Martial," VIII (1863), 556-81 (India).

888 [Allen, Robert]. "A Trip to Xanadu," IX (1864), 159-63
    (Fatehpur, India).

889 [Cowie, H.G.]. "Notes of the Late Campaign on the
    Punjab Frontier," IX (1864), 357-67.

890 [Roe, Susannah]. "A Convict's View of Penal Discipline,"
    X (1864), 722-33 (Australia).

891 Jones, Gavin S. "The Story of My Escape from Futtehghur,"
    XI (1865), 88-108 (Indian mutiny).

892 [Morris, Miss]. "Maori Sketches," XII (1865), 498-512
    (New Zealand).

893 [Forrest, R.E.T.]. "The Holy Fair of Hurdwar," XII
    (1865), 609-22 (India).

894 [Spence, Catherine H.]. "An Australian's Impressions of
    England," XIII (1866), 110-20 (comparisons between
    England and Australia).

895 [Wyllie, J.W.S.]. "A Visit to the Suez Canal," XIII
    (1866), 363-84.

896 [Roe, James]. "A Letter from a Convict in Australia
    to a Brother in England," XIII (1866), 489-512.

896a [Bertram, James G.]. "The Pearl Harvest," XIV (1866),
    161-73 (Ceylon).

897 [Kaye, J.W.]. "The Peace-Conflicts of India," XIV (1866),
    422-31 (English life in India).

898   [Browne, T.A.]. "A Kangaroo Drive," XIV (1866), 735-46
       (Australia).

899   [Hopkins, Manley]. "Coolie Labour and Coolie Immigra-
       tion," XVI (1867), 74-83 (Chinese and Indian workers
       throughout the empire).

899a   [Kaye, J.W.]. "The House That Scott Built," XVI (1867),
       356-69 (see #873; comparison of Indian Department to
       East India Company).

900   [Russell, William Howard]. "The Shootings at Kamptully,"
       XVI (1867), 376-84 (grouse shooting during famine in
       Orissa, India).

901   [Bradshaw, O.M.]. "Witch-Murders in India," XVI (1867),
       409-17.

902   [Robinson, John]. "By the Sea-Side in South-East Africa,"
       XVI (1867), 629-40 (Natal).

THE DUBLIN REVIEW

903   [Chapman, H.S.]. "The Canadian Question," III (1837),
       79-113; with postscript, 276.

904   [Chapman, H.S.]. "Principles of Colonization - New
       Zealand," IV (1838), 67-96.

905   [Chapman, H.S.]. "South Australia," VI (1839), 449-66.

906   [Chapman, H.S.]. "New Zealand," IX (1840), 189-214.

907   [Anstey, T.C.]. "Southern Africa in 1840," XI (1841), 1-
       53.

908   [Anstey, T.C.]. "Van Diemen's Land under the Prison
       System," XI (1841), 426-77 (transportation).

909   [Grimes, Thomas]. "Affghanistan," XII (1842), 386-419.

910   [Chapman, H.S.]. "Progress of Australian Discovery,"
       XIII (1842), 74-100.

911   [Sullivan, John]. "China," XVI (1844), 444-63.

912   [Wiseman, Nicholas]. "Upper Canada," XXI (1847), 494-
       509.

913   [Campbell, J.S.]. "Colonial Emigration," XXII (1847),
       388-408.

914   [Dasent, John Bury]. "The Eastern Archipelago and the
       Rajah of Sarawak," XXIV (1848), 295-316.

915   [Wenham, J.G.]. "The Church in Ceylon," XXV (1848), 71-
       117 (Roman Catholic with much on natives).

916   [Wenham, J.G.]. "The Portuguese Schism in India," XXVI
      (1849), 179-213 (struggle between Portuguese king
      and Pope about appointing Indian bishops).

917   [McCabe, W.B.]. "Ceylon - Its Ancient Traditions and
      Modern Missionaries," XXVI (1849), 273-300.

918   [Sinnett, Jane]. "Colonization and Emigration," XXVI
      (1849), 316-37.

919   [O'Reilly, Miles]. "Poor Administration at Home and
      Abroad," XXIX (1850), 324-54 (emigration).

920   [Wenham, J.G.]. "Sir Emerson Tennent's CHRISTIANITY IN
      CEYLON," XXX (1851), 410-36.

921   [Allies, T.W.]. "The Jesuit in India," XXXII (1852),
      386-407.

922   [Russell, C.W.]. "Huc's CHINESE EMPIRE," XXXVIII (1855),
      134-69.

923   [Russell, C.W.]. "Huc's CHRISTIANITY IN CHINA," XLII
      (1857), 438-80; XLIV (1858), 501-25.

924   [Wiseman, Nicholas]. "Italy and India," XLIII (1857),
      206-34 (Indian mutiny).

925   [Abraham, G.W.]. "Recent African Explorations," XLIV
      (1858), 158-80; XLV (1858), 168-87 (notes on Sierra
      Leone and South and Southeast Africa).

925a [Russell, C.W.]. "The Cornwallis Correspondence," XLVI
      (1859), 110-34 (notes on India).

926   [Abraham, G.W.]. "Ceylon," XLVII (1859-60), 445-68.

927   [Russell, C.W.]. "Christian Missions," LI (1862), 219-57.

928   "The Mexican Empire and the Canadian Confederation,"
      V N.S. and LVII O.S. (1865), 206-26.

929   [Wilburforce, H.W.]. "The Negro in Africa and the West
      Indies," VII N.S. and LIX O.S. (1866), 116-42.

930   [Wilburforce, H.W.]. "Jamaica," VII N.S. and LIX O.S.
      (1866), 362-414.

THE DUBLIN UNIVERSITY MAGAZINE

931   "The Canads and Emigration," I (1833), 287-303.

932   "Letters from Canada," I (1833), 600-11.

933   "Memoir of the Late Edward Walsh, M.D.," III (1834),
      63-80 (Canada).

934   "Martin's British Colonies - No. 1 Asia," III (1834),
      647-62 (India).

935   "Irwin on Western Australia," VII (1836), 149-62.

936   "Astoria; or, Enterprise beyond the Rocky Mountains,"
      IX (1837), 167-76 (notes on Hudson's Bay Company).

937   "Parliamentary Doings," IX (1837), 377-92 (Canada).

938   "Inland Sea in the Swan River Settlement," IX (1837),
      570-77 (Western Australia).

939   "Canada," XI (1838), 326-53.

940   "Prospects of the British Empire," XIII (1839), 3-25.

941   "Persia," XIII (1839), 26-37 (note on Russian influence).

942   [Blundell, J.W.F.]. "Eastern Colonies - Australia -
      First Article," XIII (1839), 88-95 (see #943, #947,
      and #948).

943   "Australia - Second Article - Van Diemen's Land," XIII
      (1839), 176-86 (see #942, #947, and #948).

944   "Canada - Lord Durham's Report," XIII (1839), 355-68.

945   "Colonies of the British Empire," XIII (1839), 391-404.

946   "Canada - Despatches of Sir Francis Head," XIII (1839),
      501-19.

947   "Australia - Third Article - Western Australia, or Swan
      River Settlement," XIV (1839), 84-91 (see #942, #943,
      and #948).

948   "Australia - Fourth Article - South Australia," XIV
      (1839), 196-205 (see #942, #943, and #947).

949   "New Zealand," XIV (1839), 298-311.

950   "Australian Emigration Society," XIV (1839), 329-33.

951   "State of Parties in the British Empire: the Government
      a Faction - the Faction a Government," XIV (1839),
      379-93 (imperial conditions).

952   "Thuggee in India, and Ribandism in Ireland, Compared,"
      XV (1840), 50-65.

953   "British America - THE EDINBURGH CABINET LIBRARY," XV
      (1840), 93-112.

954   "TRAVELS IN SOUTH-EASTERN ASIA," XV (1840), 176-87
      (Burma).

955   "China," XV (1840), 579-94.

956   "Letters from Gibraltar," XVI (1840), 625-37.

957   "The Life of Warren Hastings," XVIII (1841), 619-31, 693-710 (India).

958   "Central America, Ancient and Modern," XIX (1842), 189-200.

959   "The North American Indians," XIX (1842), 371-85.

960   "Affghanistan - with a Map of the Seat of the War," XIX (1842), 645-60.

961   Dunne, Col. [William Henry]. "A Narrative of the Affghan War, in a Series of Letters of the Late Colonel Dennie, C.B., Her Majesty's 13th Light Infantry Regiment, Aid-de-Camp to the Queen," XX (1842), 327-41, 459-84.

962   "Canada," XX (1842), 735-52.

963   "Successes in the East - Affghanistan - China," XXI (1843), 125-42.

964   "The North-West Boundary Question," XXI (1843), 377-94.

965   "EMIGRATION," XXI (1843), 506-20.

966   "Australia - Present and Future," XXIV (1844), 219-39.

967   Lynch, Major. "Major Lynch's Journal of a Residence among the Ghilzies in 1839-40," XXIV (1844), 326-52, 479-504, 576-94, 686-701 (Afghanistan).

968   "Ceylon," XXIV (1844), 400-12.

969   "India - Elphinstone's and Wilson's HISTORIES," XXV (1845), 630-48.

970   "THE CONQUEST OF SCINDE," XXVI (1845), 101-09.

971   "New Zealand," XXVI (1845), 405-19.

972   G., M.R. "Travelling in India," XXVI (1845), 563-70.

973   "Borneo - Captain Keppel and Mr. Brooke," XXVII (1846), 387-405.

974   "Pearce's MEMOIRS OF THE MARQUESS OF WELLESLEY," XXVII (1846), 517-35 (notes on India).

975   "Our Portrait Gallery - No. XL: Sir Henry Pottinger, Bart.," XXVIII (1846), 426-42 (China and India).

976   "THE HISTORY OF THE SIKHS," XXIX (1847), 546-58 (Punjab).

977   "Narayun Bawa, the Pseudo-Messiah of the Mahrattas," XXX (1847), 412-21 (India).

978   "Theory and Phenomena of Possession among the Hindoos:
      Part I - Demoniac Possession," XXXI (1848), 315-19;
      "Part II - Women; or, the Divine Possession," 320-30.

979   "English Adventure in Borneo," XXXI (1848), 647-61.

980   Onesiphorus [Sirr, Henry Charles]. "China and the
      Chinese," XXXII (1848), 32-48, 126-42, 295-314.

981   "Pythonic and Demoniac Possessions in India and Judea,"
      XXXII (1848), 262-75, 421-43.

982   Onesiphorus [Sirr, Henry Charles]. "Ceylon and the
      Cingalese," XXXII (1848), 563-78, 697-714; XXXIII
      (1849), 36-59, 228-37, 382-91, 463-77, 612-25, 681-
      92; XXXIV (1849), 61-78, 153-67, 293-304, 392-405,
      555-74 (see #993).

983   "British India," XXXII (1848), 607-24.

984   "Warren, or the Oracular Afflatus of the Hindoos,"
      XXXIII (1849), 307-24.

985   Smyth O'Connor, Major Luke, 1st West India Regiment.
      "A Few Words about Mosquitia and Mosquitos," XXXIV
      (1849), 172-80 (Central America).

986   "The Canadas - How Long Can We Hold Them?" XXXIV (1849),
      314-30.

987   "Notes and Suggestions on Indian Affairs," XXXIV (1849),
      592-610, 700-17.

988   "CHINA AND THE CHINESE," XXXIV (1849), 739-52.

989   "Borneo and the Pirate System," XXXV (1850), 107-16.

990   "Canada," XXXV (1850), 151-68.

991   "Expedition against the Chinese Pirates," XXXV (1850),
      521-30.

992   "Sir James Brooke - the Rajah of Sarawak," XXXV (1850),
      574-83.

993   "Sirr's CEYLON," XXXVI (1850), 241-52 (see #982).

994   "The Euphrates Expedition," XXXVI (1850), 381-92.

995   "Daimoniac [sic] Possession, Oracles, and Medical
      Thaumaturgy in India," XXXVII (1851), 52-67.

996   "Major Herbert Edwardes's YEAR ON THE PUNJAB FRONTIER,"
      XXXVII (1851), 411-26.

997   "CHRISTIANITY IN CEYLON," XXXVII (1851), 557-76.

998   "Our Portrait Gallery - No. LXVI: Sir James Emerson
       Tennent," XXXIX (1852), 84-97 (notes on Ceylon).

999   "Administration of Scinde," XXXIX (1852), 363-72.

1000   "Sir John Richardson's ARCTIC EXPEDITION," XXXIX (1852),
       458-76 (notes on Hudson's Bay Company).

1001   "Australia and Its Gold Diggings," XXXIX (1852), 607-25.

1002   "China - the War - the Peace," XL (1852), 318-32.

1003   Nicholl, Andrew. "A Sketching Tour of Five Weeks in
       the Forests of Ceylon," XL (1852), 527-40, 691-700.

1004   "The Indian Archipelago," XLI (1853), 315-31 (East
       Indies).

1005   "New South Wales and Tasmania," XLI (1853), 453-72.

1006   "THE ISTHMUS OF DARIEN," XLI (1853), 718-26 (Central
       America).

1007   An English Radical. "Our Colonies," XLI (1853), 758-76.

1008   " 'The Story of Mairwara, and the Labours of Colonel
       Hall'," XLII (1853), 69-87 (India).

1009   "A Voyage to Van Diemen's Land," XLIII (1854), 9-20,
       275-82.

1010   "VICTORIA," XLIII (1854), 192-204.

1011   "British Rule in India," XLIII (1854), 475-92.

1012   "The Himalayas," XLIII (1854), 670-84 (notes on Sikkim).

1013   "THE WEST INDIES," XLIV (1854), 29-43.

1014   "The Nott Correspondence and Memoirs," XLIV (1854),
       297-309 (Afghanistan).

1015   "Polynesia," XLVI (1855), 18-37 (notes on Maoris of
       New Zealand).

1016   "The Rail in Canada," XLVI (1855), 127-37.

1017   "Traditions, Customs, and Superstitions of the New
       Zealanders," XLVII (1856), 221-35.

1018   "Position and Prospects of Popular Education in the
       British Empire," XLVIII (1856), 240-52 (focus is
       education in Great Britain).

1019   "Our Political Relations with Persia," XLVIII (1856),
       631-46.

1020   "Our Antipodean Neighbours," XLVIII (1856), 735-48
       (Australia).

1021 "Oude, as a Kingdom," XLIX (1857), 112-28.

1022 "Travelling in China," XLIX (1857), 216-28.

1023 "Transportation," XLIX (1857), 322-34.

1024 "The Cotton Fields of India," XLIX (1857), 678-89.

1025 "The Opium Traffic," L (1857), 59-66 (China and India).

1026 "Sir Charles Napier in India," L (1857), 129-39.

1027 "The Indian Mutiny," L (1857), 236-45.

1028 "Historical Sketch of Delhi," L (1857), 352-60.

1029 "Lady Falkland's Journal in India," L (1857), 360-67.

1030 "The Revolt of the Bengal Army," L (1857), 383-94.

1031 "Recent Books on India," L (1857), 468-76.

1032 "How We Talked about the Indian Mutiny: an Extract
      from the Journal of a Public Servant," L (1857), 625-
      38, 742-57.

1033 "Livingstone's MISSIONARY TRAVELS," LI (1858), 56-74
      (notes on trade in Zambezi area).

1034 "Henry Havelock, of Lucknow," LI (1858), 197-209.

1035 "The Euphrates Valley Railway," LI (1858), 239-48.

1036 An Eastern. "Notes on India," LI (1858), 320-31.

1037 "The Hudson's Bay Company," LI (1858), 430-37.

1038 "Double Government," LI (1858), 460-70 (India).

1039 "The Defence of Lucknow: Martial Incidents in Oude,"
      LI (1858), 479-93.

1040 "Suez Ship Canal," LI (1858), 542-52.

1041 "The Indian Resolutions," LI (1858), 690-92.

1042 "Indian Commerce," LII (1858), 142-53.

1043 "The Homes of the South," LII (1858), 298-312 (Australia
      and New Zealand).

1044 "Christianity in India," LII (1858), 640-51.

1045 "A British Straw upon an Indian Stream," LIII (1859),
      47-56 (English colonial life).

1046 "M. de Montalembert on the Indian Debate," LIII (1859),
      118-28.

1047   Heard, J.B., B.A. "The Analogy between the Decline of
Paganism in the Roman Empire, and Its Present Decline
in India," LIII (1859), 129-46.

1048   "Anglo-Saxon Colonization," LIII (1859), 499-512.

1049   Heard, J.B., B.A. "Prize Essay on Christianity in
India," LIII (1859), 513-38, 641-64.

1050   "Kaye and Marshman on India," LIV (1859), 334-57.

1051   "Tennent's CEYLON," LVI (1860), 59-67.

1052   "Notes on New Books," LVI (1860), 446-58, 616-28, 741-
50 (notes on British Columbia and India).

1053   "Sketches in the West Indies," LVI (1860), 607-16.

1054   "The Maori War," LVII (1861), 175-83 (New Zealand).

1055   "The Morality of Garbled Blue Books," LVII (1861), 530-
38 (Afghanistan).

1056   "China," LVII (1861), 560-69.

1057   "Scenes and Customs in the West Indies - Jamaica,"
LVII (1861), 675-86.

1058   "Australian Life," LVIII (1861), 361-66.

1059   "Salmon Fishing in the Canadian River Moisie," LVIII
(1861), 423-31.

1060   "Ceylon and the Eastern Archipelago," LVIII (1861),
751-53.

1061   "Mr. Goldwin Smith on the Colonies," LIX (1862), 259-66.

1062   "China's Greatest River - the Yang-Tse-Kiang," LIX
(1862), 387-96 (1861 trade expedition).

1063   "Two Gossiping Books of Travel," LX (1862), 346-58
(Australia and India).

1064   "The West Indies and American Slavery," LX (1862), 465-75.

1065   "The Yang-Tsze River, and the Taepings in China," LXI
(1863), 24-33.

1066   "A Cruise about British Columbia," LXI (1863), 482-85.

1067   "Indian Adventure - Treasure Hunting," LXI (1863), 564-
68.

1068   "Emigration as an Agency of Lancashire Relief," LXI
(1863), 595-99.

1069   "A Couple of Indian Recollections," LXII (1863), 350-54.

1070   "England and Her Colonies," LXIV (1864), 483-96.

1071   "The Crisis of British Rule in India," LXV (1865), 56-68.

1072   "Indian Biography," LXX (1867), 466-72 (famous Englishmen).

THE ECLECTIC REVIEW

1073   "Insurrection in Jamaica," VII 3S. (1832), 244-60.

1074   "Landers' EXPEDITION TO THE NIGER," VII 3S. (1832), 359-97.

1075   "The Neilgherry Hills," VII 3S. (1832), 422-41 (India).

1076   "Disturbances in Jamaica," VII 3S. (1832), 544-47.

1077   "Tod's ANNALS OF RAJASTHAN," VIII 3S. (1832), 120-45 (India).

1078   "Statham's INDIAN RECOLLECTIONS," VIII 3S. (1832), 168-72 (recollections of Baptist missionary).

1079   "M'Culloch's DICTIONARY OF COMMERCE," VIII 3S. (1832), 209-26 (notes on colonial trade).

1080   "Earle's RESIDENCE IN NEW ZEALAND," VIII 3S. (1832), 239-47.

1081   "Negro Colonization and Emancipation," VIII 3S. (1832), 385-405.

1082   "Navigation of the Euphrates," IX 3S. (1833), 263-65.

1083   "The Canadas," IX 3S. (1833), 338-46.

1084   "Colonial Slavery," IX 3S. (1833), 346-57.

1085   "Eliot on CHRISTIANITY AND SLAVERY," IX 3S. (1833), 383-97 (West Indies).

1086   "On Secondary Punishments," IX 3S. (1833), 453-73 (transportation).

1087   "Free and Slave Labour," IX 3S. (1833), 544-47.

1088   "Pebrer's RESOURCES OF THE BRITISH EMPIRE," X 3S. (1833), 22-42 (notes on trade).

1089   "Owen's VOYAGES TO AFRICA, Etc.," X 3S. (1833), 181-203 (notes on South Africa).

1090   "Voyage of the AMHERST to Northern China," X 3S. (1833), 326-43.

1091 "Mrs. Carmichael on West Indian Manners," X 3S. (1833), 397-415.

1092 "The African Nations," X 3S. (1833), 480-508 (notes on natives of South Africa).

1093 "Pringle's AFRICAN SKETCHES," XI 3S. (1834), 425-41 (South Africa).

1094 "Australian Colonies," XII 3S. (1834), 123-53.

1095 "Burnes's TRAVELS INTO BOKHARA," XII 3S. (1834), 204-32 (Central Asia).

1096 "Emigration to Canada," XII 3S. (1834), 331-37.

1097 "THE NEW BRITISH PROVINCE OF SOUTH AUSTRALIA," XIII 3S. (1835), 167-87.

1098 "Abeel's RESIDENCE IN CHINA, Etc.," XIII 3S. (1835), 304-18.

1099 "Mission to the Karens," XIV 3S. (1835), 57-74 (Burma).

1100 "MEMOIRS OF RAFFLES," XIV 3S. (1835), 189-98 (Singapore).

1101 "Innes's LETTER TO LORD GLENEG," XIV 3S. (1835), 375-404 (West Indies since emancipation).

1102 "Indian Scenes and Characteristics," XIV 3S. (1835), 414-31.

1103 "Cape Colony and the Caffer War," XV 3S. (1836), 77-87 (South Africa).

1104 "Church Missionary Society's Missions: Abyssinia and New Zealand," XV 3S. (1836), 123-44.

1105 "THE BACKWOODS OF CANADA," XV 3S. (1836), 158-65.

1106 "The Serampore Mission," XV 3S. (1836), 246-56 (India).

1107 "Abolition of Slavery," XV 3S. (1836), 325-33 (West Indies).

1108 "Intercourse with China," XV 3S. (1836), 346-51.

1109 "Gardiner's JOURNEY TO THE ZOOLU COUNTRY," XV 3S. (1836), 504-12 (South Africa).

1110 "Memoir of Dr. Carey," XVI 3S. (1836), 449-64 (missionary in Bengal).

1111 "Colonial Legislation," I 4S. (1837), 188-200 (Jamaica).

1112 "Working of the Apprenticeship System," I 4S. (1837), 356-75 (West Indies).

1113   "Bacon's HINDOSTAN," I 4S. (1837), 477-91.

1114   "Jamaica: Apprenticeship - Narrative of James Williams,"
        II 4S. (1837), 86-94; with note, 341-44.

1115   "British Support of Idolatry in India," II 4S. (1837),
        233-50.

1116   "Present State of the Anti-Slavery Cause," III 4S.
        (1838), 54-77 (West Indies).

1117   "Davis' China," III 4S. (1838), 146-60.

1118   "War in Canada - Its Causes and Consequences," III 4S.
        (1838), 214-37.

1119   "Colonization of New Zealand," III 4S. (1838), 382-95.

1120   "Anti-Slavery Crisis: Policy of Ministers," III 4S.
        (1838), 458-80 (West Indies).

1121   "Division on Sir G. Strickland's Motion: Effect of
        Ministerial Policy," III 4S. (1838), 582-99 (West
        Indies).

1122   "Auber's RISE AND PROGRESS OF THE BRITISH POWER IN
        INDIA," IV 4S. (1838), 125-59.

1123   "Results of Anti-Slavery Agitation - Abolition of
        Negro Apprenticeship," IV 4S. (1838), 230-44 (West
        Indies).

1124   "The Church of England in Canada," IV 4S. (1838), 249-
        70.

1125   "CHINA: ITS STATE AND PROSPECTS," IV 4S. (1838), 271-
        80.

1126   "Aborigines Protection Society," IV 4S. (1838), 319-31
        (colonies).

1127   "Thome and Kimball's Tour in ANTIGUA, BARBADOES, AND
        JAMAICA," IV 4S. (1838), 450-60.

1128   "Hodgson's TRUTHS FROM THE WEST INDIES," IV 4S. (1838),
        532-47.

1129   "Reform of Prison Discipline," IV 4S. (1838), 568-90
        (note on transportation).

1130   "European Colonization - Its Crimes and Improvement,"
        IV 4S. (1838), 646-71.

1131   "Australian Discovery - Killing Natives by Explorers,"
        V 4S. (1839), 157-85.

1132   "Jameson's CANADA," V 4S. (1839), 331-48.

1133   "Aggressive Policy of Russia," V 4S. (1839), 457-78
        (India).

1134   "Sir Francis Head's NARRATIVE," V 4S. (1839), 556-71
        (Canada).

1135   "Polack's NEW ZEALAND," VI 4S. (1839), 31-49.

1136   "Trevelyan on Education in India," VI 4S. (1839), 393-
        407.

1137   "THE INIQUITIES OF THE OPIUM TRADE," VI 4S. (1839),
        458-68 (China).

1138   "The Prospects of Turkey," VI 4S. (1839), 707-30
        (notes on Aden, East Africa, and Egypt).

1139   "Martin's History of British India," VII 4S. (1840),
        219-27.

1140   "Present Condition of British India," VII 4S. (1840),
        304-26.

1141   "Malcolm's TRAVELS IN SOUTH-EASTERN ASIA," VII 4S.
        (1840), 334-45 (India).

1142   "Recent Missionary Works," VII 4S. (1840), 413-26
        (India).

1143   "The Opium Trade and the War," VII 4S. (1840), 699-725
        (China).

1144   "Sir William Lloyd's NARRATIVE," VIII 4S. (1840), 92-
        101 (India).

1145   "The Claims of Home and Colonial Missions," VIII 4S.
        (1840), 446-55.

1146   "The Niger Expedition," VIII 4S. (1840), 456-71.

1147   "The West Indies: Results of Emancipation," IX 4S.
        (1841), 471-85.

1148   "Beecham's ASHANTEE AND GOLD COAST," X 4S. (1841), 18-
        29.

1149   "Wesleyan Methodism," X 4S. (1841), 196-210 (Canada).

1150   "The Publication of Intelligence concerning Aborigines,"
        X 4S. (1841), 297-312 (natives in the empire).

1151   "Kidd's CHINA," XI 4S. (1842), 82-91.

1152   "The Language and Prospects of China," XI 4S. (1842),
        673-91.

1153   "MISSIONARY LABOURS AND SCENES IN SOUTHERN AFRICA,"
       XII 4S. (1842), 269-83.

1154   "Cox's History of the Baptist Mission," XII 4S. (1842),
       637-59 (Jamaica).

1155   "Bonnycastle and Jukes on Newfoundland," XIII 4S.
       (1843), 316-27.

1156   "Taylor's POPULAR HISTORY OF INDIA," XIII 4S. (1843),
       425-39.

1157   "Franklin's Works: Founding, Misruling, and Losing
       Colonies," XIV 4S. (1843), 19-38.

1158   "Chinese Missions," XIV 4S. (1843), 72-81.

1159   "Postans' PERSONAL OBSERVATIONS ON SINDH," XIV 4S.
       (1843), 324-30.

1160   "Christian Missions - Phillippo's JAMAICA," XIV 4S.
       (1843), 633-53.

1161   "Suppression of the Opium Trade," XIV 4S. (1843), 654-
       76 (China).

1162   "Backhouse's VISIT TO THE AUSTRALIAN COLONIES," XIV 4S.
       (1843), 676-87.

1163   "Knowledge of the Affairs of Aborigines Essential to
       Their Safety," XVI 4S. (1844), 223-42 (natives in
       the empire).

1164   "The Church Establishment in the Colonies," XVI 4S.
       (1844), 317-21 (Bahamas).

1165   "HISTORY OF BRITISH INDIA," XVIII 4S. (1845), 1-22.

1166   "Howitt's IMPRESSIONS OF AUSTRALIA," XVIII 4S. (1845),
       166-74.

1167   "Von Orlich's TRAVELS IN INDIA," XVIII 4S. (1845),
       272-86.

1168   "Lyell's TRAVELS IN NORTH AMERICA," XVIII 4S. (1845),
       464-82.

1169   "Dr. Wardlaw's MEMOIRS OF REV. JOHN REID," XIX 4S.
       (1846), 460-69 (missionary in India).

1170   "Borneo and the Eastern Archipelago," XIX 4S. (1846),
       552-76.

1171   "Prospects and Principles of Colonial Reforms," XIX 4S.
       (1846), 576-94.

1172 "MEMOIRS OF THE MARQUESS WELLESLEY," XIX 4S. (1846), 641-60 (India).

1173 "The Oriental Translation Society," XIX 4S. (1846), 679-92 (notes on imperial policy).

1174 "The Third Caffre Invasion of the Cape Colony," XX 4S. (1846), 385-417 (South Africa).

1175 "Discoveries in Australia," XX 4S. (1846), 622-37.

1176 "Angas's SAVAGE LIFE AND SCENES," XXI 4S. (1847), 79-95 (Australia and New Zealand).

1177 "Hinton's MEMOIR OF WILLIAM KNIBB," XXI 4S. (1847), 435-66 (Baptist missionary in Jamaica).

1178 "The Salt Monopoly of India," XXI 4S. (1847), 482-95.

1179 "The Abandonment of Transportation," XXI 4S. (1847), 749-53.

1180 "The Colonial Office, and South Africa," XXII 4S. (1847), 728-38.

1181 "Hutton's FIVE YEARS IN THE EAST," XXIII 4S. (1848), 83-93 (China and India).

1182 "Results of Emancipation - the Immigration Scheme," XXIII 4S. (1848), 197-220 (West Indies).

1183 "The White Rajah in the East," XXIII 4S. (1848), 567-91 (James Brooke in Borneo).

1184 "Marryat's EASTERN ARCHIPELAGO," XXIV 4S. (1848), 51-58.

1185 "FIVE YEARS IN KAFFIRLAND," XXIV 4S. (1848), 156-73 (South Africa).

1186 "The Niger Expedition," XXIV 4S. (1848), 416-32.

1187 "Public Title to Land in New Colonies," XXIV 4S. (1848), 579-84 (notes on New Zealand).

1188 "VIEWS IN THE INDIAN ARCHIPELAGO," XXIV 4S. (1848), 671-80 (East Indies).

1189 "THE EMIGRANT FAMILY," XXV 4S. (1849), 699-708 (Australia).

1190 "Ross's Adventures on the Columbia," XXV 4S. (1849), 746-55 (Hudson's Bay Company territory).

1191 "Colonization and Colonial Reform," XXV 4S. (1849), 755-68.

1192   "Missionary Life in Jamaica - Thomas Burchell," XXVI 4S. (1849), 159-76.

1193   "Ceylon: Its People and Its Resources," XXVI 4S. (1849), 183-94.

1194   "Power's SKETCHES IN NEW ZEALAND," XXVI 4S. (1849), 414-22.

1195   "The Fine Arts in the Colonies," XXVI 4S. (1849), 423-27 (natives in the empire).

1196   "Sturt's EXPEDITION INTO CENTRAL AUSTRALIA," XXVI 4S. (1849), 599-611.

1197   "The Borneo Slaughtering," XXVII 4S. (1850), 137-57.

1198   "Exhibition of Industry, 1851," XXVII 4S. (1850), 557-63 (notes on native rights).

1199   "Warburton's CONQUEST OF CANADA," XXVII 4S. (1850), 657-71.

1200   "Ship-Passage in Central America to the Pacific," XXVII 4S. (1850), 711-20.

1201   "The Hunter in South Africa," XXVIII 4S. (1850), 476-90.

1202   "Emigration: Its Distribution and Importance," I 5S. (1851), 179-90.

1203   "Rovings in the Pacific," I 5S. (1851), 601-11 (Australia and New Zealand).

1204   "The Caffre War," I 5S. (1851), 611-27 (South Africa).

1205   "Progress of Australia," II 5S. (1851), 158-72.

1206   "Arab Travels in Central Africa," II 5S. (1851), 535-49 (Egypt).

1207   "South African Missions: Freeman and Dr. Gray," II 5S. (1851), 591-607.

1208   "Colonel Dixon's SKETCH OF MAIRWARA," II 5S. (1851), 674-83 (India).

1209   "Railway to India," III 5S. (1852), 135-46 (notes on Egypt and Euphrates).

1210   "India and Our Supply of Cotton," III 5S. (1852), 391-409; IV 5S. (1852), 129-45.

1211   "Squier's CENTRAL AMERICA," IV 5S. (1852), 307-16.

1212   "Australia: Its Capabilities and Prospects," IV 5S. (1852), 389-407.

1213   "Australian Progress," IV 5S. (1852), 565-78.

1214   "Horace St. John's British India," IV 5S. (1852), 595-606.

1215   "British South Africa," V 5S. (1853), 49-73.

1216   "St. John's INDIAN ARCHIPELAGO," V 5S. (1853), 677-94 (East Indies).

1217   "India: Its Government and Resources," VI 5S. (1853), 100-24.

1218   "Russell's TOUR IN CEYLON AND INDIA," VI 5S. (1853), 192-96.

1219   "Colonial Reforms beyond Sea," VI 5S. (1853), 458-79.

1220   "The Insurrection in China," VII 5S. (1854), 39-55 (Taipings).

1221   "Progress of the British West Indies," VIII 5S. (1854), 47-58.

1222   "Huc's TRAVELS in China," IX 5S. (1855), 309-20.

1223   "Dalton's BRITISH GUIANA," IX 5S. (1855), 708-17.

1224   "The Colony of Natal," X 5S. (1855), 51-60.

1225   "Government Education in India," X 5S. (1855), 227-37.

1226   "Howitt's TWO YEARS IN VICTORIA," X 5S. (1855), 422-37.

1227   "Captain Allen's NEW ROUTE TO INDIA," X 5S. (1855), 454-66 (Euphrates).

1228   "A VOICE FROM THE WEST INDIES," X 5S. (1855), 514-18.

1229   "Eastern and Western Africa," XI 5S. (1856), 372-82.

1230   "China: Its Civilization and Philosophy," XI 5S. (1856), 550-60.

1231   "Sir John Malcolm," I 6S. (1857), 189-200 (India).

1232   "The Indian Archipelago," I 6S. (1857), 269-84 (East Indies).

1233   "The Euphrates Valley Route to India," I 6S. (1857), 320-26.

1234   "Travels in Australasia," I 6S. (1857), 426-35 (Australia).

1235   "Over Darien by a Ship-Canal, I 6S. (1857), 443-47 (Central America).

1236   "Christianity and Hinduism," I 6S. (1857), 515-33
        (India).

1237   "EUSTACE CAREY," I 6S. (1857), 626-30 (missionary in
        India).

1238   "Indian Irrigation and the Culture of Cotton," II 6S.
        (1857), 104-18.

1239   "LIFE IN CHINA," II 6S. (1857), 263-71.

1240   "AUTOBIOGRAPHY OF LUTFULLAH," II 6S. (1857), 365-72
        (Muslim gentleman in India).

1241   "Westgarth's AUSTRALIA," II 6S. (1857), 372-80.

1242   "The Theory and Practice of Irrigation," II 6S. (1857),
        409-24 (notes on India).

1243   "The Theory and Practice of Caste," II 6S. (1857), 445-
        52 (India).

1244   "Livingstone's African Travels," II 6S. (1857), 505-24
        (Southeast Africa).

1245   "The Indian Mutiny," II 6S. (1857), 524-44.

1246   "The Kingdom of Oude," III 6S. (1858), 352-60.

1247   "Sir Henry Havelock," III 6S. (1858), 371-77 (India).

1248   "The Future Government of India," III 6S. (1858), 443-
        57.

1249   "Snow's TWO YEARS' CRUISE OFF TIERRA DEL FUEGO," IV 6S.
        (1858), 176-78 (Falkland Islands).

1250   "Lord Metcalfe," IV 6S. (1858), 232-42 (Canada, India,
        and Jamaica).

1251   "The Indian Mutiny," IV 6S. (1858), 332-46.

1252   "Fiji and the Fijians," IV 6S. (1858), 520-35.

1253   "Isthmus of Suez Ship Canal," IV 6S. (1858), 541-45.

1254   "The Queen's Government and the Religions of India,"
        I 7S. (1859), 125-48.

1255   "Our New Colony - British Columbia and Vancouver's
        Island," I 7S. (1859), 501-06.

1256   "The Gospel among the Karens," II 7S. (1859), 258-73
        (Burma).

1257   "General Havelock," IV 7S. (1860), 192-201 (India).

1258   "The Opium Revenue of India," V 7S. (1861), 39-47.

1259 "Underhill's WEST INDIES - a Visit to a Ruined Colony," II 8S. (1862), 245-60 (Jamaica).

1260 "Lacroix of Calcutta," II 8S. (1862), 289-302 (missionary).

1261 "Education in British India," IV 8S. (1863), 535-54.

1262 "MEMORIES OF NEW ZEALAND LIFE," VI 8S. (1864), 205-18.

1263 "Tropical Production - the Labour Supply," VII 8S. (1864), 390-96 (West Indies).

1264 "Australian Explorations," VII 8S. (1864), 407-18.

1265 "New South Wales," VII 8S. (1864), 626-36.

1266 "The Problem of Jamaica," IX 8S. (1865), 235-70.

1267 "The Jeopardy of Jamaica," IX 8S. (1865), 359-77.

1268 "The Zambesi - Livingstone and Mackenzie," X 8S. (1866), 47-62.

1269 "Recent Missionary Literature," X 8S. (1866), 315-35 (Pacific).

1270 "CHRISTIANITY AMONG THE NEW ZEALANDERS," XII 8S. (1867), 443-58.

THE EDINBURGH REVIEW

1271 [Mangles, R.D.]. "Government of British India - Revenue Systems," LV (1832), 79-108.

1272 [Malden, Henry]. "Jeremie ON COLONIAL SLAVERY," LV (1832), 144-81 (West Indies).

1273 [Murray, Hugh]. "Lander's VOYAGE AND DISCOVERIES ON THE NIGER," LV (1832), 397-421.

1274 [Erskine, William]. "Colonel Tod ON THE HISTORY AND CHARACTER OF THE RAJPOOTS," LVI (1832-33), 73-98 (India).

1275 "Earle's ACCOUNT OF NEW ZEALAND," LVI (1832-33), 333-49.

1276 [Erskine, William]. "Captain Head's STEAM NAVIGATION TO INDIA," LVII (1833), 313-29.

1277 [Empson, William]. "Recent Travels in Upper India," LVII (1833), 358-70.

1278 [Grey, Charles]. "Secondary Punishments - Transportation," LVIII (1833-34), 336-62.

1279   [Pringle, Thomas]. "Kay's TRAVELS IN CAFFRARIA," LVIII
        (1833-34), 363-87 (South Africa).

1280   [Lister, T.H.]. "JOURNAL OF A WEST INDIAN PROPRIETOR,"
        LIX (1834), 404-25.

1281   "Conolly's JOURNEY TO THE NORTH OF INDIA," LX (1834-
        35), 54-66.

1282   [Cooley, W.D.]. "Burnes's TRAVELS INTO BOKHARA," LX
        (1834-35), 395-442 (Afghanistan, Punjab, and Sind).

1283   [Peacock, T.L.]. "On Steam Navigation to India," LX
        (1834-35), 445-82.

1284   [Cooley, W.D.]. "Cape of Good Hope - the Late Caffre
        War," LXII (1835-36), 455-70.

1285   [Brougham, Henry]. "Marquess Wellesley's INDIAN ADMIN-
        ISTRATION," LXIII (1836), 537-59.

1286   [Trevelyan, Charles E.]. "The Thugs; or, Secret Murder-
        ers of India," LXIV (1836-37), 357-95.

1287   [Browne, James]. "Modern Egypt and the Modern Egyptians,"
        LXV (1837), 146-73 (notes on Ionian Islands).

1288   [Brougham, Henry]. "The Marquess of Wellesley's Des-
        patches," LXVI (1837-38), 151-55 (India).

1289   [Cooley, W.D.]. "Laird and Oldfield's EXPEDITION INTO
        AFRICA," LXVI (1837-38), 326-57 (West Africa).

1290   [Spedding, James]. "The Negro Apprenticeship System,"
        LXVI (1837-38), 477-522 (West Indies).

1291   [Stephen, James]. "Life of William Wilberforce," LXVII
        (1838), 142-80 (notes on West Indies).

1292   [Brougham, Henry]. "Lord Brougham's SPEECHES ON
        SLAVERY," LXVII (1838), 198-201 (West Indies).

1293   [Murray, George]. "Duke of Wellington's Indian Des-
        patches," LXVIII (1838-39), 1-46.

1294   [Cooley, W.D.]. "Ruschenberger's VOYAGE ROUND THE
        WORLD," LXVIII (1838-39), 46-75 (notes on Ceylon and
        opium trade).

1295   [Hall, Basil]. "Voyages of Captains King and Fitzroy,"
        LXIX (1839), 467-93 (notes on Falkland Islands).

1296   [Spedding, James]. "The Jamaica Question," LXIX (1839),
        527-56.

1297   [Macaulay, T.B.]. "Sir John Malcolm's LIFE OF LORD
        CLIVE," LXX (1839-40), 295-362 (India).

1298   [Mangles, R.D.]. "Revenue System of British India," LXX
        (1839-40), 391-426.

1299   [Merivale, Herman]. "Court and Camp of Runjeet Singh,"
        LXXI (1840), 263-75 (Punjab).

1300   [Mangles, R.D.]. "Present State and Prospects of Brit-
        ish India," LXXI (1840), 327-70.

1301   [Spedding, James]. "New Theory of Colonization," LXXI
        (1840), 517-44 (Wakefield plan).

1302   [Brougham, Henry]. "The Foreign Slave Trade," LXXII
        (1840-41), 179-93 (notes on "free" immigration).

1303   [Mangles, R.D.]. "Wrongs and Claims of Indian Commerce,"
        LXXII (1840-41), 340-83.

1304   [Spedding, James]. "The Expedition to the Niger -
        Civilization of Africa," LXXII (1840-41), 456-77.

1305   [Mangles, R.D.]. "Administration of Justice in British
        India," LXXIII (1841), 425-60.

1306   [Macaulay, T.B.]. "Warren Hastings," LXXIV (1841-42),
        160-255 (India).

1307   [Senior, N.W.]. "France, America, and Britain," LXXV
        (1842), 1-48 (notes on the empire).

1308   [Spedding, James]. "South Australia," LXXV (1842), 140-
        62.

1309   [Mangles, R.D.]. "Government of India - Its Constitution
        and Departments," LXXVI (1842-43), 171-202.

1310   [Mangles, R.D.]. "Ministerial Misrepresentations regard-
        ing the East," LXXVII (1843), 261-300 (Afghanistan).

1311   [Merivale, Herman]. "Mexico and the Great Western
        Prairies," LXXVIII (1843), 157-92 (notes on Hudson's
        Bay Company territory).

1312   [Strachey, William]. "CONQUEST OF SCINDE," LXXIX (1844),
        476-544.

1313   [Merivale, Herman]. "British Mission to Shoa," LXXX
        (1844), 43-67 (notes on Aden and East Africa).

1314   [McNeill, John]. "The Bokhara Victims," LXXXII (1845),
        132-71 (Central Asia).

1315   [Senior, N.W.]. "The Oregon Question," LXXXII (1845), 238-65.

1316   "Wilkes' EXPLORING EXPEDITION," LXXXIII (1846), 431-52 (Pacific and Singapore).

1317   [Senior, N.W.]. "Lewis, ON THE GOVERNMENT OF DEPEND-ENCIES," LXXXIII (1846), 512-54.

1318   "Borneo and the Indian Archipelago," LXXXIV (1846), 147-75.

1319   [Lewis, G.C.]. "Colonial Protection," LXXXIV (1846), 236-66 (trade).

1320   [Mangles, R.D.]. "Government of British India," LXXXIV (1846), 452-79.

1321   [Buller, Charles]. "Sir Francis Head's EMIGRANT: Canada," LXXXV (1847), 358-97.

1322   [Rogers, Henry]. "What is To Be Done with Our Crimi-nals?" LXXXVI (1847), 214-72 (transportation).

1323   [Porter, G.R.]. "Navigation Laws," LXXXVI (1847), 273-306.

1324   [St. John, J.A.]. "Piracy in the Oriental Archipelago," LXXXVIII (1848), 63-94 (East Indies).

1325   [Carpenter, William Benjamin]. "Ethnology, or the Science of Races," LXXXVIII (1848), 429-87 (notes on natives in the empire).

1326   [Woodham, H.A.]. "The Punjab," LXXXIX (1849), 184-221.

1327   [O'Brien, W.]. "Transportation as It Now Is," XC (1849), 1-39.

1328   [Porter, G.R.]. "Free Trade," XC (1849), 133-55.

1329   [DeVere, Aubrey]. "Colonization," XCI (1850), 1-62.

1330   [Chapman, H.S.]. "The Polynesians: and New Zealand," XCI (1850), 443-71.

1331   [Buxton, Charles]. "The African Squadron," XCII (1850), 241-62 (notes on West Indies).

1332   [Fergusson, James]. "The Euphrates Expedition," XCII (1850), 436-67.

1333   [Burton, J. Hill]. "Emigration and Industrial Train-ing," XCII (1850), 491-504.

1334   [Greg, W.R.]. "Shall We Retain Our Colonies?" XCIII (1851), 475-98.

1335 [Greg, W.R.]. "Johnston's NOTES ON NORTH AMERICA,"
      XCIV (1851), 46-64 (Canada and New Brunswick).

1336 "Campbell's MODERN INDIA," XCVI (1852), 33-35.

1337 [Knox, A.A.]. "Dutch Diplomacy and Indian Piracy,"
      XCVI (1852), 54-94 (East Indies).

1338 [Greg, W.R.]. "Representative Reform," XCVI (1852),
      452-508 (colonists in Parliament).

1339 [Colborne, John]. "Jervis's HISTORY OF CORFU AND THE
      IONIAN ISLANDS," XCVII (1853), 41-86.

1340 [Gleig, G.R.]. "The Indian Army," XCVII (1853), 183-220.

1341 [Crawfurd, John]. "The Nations of India and Their Man-
      ners," XCVIII (1853), 33-61.

1342 [Lewis, G.C.]. "Lord Grey's COLONIAL ADMINISTRATION,"
      XCVIII (1853), 62-98.

1343 [Beaumont, Joseph]. "Relations of England with China,"
      XCVIII (1853), 98-131.

1344 [Howell, T. James]. "Quarantine, Small Pox, and Yellow
      Fever," XCVIII (1853), 191-215 (notes on West Indies).

1345 [Devereux, H.B.]. "Public Works in the Presidency of
      Madras," XCIX (1854), 130-57.

1346 [Forster, W.E.]. "Kafir Wars and Cape Policy," C (1854),
      115-63 (South Africa).

1347 [Mansfield, W.R.]. "The Russian War of 1854," C (1854),
      264-302 (notes on India).

1348 [Greg, W.R.]. "The Management and Disposal of Our
      Criminal Population," C (1854), 563-632 (notes on
      transportation).

1349 [Rogers, Henry]. "M. Huc's TRAVELS in China," CI (1855),
      415-42.

1350 [Johnston, J.F.W.]. "Indian Substitutes for Russian
      Produce," CII (1855), 40-59.

1351 [Mangles, R.D.]. "Statesmen of India," CII (1855), 147-
      78.

1352 [Milne, W.C.]. "Political Disturbances in China," CII
      (1855), 346-77 (Taipings).

1353 [Mangles, R.D.]. "The Court of Oude," CII (1855), 404-
      17.

1354   [Forbes, J.D.]. "Himalayan Journals," CIII (1856), 55-
         81 (Nepal and Sikkim).

1355   [Russell, C.W. and Smith, Maj.]. "The Use of Torture
         in India," CIII (1856), 153-80.

1356   [Fergusson, James]. "The Suez Canal," CIII (1856),
         235-67; with anonymous note, 298-300.

1357   [Bulwer, W.H.L.]. "Great Britain and the United States,"
         CIV (1856), 267-98 (Central America).

1358   [Kaye, J.W.]. "India, Persia, and Afghanistan," CV
         (1857), 266-304.

1359   [Alcock, Rutherford]. "British Relations with China,"
         CV (1857), 517-51.

1360   [Kaye, J.W.]. "Napier," CVI (1857), 322-55 (notes on
         Sind).

1361   [Kaye, J.W.]. "India," CVI (1857), 544-94.

1362   [Reeve, Henry]. "Prospects of the Indian Empire,"
         CVII (1858), 1-50.

1363   [Kaye, J.W.]. "The Conquest of Oude," CVII (1858), 513-
         40.

1364   [Lewis, G.C.]. "The Second Derby Ministry," CVII
         (1858), 540-82.

1364a   [Cowell, E.B.]. "The Hindu Drama," CVIII (1858), 253-
         70.

1365   [Lowe, Robert]. "The Hudson's Bay Territory," CIX
         (1859), 122-56.

1365a   [Lewis, G.C.]. "Life and Correspondence of Lord
         Cornwallis," CIX (1859), 387-421 (notes on India).

1366   [Buxton, Charles]. "The West Indies, as They Were and
         Are," CIX (1859), 421-60.

1366a   [Stephen, Fitzjames]. "Major Hodson's LIFE," CIX
         (1859), 545-58 (Indian mutiny).

1367   [Owen, Richard]. "Sir Emerson Tennent's CEYLON," CX
         (1859), 343-75.

1368   [Reeve, Henry]. "Lord Elgin's MISSION TO CHINA AND
         JAPAN," CXI (1860), 96-118.

1369   [Cairnes, J.E.]. "Chevalier on THE PROBABLE FALL IN
         THE VALUE OF GOLD," CXII (1860), 1-33 (effects on
         the empire).

1370 [Galton, Douglas]. "Ocean Telegraphy," CXIII (1861),
113-43 (use to connect the empire).

1371 [Bayley, C.H.]. "Sewell's ORDEAL OF FREE LABOUR," CXV
(1862), 42-66 (West Indies).

1372 [Lewis, G.C.]. "Military Defense of the Colonies," CXV
(1862), 104-26.

1373 [Taylor, Meadows]. "Cotton Culture in India," CXV
(1862), 478-509.

1374 [Thynne, Robert]. "The Explorers of Australia," CXVI
(1862), 1-46.

1375 [Martineau, Harriet]. "The English in the Eastern Seas,"
CXVI (1862), 398-417 (Borneo).

1376 [Campbell, G.D.]. "India under Lord Dalhousie," CXVII
(1863), 1-42.

1377 [Thynne, Robert]. "Goldfields and Goldminers," CVXII
(1863), 82-116 (Australia).

1378 [Martineau, Harriet]. "Convict System in England and
Ireland," CXVII (1863), 241-68 (notes on transportation).

1379 [Campbell, G.D.]. "India under Lord Canning," CXVII
(1863), 444-97.

1380 [Thynne, Robert]. "Queensland," CXVIII (1863), 305-41.

1381 [Ball, James]. "Chinchona Cultivation in India,"
CXVIII (1863), 507-22.

1382 [Merivale, Herman]. "The Colonial Episcopate," CXVIII
(1863), 552-87.

1383 [Mangles, R.D.]. "The Progress of India," CXIX (1864),
95-136.

1384 [Taylor, Meadows]. "Human Sacrifice and Infanticide in
India," CXIX (1864), 389-412.

1385 [Thynne, Robert]. "British North America," CXIX (1864),
441-80.

1386 [Lowe, Robert]. "Criminal Law Reform," CXXI (1865),
109-35 (notes on transportation).

1387 [Mills, Arthur]. "The British North American Federation," CXXI (1865), 181-99.

1388 [Thynne, Robert]. "The Australian Colonies," CXXI
(1865), 349-83.

1389   [Alcock, Rutherford]. "China and Japan," CXXII (1865), 175-202.

1390   [Taylor, Meadows]. "The Rock-cut Temples of India," CXXII (1865), 371-95 (notes on history and religion of the Deccan).

1391   [Mangles, R.D.]. "Kaye's HISTORY OF THE SEPOY WAR," CXXIV (1866), 299-340 (Indian mutiny).

1392   [Wyllie, J.W.S.]. "Foreign Policy of Sir John Lawrence," CXXV (1867), 1-47 (Indian defense).

1393   [Taylor, Meadows]. "Indian Costumes and Textile Fabrics," CXXVI (1867), 125-50.

THE FOREIGN QUARTERLY REVIEW

1394   [Courtenay, T.P.]. "The Reciprocity System," IX (1832), 261-89.

1395   [Southern, Henry]. "Penal Colonies," IX (1832), 422-37 (transportation).

1396   [Taylor, W.C.]. "Jacquemont's LETTERS FROM INDIA," XIII (1834), 107-32.

1397   [Devereux, Humphrey B.]. "Judicial System of British India," XIII (1834), 406-41.

1398   [Taylor, W.C.]. "Central Asia," XIV (1834), 58-92.

1399   [Clarkson, Edward]. "Steam Navigation to India," XVIII (1836-37), 342-92 (Egypt and Euphrates).

1400   "The Thugs, or Phansigars," XXI (1838), 1-32 (India).

1401   [Courtenay, T.P.]. "Canada," XXI (1838), 191-220.

1402   "Russian Position and Policy towards Turkey, Circassia, Persia, and Hindostan," XXII (1838-39), 183-213.

1403   [Pote, B.E. and a collaborator]. "Late Proceedings in India: English Usurpation of Oude," XXIII (1839), 93-116.

1404   "Russian Actual Policy: Persia, Hindostan, and Central Asia," XXIII (1839), 161-212 (also Afghanistan and Punjab).

1405   [Pote, B.E. and a collaborator]. "Russia, Persia, Turkey, and France," XXIII (1839), 413-43 (also Afghanistan and Punjab).

1406   "The Opium Trade with China," XXIV (1839-40), 106-38.

1407   [Pote, B.E.]. "Turkey, Egypt, France, Russia, Asia,
        and the British Ministry," XXIV (1839-40), 386-421
        (notes on Afghanistan and China).

1408   "War with China," XXV (1840), 188-206.

1409   [Worthington, J.W.]. "South Australia," XXV (1840),
        374-93.

1410   [Bannister, Saxe]. "Herder, the Protector of Aboriginal
        People," XXVI (1840-41), 80-94 (notes on natives in
        the empire).

1411   [Clarkson, Edward]. "France and England," XXVI (1840-
        41), 428-56 (notes on Egypt and defense of region).

1412   "Clot-Bey's GENERAL OBSERVATIONS ON EGYPT," XXVII (1841),
        362-93 (notes on trade route to India).

1413   "Hugel's TRAVELS IN CASHMERE," XXVIII (1841-42), 45-63.

1414   "Sinde, Its Amirs and Its People," XXXII (1843-44), 491-
        524.

1415   [St. John, Bayle and St. John, J.A.]. "English and
        French Rivalry in Eastern Africa," XXXIII (1844), 79-
        111 (also Aden).

1416   "Problematic Invasion of British India," XXXIII (1844),
        213-29.

1417   [St. John, J.A.]. "Fontanier's Eastern Mission," XXXIII
        (1844), 299-320 (India).

1418   "The Anglo-Indian Army," XXXIII (1844), 388-432.

1419   "The Punjab," XXXIV (1844-45), 70-104.

1420   [St. John, Bayle]. "French Aggressions in the Pacific,"
        XXXIV (1844-45), 165-94 (notes on reasons for an
        empire).

1421   "Sacrifice of British Ambassadors in Central Asia,"
        XXXIV (1844-45), 221-38 (defense against Russia).

1422   "RAMBLES AND RECOLLECTIONS OF AN INDIAN OFFICIAL,"
        XXIV (1844-45), 369-89.

1423   [St. John, Bayle and ?St. John, Percy]. "Projected
        Ship Canal across the Great American Isthmus." XXXIV
        (1844-45), 389-400 (Central America).

1424   "Field Sports of South Africa," XXXIV (1844-15), 421-31.

1425   [St. John, Bayle]. "British Intercourse with China,"
        XXXIV (1844-45), 432-49.

1426   "Lord Ellenborough's Indian Policy," XXXIV (1844-45), 479-514.

1427   "The History of British India," XXXV (1845), 34-55.

1428   "Railways in India," XXXV (1845), 382-409.

1429   [St. John, J.A.]. "The Surveys of the Indian Navy," XXXV (1845), 454-88.

1430   "The Oregon Territory," XXXV (1845), 489-517.

1431   "TRAVELS IN KASHMIR AND THE PANJAB," XXXVI (1845-46), 196-231.

1432   "Indian Railways and the Indian Press," XXXVI (1845-46), 306-23.

1433   "The Political Prospects of Our Empire in the East," XXXVI (1845-46), 486-505 (India).

1434   [St. John, J.A.]. "The English in Borneo," XXXVII (1846), 63-105.

1435   "The Governor General of India, and the War in the Punjab," XXXVII (1846), 212-34.

1436   "Stokes's DISCOVERIES IN AUSTRALIA," XXXVII (1846), 257-80.

1436a   [St. John, J.A.]. "The Diffusion of Christianity," XXXVII (1846), 494-528 (notes on the empire with emphasis on Borneo).

THE FORTNIGHTLY REVIEW

1437   Bowring, John. "Chinese Characteristics," I (1865), 561-71.

1438   Pelly, Lewis. "British India," II (1865), 31-42.

1439   Jennings, L.J. "The Calcutta Cyclone of 1864," II (1865), 424-31.

1440   Lusk, Hugh. "Maori Mahommedanism," II (1865), 731-37 (New Zealand).

1441   Macfie, Matthew. "The True North-West Passage," III (1865-66), 227-39 (British North America).

1441a   Cooley, W.D. "Dr. Livingstone's Errors," IV (1866), 96-110 (notes on Southeast Africa).

1442   Mackay, Charles. "A Week in Prince Edward Island," V (1866), 143-57.

1443   Morley, John. "England and the Annexation of Mysore,"
        VI (1866), 257-71 (India).

1444   Wynne, G.R. "The Theory of Missionary Effort," VI
        (1866), 714-28 (activities in the empire).

1445   Grant, Alexander. "Tukaram: a Study of Hinduism,"
        VII O.S. and I N.S. (1867), 27-40 (note on need to
        study Indian literature).

1446   Herbert, Auberon. "The Canadian Confederation," VII O.S.
        and I N.S. (1867), 480-90.

FRASER'S MAGAZINE

1447   Z. "The British North American Provinces," V (1832),
        77-84.

1448   "Voyages and Travels: Captain Basil Hall and the
        Landers," V (1832), 462-74 (notes on Niger River
        expedition).

1449   [Maginn, William]. "Canada, by Tiger (William Dunlop) -
        Galt - Picken," V (1832), 633-42.

1450   "The Canada Corn Trade," VI (1832), 362-65.

1451   "The Colonies," VI (1832), 437-45.

1452   Galt, John. "The Free-Trade Question," VI (1832), 593-
        98; VII (1833), 106-11.

1453   Galt, John. "The Whole West Indian Question," VIII
        (1833), 81-90.

1454   "India and England," VIII (1833), 593-603.

1455   "Holman's VOYAGE ROUND THE WORLD," XI (1835), 653-66
        (notes on various dependencies).

1456   Galt, John. "The Metropolitan Emigrant," XII (1835),
        291-99.

1457   [Dunlop, William]. "Authentic Narrative of Facts Which
        Occurred during a March in India: from an Officer's
        Sketch-Book," XII (1835), 664-72.

1458   [Dunlop, William]. "Sketches of Savage Life," XIII
        (1836), 169-76, 316-23, 499-511 (British North
        America).

1459   "Capt, Gardiner's JOURNEY TO THE ZOOLU COUNTRY," XIV
        (1836), 332-48 (South Africa).

1460   "The Life of Lord Clive," XVI (1837), 433-50 (India).

1461   A Sixteen Years' Resident [Brown, John B.]. "Emigration and the United States," XVI (1837), 562-77 (contrasted with British dependencies).

1462   A Sixteen Years' Resident [Brown, John B.]. "Emigration and the Canadas," XVI (1837), 683-96.

1463   "State of Lower Canada," XVII (1838), 233-42.

1464   "The Rehearsal," XVII (1838), 255-58 (Canada and Ireland compared).

1465   "The Bayadères," XVIII (1838), 729-32 (Indian dancers).

1466   "Saints and Sinners in Far Cathay," XIC (1839), 105-14 (Chinese and opium).

1467   [Cumming, John]. "Statistics of Popery in Great Britain and the Colonies," XIX (1839), 261-77, 387-407.

1468   "Voyaging in Hindostan," XIX (1839), 359-66; XX (1839), 42-64.

1469   "The Opium Trade with China," XX (1839), 572-88.

1470   [McDonnell, Richard Graves]. "Poland, England, and Russia," XXI (1840), 177-90 (notes on defense of India and on Central Asia).

1471   "The Opium Question, and the Suspended Trade with China," XXI (1840), 365-75.

1472   "North American Boundary," XXII (1840), 346-58.

1473   [McDonnell, Richard Graves]. "The Russian Alliance," XXII (1840), 592-604 (defense of Central Asia and India).

1474   [McDonnell, R.G.]. "What Does Our Russian Ally Mean To Do?" XXIII (1841), 1-14 (defense of Central Asia, China, and India).

1475   [McDonnell, R.G.]. "Our Foreign Policy, and Home Prospects," XXIII (1841), 235-52 (defense of China and India).

1476   "The Chinese and Our 'Great Plenipotentiary'," XXIV (1841), 612-27 (Sir Charles Elliott).

1477   "Excursion to Port Arthur," XXVI (1842), 281-98 (Van Diemen's Land).

1478   "Affghanistan," XXVI (1842), 493-504, 505-13.

1479   "The Ashburton Treaty," XXVI (1842), 579-94 (see #1481; British North America).

1480 "Our Eastern Policy," XXVII (1843), 108-23 (Afghanistan and China).

1480a A Barbarian Eye. "Wan Tang Jin Wuh," XXVII (1843), 176-84 (China).

1481 "The Ashburton Treaty Again," XXVII (1843), 272-89 (see #1479; British North America).

1482 "The North-West (American) Boundary Question," XXVII (1843), 484-502.

1483 "Colonisation - the Only Cure for National Distress: Mr. Charles Buller's Speech," XXVII (1843), 735-70.

1484 "New South Wales: Colonial Immigration - the Bounty System, and Its Frauds," XXVIII (1843), 426-41.

1485 "The Christian Highlands of Aethiopia," XXIX (1844), 442-49 (East Africa as defense against Franch expansion).

1486 "Lord Ellenborough, and the Affairs of India," XXIX (1844), 472-84.

1487 Morgan Rattler [Banks, P.W.]. "Of the Red Indian," XXIX (1844), 655-76 (British North America).

1488 [Campbell, R. Calder]. "The Suniassie," XXX (1844), 280-87 (Indian mendicants).

1489 "British India - Its State and Prospects," XXX (1844), 743-50.

1490 Anglomane [Gallenga, Antonio]. "England and Yankee-Land," XXXII (1845), 485-96 (notes on Oregon boundary question).

1491 "A Day's Excursion in Newfoundland," XXXII (1845), 740-42.

1492 "The Sikhs - Their Rise and Progress," XXXIII (1846), 478-87 (Punjab).

1493 "Elephant Shooting in Ceylon," XXXIII (1846), 561-76.

1494 "The Sikhs and the Late Campaign," XXXIII (1846), 606-21 (Punjab).

1495 "The BEAGLE's Discoveries in Australia," XXXIV (1846), 105-17.

1496 "Commercial Relations of the Indian Archipelago," XXXIV (1846), 378-91 (East Indies).

1497   Morgan Rattler, Esquire, M.A., An Apprentice of the
       Law [Banks, P.W.]. "Touching Head's Book, and
       Canada," XXXV (1847), 96-110.

1498   Morgan Rattler [Banks, P.W.]. "Touching Canada," XXXV
       (1847), 467-82.

1499   "Lord Grey and His Plans for Colonisation," XXXV (1847),
       738-49.

1500   "What Will the Government Do?" XXXVI (1847), 743-50.

1501   "THE BUSHMAN," XXXVII (1848), 343-56 (Western Austral-
       ia).

1502   "Railway Prospects of India," XXXVII (1848), 414-25.

1503   "Australian Colonies or Republics?" XXXVII (1848), 566-
       78.

1504   South, Lieutenant Michael [Hamley, E.B.]. "Snow Pic-
       tures," XXXIX (1849), 45-58 (Canada).

1505   [Tremenheere, J.H.]. "New Zealand and Its Recent Prog-
       ress under Governor Grey," XXXIX (1849), 78-89.

1506   "The National Debt and Colonization," XXXIX (1849), 90-
       92.

1507   "Wakefield's VIEW OF THE ART OF COLONIZATION," XXXIX
       (1849), 245-58.

1508   "Military Policy - the Late Reductions," XXXIX (1849),
       586-98 (notes on impact for the empire).

1509   "The Macedonian and the English Campaigns in the
       Punjaub," XXXIX (1849), 618-24.

1510   "Roebuck on the Colonies," XXXIX (1849), 624-38.

1511   [Carlyle, Thomas]. "Occasional Discourse on the Negro
       Question," XL (1849), 670-79 (West Indies).

1512   D. [Mill, John Stuart]. "The Negro Question," XLI
       (1850), 25-31 (West Indies).

1513   "Colonial Reform," XLI (1850), 366-78.

1514   "The Island of Cuba," XLII (1850), 107-18 (relationship
       to Central American and West Indian defense and
       trade).

1515   "Canterbury, New Zealand," XLII (1850), 463-72.

1516   [Ludlow, J.M.]. "Captain Hervey's TEN YEARS IN INDIA,"
       XLII (1850), 479-95.

1517 "Commerce with Africa," XLIII (1851), 30-36.

1518 Hardbargain, Captain. "A Jungle Recollection," XLIV
      (1851), 18-25 (see #1535; India).

1519 "Our Wars in Central Asia," XLIV (1851), 537-50
      (Afghanistan).

1520 "What Has the British Tax-Payer To Do with Colonial
      Wars or Constitutions?" XLIV (1851), 575-90.

1521 [Broderip, W.J.]. "The Naturalist in Jamaica," XLV
      (1852), 379-98 (notes on sugar production).

1522 "The East and the West," XLV (1852), 472-84 (British
      North America and Central America).

1523 "Gold and Emigration," XLVI (1852), 127-38.

1524 "Bear Hunting in India," XLVI (1852), 373-85.

1525 [Craufurd, John]. "The Ionian Islands and Their Govern-
      ment," XLVI (1852), 593-608.

1526 "How India is Governed," XLVI (1852), 713-28.

1527 "Bison Hunting in India," XLVII (1853), 39-48.

1528 "Indian Teas and Chinese Travellers," XLVII (1853),
      88-99 (governance of India).

1529 Utrinque. "Concerning Free British Negros; to the
      Editors of FRASER'S MAGAZINE," XLVII (1853), 114-26
      (West Indies).

1530 [Bright, H. Arthur]. "Canada," XLVII (1853), 183-90.

1531 [Arnold, W.D.]. "Progress on the India Question," XLVII
      (1853), 473-84.

1532 "Lord Grey's COLONIAL ADMINISTRATION," XLVII (1853),
      485-99.

1533 "Turkey and the East of Europe in Relation to England
      and the West," XLVII (1853), 562-73 (notes on India
      and Ionian Islands).

1534 "Lieutenant Governor Gore and Upper Canada," XLVII
      (1853), 627-39.

1535 Hardbargain, Captain. "My First Night in the Jungle,"
      XLVIII (1853), 156-64 (see #1518; India).

1536 [Arnold, W.D.]. "What Is the Indian Question?" XLVIII
      (1853), 234-58.

1537 "Extracts from the Journal of a Visit to New South
      Wales in 1853," XLVIII (1853), 506-18, 634-47.

1538 "The North American Fisheries," XLVIII (1853), 587-95.

1539 "The Insurrection in China," XLVIII (1853), 596-606.

1540 "Wolf Nurses in India," XLIX (1854), 587-90 (children
      reared in wilds).

1541 [Arnold, William D.]. "What Is the India Question Now?"
      L (1854), 454-65.

1542 "Kaye's LIFE OF LORD METCALFE," L (1854), 701-10
      (India).

1543 [Marx, Francis]. "The Latest Acquisition of Russia: the
      River Amoor," LI (1855), 10-14 (China).

1544 W-M., G. [Whyte-Melville, George]. "The Old World and
      the New," LI (1855), 291-306 (notes on Australia).

1545 W-M., G. [Whyte-Melville, George]. "Huc's CHINA," LI
      (1855), 409-21.

1546 A., W.D. [Arnold, W.D.]. "Lord Dalhousie," LII (1855),
      123-35 (India).

1547 S-K., W.S. [Seton-Karr, Walter Scott]. "Six Months in
      India," LIII (1856), 92-104, 198-211.

1548 "The United States, Cuba, and Canada," LIII (1856),
      522-33.

1549 "The American Questions," LIV (1856), 121-26 (Central
      America).

1550 "Prospects of the Indian Civil Service: the 'Open'
      System," LIV (1856), 270-85.

1551 A., W.D. [Arnold, W.D.]. "Jack Sepoy," LIV (1856), 359-
      62 (India).

1552 "Communications with the Far East," LIV (1856), 574-81
      (Egypt and Euphrates).

1553 A., W.D. [Arnold, W.D.]. "The Night Mail Train in
      India," LIV (1856), 680-84.

1554 "Mr. Justice Willes on Tickets of Leave and Transporta-
      tion," LV (1857), 216-17.

1555 "The War with China," LV (1857), 239-48.

1556 Beta Mikron [Keppel, W.C.]. "A Few Notes on Canadian
      Matters," LV (1857), 312-28, 554-68; LVI (1857), 90-
      105.

1557 S., G. [Smith, Goldwin]. "Imperialism," LV (1857), 493-506.

1558 "Blackey at School," LV (1857), 679-84 (India).

1559 "Our Past, Present, and Future Policy in Persia," LVI (1857), 127-40.

1560 A., A. [Andrews, Augustus]. "The Indian Army," LVI (1857), 164-72.

1561 "The Indian Mutinies," LVI (1857), 238-41.

1562 "The Indian Mutinies," LVI (1857), 627-30.

1563 R., J.W. [Russell, Jesse Watts]. "Antiquities of the Jumnah," LVI (1857), 672-74 (history of region of India).

1564 [Arnold, W.D.]. "India in Mourning," LVI (1857), 737-50.

1565 S., T.C. [Sandars, T.C.]. "Livingstone's TRAVELS IN SOUTH AFRICA," LVII (1858), 118-32.

1566 LeBas, C.T. "How We Escaped from Delhi," LVII (1858), 184-89 (Indian mutiny).

1567 Shirley [Skelton, John]. "Charles James Napier: a Study of Character," LVII (1858), 254-68 (notes on Sind).

1568 The Author of "India in Mourning" [Arnold, W.D.]. "An Anglo-Indian View of the Indian Crisis," LVII (1858), 268-82, 473-84.

1569 "Extent of the Indian Mutinies," LVII (1858), 358-62.

1570 H., A. [Helps, Arthur]. "The India Bill: a Letter to the Editor on the Proposed Council of Eight," LVII (1858), 371-76.

1571 "The Indian Mutinies: Our Past and Future Policy, in Religion and Colonization," LVII (1858), 544-49.

1572 [Arnold, W.D.]. "An Anglo-Indian Lament for John Company," LVII (1858), 635-42.

1573 "Political and Social Prospects of the Australian Colonies," LVII (1858), 659-70.

1574 "The Men of the Indian Mutinies," LVII (1858), 686-90.

1575 A., S. [Austin, Sarah]. "A Mutiny of Provincial Troops; from Tacitus," LVII (1858), 729-36 (comparison of causes between ancient and 1858 Indian mutinies).

1576   "Delhi as It Is," LVIII (1858), 59-64.

1577   "The Indian Mutinies: I. Native Feeling and Knowledge
       of Natives by Englishmen; II. The Company VERSUS the
       Crown," LVIII (1858), 245-49, 249-52.

1578   "The Oude Proclamation and the Proprietors of the Land,"
       LVIII (1858), 354-58.

1579   F., T.G. [Faussett, Thomas Godfrey]. "How I Killed a
       Cariboo," LVIII (1858), 470-78 (New Brunswick).

1580   Beta Mikron [Keppel, W.C.]. "British Columbia and
       Vancouver's Island," LVIII (1858), 493-504.

1581   "The Indian Rebellion: the Village System and the Policy
       of Annexation," LVIII (1858), 609-14.

1582   The Author of "India in Mourning" [Arnold, W.D.].
       "India in a Mess," LVIII (1858), 730-41.

1583   A., W.D. [Arnold, W.D.]. "How Queen Victoria was Pro-
       claimed at Peshawar," LIX (1859), 120-26 (India).

1584   Hughes, Thomas. "Hodson of Hodson's Horse," LIX (1859),
       127-45 (notes on Indian mutiny).

1585   "Sketches of the Antipodes: New Zealand," LIX (1859),
       159-69.

1586   K., H. [Kingsley, Henry]. "Wild Sports of the Far
       South," LIX (1859), 587-97 (Australia).

1587   Cairnes, John E. "Essay towards a Solution of the Gold
       Question," LX (1859), 267-78 (Australia).

1588   S. "Indian Finance," LX (1859), 534-43.

1589   Mill, John Stuart. "A Few Words on Non-Intervention,"
       LX (1859), 766-76 (imperial policy).

1590   "Egypt and the Suez Canal," LXI (1860), 134-50.

1591   Harlin, T. "CEYLON," LXI (1860), 624-42.

1592   F., T.G. [Faussett, T.G.]. "A Snow Picnic," LXII (1860),
       526-38 (Canada).

1593   W., S. "Recollections of Ceylon: Its Forests and Its
       Pearl Fishery," LXII (1860), 753-67.

1594   [Bullock, T.H.]. "A Blue Mutiny," LXIII (1861), 98-107
       (indigo in Bengal).

1595   M., F. [Marx, Francis]. "Another Chapter on the
       Amoor," LXIII (1861), 318-28 (China).

1596 [Sandars, T.C.]. "Chronicle of Current History," LXIV
     (1861), 125-34 (notes on imperial policy).

1597 [Arnold, Thomas]. "Reminiscences of New Zealand," LXIV
     (1861), 246-56.

1598 [Newman, F.W.]. "Duties of England to India," LXIV
     (1861), 674-89.

1599 [Bullock, T.H.]. "The Non-Regulation Provinces of
     India," LXV (1862), 285-303.

1600 "The Colonies," LXV (1862), 551-64.

1601 [Bullock, Thomas Henry]. "Indigo-Planting in Bengal,
     and the Breach-of-Contract Bill," LXV (1862), 610-26.

1602 [Bullock, T.H.]. "Public Works in India: the Navigation
     of the Godavery River, Etc.," LXVI (1862), 77-93.

1603 [Grant, Alexander]. "The Opium Revenue of India Con-
     sidered in Connexion with Mr. Laing's Last Budget,"
     LXVI (1862), 399-417.

1604 R., R. "Laurel and Cypress: a Chapter in the History
     of Australian Exploration," LXVI (1862), 726-41.

1605 B., T.H. [Bullock, Thomas Henry]. "The Sale of Waste
     Lands and Redemption of Land-Tax in India, Etc.,
     Considered," LXVII (1863), 1-16.

1606 An F.R.G.S. [Burton, Richard F.]. "My Wanderings in
     West Africa: a Visit to the Renowned Cities of Wari
     and Benin," LXVII (1863), 135-57, 273-89, 407-22.

1607 B., T.H. [Bullock, T.H.]. "Some Remarks on Mr. Laing's
     ENGLAND'S MISSION IN THE EAST," LXVII (1863), 528-
     39 (India).

1608 "Indian Prospects," LXVIII (1863), 1-14.

1609 [Price, Bonamy]. "England and Her Colonies," LXVIII
     (1863), 454-70.

1610 [Knighton, William]. "Village Life in Oudh," LXIX
     (1864), 187-98, 316-27.

1611 "Indian Barracks and Hospitals," LXIX (1864), 691-703.

1612 B., T.H. [Bullock, T.H.]. "The Land Revenue of India -
     the Perpetual Settlement," LXX (1864), 37-51.

1613 B., P.C. [Beaton, P.C.]. "From Auckland to Awamutu,"
     LXX (1864), 407-24 (New Zealand).

1614   B., P.C. [Beaton, P.C.]. "A Chapter Showing How We
       Live at Awamutu," LXX (1864), 606-26 (New Zealand).

1615   [Stephen, J.F.]. "Kaye's HISTORY OF THE INDIAN MUTINY,"
       LXX (1864), 757-74.

1616   "Rebellion, Diplomacy, and Progress in China," LXXI
       (1865), 135-53.

1617   G., W.R. [Greg, W.R.]. "England's Future Attitude
       towards Europe and the World," LXXI (1865), 719-35
       (survey of the empire).

1618   B., T.H. [Bullock, T.H.]. "The Right of Occupancy in
       Oude and Bengal: the Rent Case - Hills v. Issar Ghos,"
       LXXII (1865), 77-91.

1619   B., P.C. [Beaton, P.C.]. "A Chapter on Pai Marire, the
       New Religion of the Maoris," LXXII (1865), 423-38
       (see #1649; New Zealand).

1620   "The Military Situation in India," LXXII (1865), 710-18.

1621   A., S. [Austin, Sarah]. "The Cholera in Malta," LXXIII
       (1866), 93-103.

1622   "How We Retook Dewangiri," LXXIII (1866), 120-29
       (India).

1623   A Late Resident in the Island. "Jamaica, and the Recent
       Insurrection There," LXXIII (1866), 161-79.

1624   Trevelyan, G.O. "The Dawk Bungalow: or,'Is His Appoint-
       ment Pucka?' " LXXIII (1866), 215-31, 382-91 (India).

1625   [Greg, W.R.]. "The Jamaica Problem," LXXIII (1866),
       277-305.

1626   "The Native Army in India," LXXIII (1866), 466-76.

1626a P., L.J. [Proctor, L.J.]. "Native Tribes on the Zambesi
       River: an East African Sketch," LXXIII (1866), 531-
       48 (also notes on Southeast Africa).

1627   "The English Troops in the East," LXXIII (1866), 558-
       68 (Burma, Ceylon, China, and India).

1628   Cobbe, Frances Power. "The Brahmo Samaj," LXXIV (1866),
       199-211 (culture conflicts for educated Indians).

1629   "The Indian Civil Service," LXXIV (1866), 427-42.

1630   "Village Sketches in Oude: Village Joys and Festivities,"
       LXXV (1867), 301-15; LXXVI (1867), 30-41.

1631   B., T.H. [Bullock, T.H.]. "Prevention of Famine in
       India," LXXV (1867), 358-69.

1632   Fraser, Lieut. Col. A[lexander], R.E., C.B. "On the
       Defence of India," LXXV (1867), 557-69.

1633   R.A.J.A. "Sport in Nepaul with Maharaja Sir Jung
       Bahadoor, G.C.B.," LXXVI (1867), 337-46.

1634   "The Famine in Orissa," LXXVI (1867), 373-82 (India).

1635   "Kaye's LIVES OF INDIAN OFFICERS," LXXVI (1867), 587-
       600.

GOOD WORDS

1636   "Incident in the Sikh War," I (1860), 246-47 (Punjab).

1637   L., J.M. [Ludlow, J.M.]. "Aspects of Indian Life during
       the Rebellion," I (1860), 250-53, 268-71, 322-26,
       347-50, 356-60, 394-97.

1638   "What Has Been Done in the Fiji Islands," I (1860),
       337-40, 361-64, 408-11.

1639   "The Serampore Missionaries," I (1860), 419-23 (India).

1640   Stevenson, W.F. "The Gospel in Chota Nagpore," II
       (1861), 35-38 (India).

1641   Smith, Thomas. "All about the Indigo," III (1862), 43-
       48 (Bengal).

1642   Leitch, William. "A Winter in Canada," III (1862),
       722-29.

1643   Oliphant, Laurence. "A Visit to the Taipings," IV
       (1863), I86-90 (China).

1644   Bidie, G., M.B. "The Undeveloped Fibres of India," IV
       (1863), 656-63 (cotton and other products).

1645   B., P.C., An Army Chaplain [Beaton, P.C.]. "Our First
       Week in New Zealand: March, 1864," V (1864), 621-24.

1646   Kaye, John William. "Our Indian Heroes," VI (1865),
       69-80, 165-76, 246-56, 327-36, 398-408, 467-78, 543-
       52, 621-32, 699-708, 771-80, 841-52, 925-34.

1647   Stewart, James. "On the Zambesi: a Short Sketch of a
       Long Journey," VI (1865), 133-41 (Southeast Africa).

1648   Winkworth, Catherine. "Our Convicts," VI (1865), 446-
       53 (Norfolk Island).

1649   B., P.C., An Army Chaplain [Beaton, P.C.]. "Pai Marire,
       the New Religion of the Maoris," VI (1865), 726-32
       (see #1619; New Zealand).

1650   A Government Commissioner. "A Visit to the Andaman
       Islands (the Convict Settlement for India)," VII
       (1866), 305-14.

1651   Bayliss, Daniel. "A Glimpse of Shepherd-Life in New
       Zealand," VII (1866), 620-22.

1652   Ludlow, J.M. "The Cornwall Agricultural and Commercial
       Association of Jamaica," VII (1866), 672-80.

1653   B., P.C., An Army Chaplain [Beaton, P.C.]. "Two Years'
       Experience of the Maories," VII (1866), 696-701
       (New Zealand).

1654   Walker, Lucilla. "Out in the Mofussil," VIII (1867),
       335-41 (colonial life in India).

1655   Ellis, Margaret. "From India," VIII (1867), 550-56
       (travel in the hill country).

1656   Gilbert, William. "Our Discharged Convicts," VIII (1867),
       622-26 (convicts helped to emigrate from Britain).

1657   M., H.C. "A Bengali Will," VIII (1867), 669-73.

1658   Moncrieff, C.C. Scott. "The Canals of Northern India,"
       VIII (1867), 807-11.

HOGG'S (WEEKLY) INSTRUCTOR

1659   "Chapters from the Diary of an Officer in the East
       India Company's Service," I (1845), 203-05, 212-15.

1660   "John Galt," I (1845), 259-62 (Canada Company).

1661   "Travels in India," II (1845-46), 395-97, 408-10.

1662   "The Country of the Seikhs," III (1846), 81-83 (Punjab).

1663   "The People of the Seikhs," III (1846), 97-99 (Punjab).

1664   "Life in the Eastern Archipelago," III (1846), 172-75
       (Borneo).

1665   "Sir Robert Sale's Defence of Jellalabad," IV (1846-47),
       12-15 (Afghanistan).

1666   "Enterprise in Tropical Australia," IV (1846-47), 60-63.

1667   "Present State of the Island of Borneo," IV (1846-47),
       86-88.

1668   "Adventures of Lady Sale," IV (1846-47), 139-42
       (Afghanistan).

1669   "HOCHELAGA; OR ENGLAND IN THE NEW WORLD," IV (1846-47),
       179-83, 205-08 (Canada).

1670   Howitt, Richard. "Australia Felix in 1841 - Colonial
       Coilers," IV (1846-47), 211-13 (poor at bushstations).

1671   "The Tea-Plant," IV (1846-47), 274-76 (China and India).

1672   "The Cape Colony," IV (1846-47), 390-91; V (1847), 155.

1673   "The Tea Duty," V (1847), 5-6 (China).

1674   "Notes on Gibraltar," V (1847), 51-54.

1675   "THREE YEARS' WANDERINGS IN THE NORTHERN PROVINCES OF
       CHINA," V (1847), 205-08, 218-21.

1676   "Recent Explorations in Central and Northern Australia,"
       V (1847), 376-79.

1677   "Sir James Ross's Voyage to the Southern Seas," VI
       (1847-48), 28-32, 37-40 (notes on Falkland Islands
       and New Zealand).

1678   "Free Church of Scotland Colony at Otago," VI (1847-
       48), 87-88 (New Zealand).

1679   "Notes on China," VI (1847-48), 302-03.

1680   "Singular Discovery in Connection with the Aborigines
       of America," I N.S. (1848), 141.

1681   "Floating Gardens of Cashmere," I N.S. (1848), 164-65
       (notes on natives).

1682   "Snake-Charmers," I N.S. (1848), 180-81 (India and
       South Africa).

1683   Arthur, Rev. William. "The British Empire," (published
       YMCA lecture), I N.S. (1848), 260-65.

1684   "The Cave of Elephanta," I N.S. (1848), 351-52 (Indian
       history).

1685   "British Guiana and Its Missionaries," I N.S. (1848),
       378-83.

1686   "The British Colonies and Emigration," II N.S. (1849),
       51-53.

1687   "Indian Railways," II N.S. (1849), 101-02.

1688   "The Mahogany-Tree," II N.S. (1849), 250-51 (British
       Honduras).

1689   "Cities of India: Hurdwaar," II N.S. (1849), 356-57.

1690   "The Potters' Emigration Society," II N.S. (1849), 365-67.

1691   "Need of Missions," III N.S. (1849), 252-53, 315-18.

1692   "The Owner of Niagara," IV N.S. (1850), 71-72 (Canada).

1693   "Road-Surveying in North America," IV N.S. (1850), 239-40.

1694   "Notes of a Ten Years' Residence in New South Wales," V N.S. (1850), 129-33, 147-50.

1695   "The Hindu Pantheon," V N.S. (1850), 347-49 (religion in India).

1696   "Hindu Gods," V N.S. (1850), 372-74 (religion in India).

1697   "Life in the Bush," V N.S. (1850), 383-84 (Canada).

1698   A Clergyman Now Resident in That Colony. "Canada," VI N.S. (1851), 1-3, 129-32, 177-80, 241-44, 321-25; VII N.S. (1851), 200-04; VIII N.S. (1852), 209-12; IX N.S. (1852), 36-41, 321-25; X N.S. (1853), 353-56.

1699   "The Agricultural Capabilities of New Brunswick," VI N.S. (1851), 84-86.

1700   "The Ojibway Indians of North America," VI N.S. (1851), 338-41.

1701   "Culture of Tea in the Himalayan Mountains," IX N.S. (1852), 84-85 (India).

1702   "The Cultivation of the Poppy," IX N.S. (1852), 213-15 (opium in India).

1703   "The Manufacture of Opium," IX N.S. (1852), 236-37 (India).

1704   "Missionary Operations of India: CALCUTTA REVIEW, Sept., 1851," IX N.S. (1852), 343-44.

1705   "SPECIMENS OF OLD INDIAN POETRY," X N.S. (1853), 38-40 (comments on culture).

1706   "The Koh-i-noor," X N.S. (1853), 221-22 (Indian history related to the stone).

1707   DeQuincey, Thomas. "On the Final Catastrophe of the Gold-Digging Mania," X N.S. (1853), 401-04.

1708   "Scraps from Australia," X N.S. (1853), 411-12.

1709   "Portable Houses for Australia," X N.S. (1853), 544.

1710   "Burmah," I 3S. (1853), 17-22.

1711   "Recent Discoveries in South Africa," I 3S. (1853),
        426-33.

1712   "Cotton, Slaves, and Slavery," III 3S. (1854), 209-18
        (cotton sources in the empire).

1713   "A Letter from Mauritius," III 3S. (1854), 249-53.

1714   A British Officer. "A Glance at Corfu, and the Funeral
        of a Greek Archbishop," III 3S. (1854), 328-32.

1715   "Steam Navigation on Australian Rivers," III 3S. (1854),
        519-28.

1716   "Bengal as a Field of Missions," V 3S. (1855), 165-76.

THE HOME AND FOREIGN REVIEW

1717   [Ornsby, Robert]. "Savage Life in Africa," I (1862),
        129-45 (notes on natives in South and Southeast
        Africa).

1718   [Lathbury, D.C.]. "Cotton Cultivation and Supply,"
        II (1863), 1-31 (cotton sources in the empire).

1719   [Moule, Henry]. "Emigration in the Nineteenth Century,"
        III (1863), 472-96.

1720   [?Lottner, Friedrich]. "Indian Epic Poetry," IV (1864),
        512-52 (notes on culture).

HOUSEHOLD WORDS

1721   [Dickens, Charles and Chisholm, Caroline]. "A Bundle
        of Emigrants' Letters," I (1850), 19-24 (Australia).

1722   [Weir, William and Wills, W.H.]. "Short Cuts across
        the Globe," I (1850), 65-68 (Central America).

1723   [Weir, William and Wills, W.H.]. "Short Cuts across
        the Globe: the Isthmus of Suez," I (1850), 167-68.

1724   [Mackay, Alexander]. "How We Went Fishing in Canada,"
        I (1850), 243-45.

1725   [Chisholm, Caroline and Horne, Richard H.]. "Pictures
        of Life in Australia," I (1850), 307-10.

1726   [Mackay, Alexander]. "How We Went Hunting in Canada,"
        I (1850), 364-68.

1727   [Wills, W.H.]. "A Mightier Hunter than Nimrod," I
        (1850), 399-402 (R. Gordon Cumming in South Africa).

1728   [Sidney, Samuel]. "An Exploring Adventure," I (1850), 418-20 (Australia).

1729   [Gwynne, Francis and Wills, W.H.]. "Two Letters from Australia," I (1850), 475-80 (from immigrants).

1730   [Sidney, Samuel]. "Family Colonisation Loan Society," I (1850), 514-15 (Australia).

1731   [Mackay, Alexander]. "An Emigrant Afloat," I (1850), 534-39 (en route to British North America).

1732   [Sidney, Samuel]. "The Good Governor," I (1850), 547-49 (Bermuda).

1733   [Cox, Miss and Wills, W.H.]. "Easy Spelling and Hard Reading," I (1850), 561-62 (Australian immigrants).

1734   [Cole, Alfred Whatley]. "Cape Sketches," I (1850), 588-91, 607-10; II (1850-51), 118-20, 165-67 (Cape Colony).

1735   [Cole, Alfred Whatley]. "How We Went Whaling off the Cape of Good Hope," II (1850-51), 58-59.

1736   [Sidney, Samuel]. "Father Gabriel; or, the Fortunes of a Farmer," II (1850-51), 67-71 (Australia).

1737   [Sidney, Samuel]. "Father Gabriel's Story," II (1850-51), 85-90 (Australian farmer).

1738   [Sidney, Samuel]. "Letters of Introduction to Sydney," II (1850-51), 187-88 (New South Wales).

1739   [Sidney, Samuel]. "Land Ho! - Port Jackson," II (1850-51), 276-77 (Australia).

1740   [Jerrold, William Blanchard]. "The Wealth of the Woods," II (1850-51), 282-84 (New Brunswick).

1741   [Siddons, Joachim Heyward]. "Christmas in India," II (1850-51), 305-06.

1742   [Morley, Henry]. "Our Phantom Ship: Negro Land," II (1850-51), 400-07 (West Africa).

1743   [Morley, Henry]. "Our Phantom Ship: Central America," II (1850-51), 516-22.

1744   [Capper, John]. "A Cinnamon Garden," II (1850-51), 546-48 (cinnamon trade in Ceylon).

1745   [Capper, John]. "The Cocoa-Nut Palm," II (1850-51), 585-89 (notes on natives in Ceylon).

1746   [Sidney, Samuel]. "Indian Railroads and British Commerce," II (1850-51), 590-95.

1747   [Morley, Henry]. "The Cape and the Kaffirs: a History,"
        III (1851), 30-35 (Cape Colony).

1748   [Capper, John]. "My Pearl-Fishing Expedition," III
        (1851), 75-80 (Ceylon).

1749   [Sidney, Samuel]. "News of Natal," III (1851), 83-85.

1750   [Capper, John]. "Coffee Planting in Ceylon," III (1851),
        109-14.

1751   [Wills, W.H.]. "Safety for Female Emigrants," III
        (1851), 228.

1752   [Sidney, Samuel]. "Profitable Investment of Toil -
        New Zealand," III (1851), 228-29.

1753   [per Bell, R.]. "Life in the Burra Mines of South
        Australia," III (1851), 250-52.

1754   [Capper, John]. "A Peep at the 'Peraharra'," III (1851),
        252-56 (festival in Ceylon).

1755   [Peppe]. "A Fuqueer's Curse," III (1851), 310-12 (fakir
        in India).

1756   [Morley, Henry]. "Our Phantom Ship - China," III (1851),
        325-31.

1757   [Ross, Thomasina]. "The 'Mouth' of China," III (1851),
        348-53 (Hong Kong).

1758   [Macpherson, Ossian]. "A Few Facts about Salt," III
        (1851), 353-55 (India).

1759   [Horne, Richard H. and Dickens, Charles]. "The Great
        Exhibition and the Little One," III (1851), 356-60
        (comparison between England and China re trade).

1760   [Gore, Augustus Frederick]. "Shots in the Jungle," III
        (1851), 402-04 (notes on natives in Ceylon).

1761   [Cunningham, Peter]. "Superstitious Murder," IV (1851-
        52), 92 (murder by sect in India).

1762   [Morley, Henry]. "Indian Furlough Regulations," IV
        (1851-52), 107-09.

1763   [Keene, John or James and Wills, W.H.]. "A Golden
        Newspaper," IV (1851-52), 207-08 (Sydney MORNING
        HERALD with much news on gold diggings).

1764   [Bell, Robert]. "The Overland Mail Bag," IV (1851-52),
        229-34 (notes on Russian threat to India from Persia).

1765   [Michie, Archibald and Morley, Henry]. "Going Circuit
        at the Antipodes," IV (1851-52), 344-48 (Australia).

1766   [Capper, John]. "The Peasants of British India," IV
        (1851-52), 389-93.

1767   [Morley, Henry]. "A Rainy Day on 'The Euphrates'," IV
        (1851-52), 409-15 (conditions aboard emigrant ship).

1768   [Sidney, Samuel]. "Three Colonial Epochs," IV (1851-
        52), 433-38 (Australia).

1769   [Capper, John]. "An Indian Wedding," IV (1851-52), 505-
        10 (in Ceylon).

1770   [Sidney, Samuel]. "Better Ties than Red Tape Ties," IV
        (1851-52), 529-34 (emigration).

1771   [Michie, Archibald]. "A Visit to the Burra Burra Mines,"
        IV (1851-52), 567-68 (South Australia).

1772   [George, Frances and Morley, Henry]. "From a Settler's
        Wife," IV (1851-52), 585-88 (New Zealand).

1773   [Dickens, Charles]. "The Fine Arts in Australia," IV
        (1851-52), 597 (Sydney reaction to Marshall Claxton
        painting).

1774   [Knighton, William and Morley, Henry]. "The Buried
        City of Ceylon," V (1852), 25-27 (Anuradhapura with
        notes on ancient culture).

1775   [Morley, Henry and Irwin]. "Norfolk Island," V (1852),
        141-45.

1776   [Wills, W.H.]. "Official Emigration," V (1852), 155-56.

1777   [Napier]. "Bombay," V (1852), 181-86.

1778   [Morley, Henry, Macpherson, Ossian, prob., and Mulock].
        "The Harvest of Gold," V (1852), 213-18 (Australia).

1779   [Capper, John]. "The Great Chowsempor Bank," V (1852),
        237-40 (India).

1780   [Morley, Henry]. "Highland Emigration," V (1852), 324-
        25 (notes on Australia).

1781   [St. John, James Augustus]. "A Chinaman's Ball," V
        (1852), 331-32 (notes on Chinese in Singapore).

1782   [Capper, John]. "Law in the East," V (1852), 347-52
        (Ceylon).

1783   [Sidney, Samuel]. "What To Take to Australia," V
        (1852), 364-66.

1784   [Morley, Henry]. "China with a Flaw in It," V (1852),
        368-74.

1785   [Sidney, Samuel]. "Climate of Australia," V (1852),
        391-92 (effects on British).

1786   [Mulock]. "We, and Our Man Tom," V (1852), 396-98
        (farming in Victoria).

1787   [Capper, John]. "Off to the Diggings!" V (1852), 405-
        10 (Australia).

1788   [Thomas, William Moy]. "Transported for Life," V (1852),
        455-64, 482-89 (Norfolk Island).

1789   [Capper, John]. "Monsters of Faith," V (1852), 506-08
        (Indian fakirs).

1790   [Capper, John]. "The Garden of Flowers," V (1852), 556-
        61 (Ceylon).

1791   [Wills, W.H.]. "Transportation for Life," V (1852),
        566-67 (Norfolk Island).

1792   [Sala, George A.]. "Cheerily, Cheerily!" VI (1852-53),
        25-31 (emigration).

1793   [Elliot, Hugh Hislop]. "A Tiger's Jaws," VI (1852-53),
        69 (tiger hunting in India).

1794   [Maxwell, H.H.]. "An Opium Factory," VI (1852-53), 118-
        20 (India).

1795   [Morley, Henry]. "Silk from the Punjaub," VI (1852-53),
        388-90.

1796   [Horne, Richard H. and Hogarth, Jr.]. "Look before You
        Leap," VI (1852-53), 497-99 (immigration to Victoria
        for gold).

1797   [Lang, John]. "An Inundation in Bengal," VII (1853),
        53-54 (floods and famine).

1798   [Sidney, Samuel]. "Lost and Found in the Gold Fields,"
        VII (1853), 84-88 (Australia).

1799   [Lang, John]. "Starting a Paper in India," VII (1853),
        94-96.

1800   [Webb, Jonathan]. "Aground up the Ganges," VII (1853),
        165-68 (India).

1801   [Rinder, Samuel]. "Four-Legged Australians," VII (1853),
        208-14 (animals with notes on natives and colonists).

1802   [Dickens, Charles]. "The Noble Savage," VII (1853), 337-39 (notes on natives in the empire).

1803   [Horne, Richard H.]. "Canvass Town," VII (1853), 361-67 (Australian gold digging sites).

1804   [Clarke, W.H.]. "The Gwalior Janissaries," VII (1853), 375-76 (India).

1805   [Siddons, Joachim Heyward]. "Justice for 'Natives'," VII (1853), 397-402 (India).

1806   [Horne, Richard H.]. "Digging Sailors," VII (1853), 425-26 (Australia).

1807   [Capper, John and Wills, W.H.]. "A Pull at the Pagoda Tree," VII (1853), 433-37 (East India Company operations).

1808   [Maxwell, H.H. and Morley, Henry]. "Good Lac," VII (1853), 463-66 (factory in India).

1809   [Horne, Richard H.] "A Digger's Wedding," VII (1853), 511-12 (Australia).

1810   [Capper, John]. "Honourable John," VII (1853), 516-18 (East India Company).

1811   [Capper, John]. "Number Forty-Two," VIII (1853-54), 17-20 (shopping in Colombo, Ceylon).

1812   [Capper, John and Wills, W.H.]. "First Stage to Australia," VIII (1853-54), 42-45.

1813   [Horne, Richard H.]. "Convicts in the Gold Regions," VIII (1853-54), 49-54 (Australia).

1814   [Capper, John]. "The Great Indian Bean-Stalk," VIII (1853-54), 60-64 (natives employed by East India Company).

1815   [Morley, Joseph and Morley, Henry]. "Bad Luck at Bendigo," VIII (1853-54), 133-39 (Victoria gold digging site).

1816   [Capper, John]. "A Great Screw," VIII (1853-54), 181-84 (effect of screw propeller on travel to Australia).

1817   [Clarke, W.H.]. "An Ashantee Palaver," VIII (1853-54), 241-46 (Gold Coast).

1818   [Michelsen, Edward Henry]. "Chinese Players," VIII (1853-54), 281-83 (East Indies).

1819   [Hogarth, Jr. and Morley, Henry]. "The Cradle and the Grave," VIII (1853-54), 317-25 (Australian gold sites).

1820 [Clark]. "By Dawk to Delhi," VIII (1853-54), 365-70
      (travel in India).

1821 [Arnold, William Delafield]. "The Steam Whistle in
      India," VIII (1853-54), 440-42 (railroad).

1822 [Capper, John]. "The Stop the Way Company," VIII (1853-
      54), 449-54 (Hudson's Bay Company).

1823 [Capper, John]. "Regular Trappers," VIII (1853-54), 471-
      76 (Hudson's Bay Company).

1824 [Irwin]. "The Antecedents of Australia," VIII (1853-54),
      476-77 (transportation).

1825 [Capper, John]. "Lancashire Witchcraft," VIII (1853-54),
      549-51 (cotton and India).

1826 [von Wenchstern, Otto]. "Troops and Jobs in Malta," IX
      (1854), 266-68.

1827 [Capper, John]. "Waste," IX (1854), 390-93 (imperial
      products undeveloped).

1828 [Costello, Dudley]. "Called to the Savage Bar," IX
      (1854), 531-33 (capture by Iroquois in British North
      America).

1829 [Sala, G.A.]. "Convicts, English and French," XI (1855),
      85-88 (transportation).

1830 [Capper, John]. "Trade," XI (1855), 323-26.

1831 [Rinder, Samuel]. "Australian Carriers," XI (1855),
      420-27 (travel between Melbourne and gold diggings).

1832 [Capper, John and/or Sidney, Samuel]. "India Pickle,"
      XI (1855), 446-53 (problems in India).

1833 [Capper, John]. "Rice," XI (1855), 522-26 (Ceylon and
      India).

1834 [Sala, G.A.]. "Unfortunate James Daley," XI (1855),
      582-84 (convict who may have discovered gold, 1788).

1835 [Meason, Malcolm Ronald Laing]. "Regulars and Irregu-
      lars," XII (1855-56), 58-60 (Indian troops).

1836 [Blanchard, Sidney Laman]. "The Santals," XII (1855-56),
      347-49 (India).

1837 [Howitt, William]. "The Old and New Squatter," XII
      (1855-56), 433-41 (Australia).

1838 [Blanchard, Sidney Laman]. "The Road to India," XII
      (1855-56), 517-21 (travel conditions).

1839   [Russell, Charles William]. "Rent Days round Madras,"
        XIII (1856), 276-79.

1840   [Whitty, Edward Michael]. "Post to Australia," XIII
        (1856), 305-06.

1841   [Capper, John]. "The Mofussil," XIII (1856), 556-59
        (India).

1842   [Fawkner, John Pascoe]. "A Colonial Patriot," XIV
        (1856), 130 (ties between Australian colonists and
        Britain).

1843   [Dixon, Edmund Saul]. "An Indian Court Circular," XIV
        (1856), 308-12 (Oudh).

1844   [Lang, John]. "The Himalaya Club," XV (1857), 265-72
        (sanitarium for British in India).

1845   [Meredith, Louisa Anne]. "Shadows of the Golden Image,"
        XV (1857), 313-18 (impact of gold on life in Tasmania).

1846   [Milne, William Charles]. "Canton-English," XV (1857),
        450-52.

1847   [Lang, John]. "Tracks in the Bush," XVI (1857), 93-96
        (notes on natives in Australia).

1848   [Dodd, George]. "Opium," XVI (1857), 104-08, 181-85
        (China and India).

1849   [Townsend, E.]. "A Mutiny in India," XVI (1857), 154-56.

1850   [prob. Robertson, John]. "Sepoy Symbols of Mutiny," XVI
        (1857), 228-32 (India).

1851   [Townsend, E.]. "Indian Irregulars," XVI (1857), 244-46.

1852   [Markham, Clements Robert]. "The First Sack of Delhi,"
        XVI (1857), 276-79 (Nadir Shah).

1853   [Capper, John]. "A Very Black Act," XVI (1857), 293-94
        (gag on India press).

1854   [Townsend, E. and Hamilton, Alexander Henry Abercromby].
        "Indian Recruits and Indian English," XVI (1857),
        319-22.

1855   [Mitchell, Andrew]. "The Snow Express," XVI (1857),
        367-72 (British North America).

1856   [von Corvin, Otto and Morley, Henry]. "Canton City,"
        XVI (1857), 376-81.

1857   [Capper, John]. "Calcutta," XVI (1857), 393-97.

1858   [Lang, John]. "Wanderings in India," XVI (1857), 457-
       63, 505-11; XVII (1857-58), 12-20, 64-70, 87-94, 112-
       18, 135-44, 148-56, 179-86, 212-16, 220-24, 254-60.

1859   "The New Colonists of Norfolk Island," XVI (1857), 476-
       77 (Pitcairn Islanders).

1860   [Townsend, E.]. "Lutfullah Khan," XVI (1857), 490-96
       (Muslim gentleman in India).

1861   [Vincent, Frank]. "Coo-EE!" XVII (1857-58), 232-36
       (trip in Australian bush).

1862   [Collins, Wilkie]. "A Sermon for Sepoys," XVII (1857-
       58), 244-47 (India).

1863   [Capper, John]. "A Nautch," XVII (1857-58), 270-73
       (Indian dancer).

1864   [Townsend, E.]. "Indian Hill Stations," XVII (1857-58),
       316-19.

1865   [Craig, George]. "Blown Away!" XVII (1857-58), 348-50
       (capital punishment for mutinous sepoys in India).

1866   [Milne, William Charles]. "Chinese Charms," XVII (1857-
       58), 370-72.

1867   [Vincent, Frank and Morley, Henry]. "John Chinaman in
       Australia," XVII (1857-58), 416-20.

1868   [Robertson, John]. "The Blue Dye Plant," XVII (1857-58),
       436-38 (indigo in Bengal).

1869   [Vincent, Frank]. "Australian Jim Walker," XVII (1857-
       58), 500-04 (former shepherd in Australia with notes
       on natives).

1870   [Edgeworth]. "At the Siege of Delhi," XVIII (1858), 56-
       60.

1871   [Hollingshead, John]. "Nine Kings," XVIII (1858), 118-
       20 (Hudson's Bay Company).

1872   [Payn, James]. "A Reminiscence of Battle," XVIII (1858),
       128-30 (Indian mutiny).

1873   [Morley, Henry]. "Sarawak," XVIII (1858), 130-36.

1874   [Morley, Henry]. "A Postscript upon Sarawak," XVIII
       (1858), 147-48.

1875   [Payn, James]. "The Savage Muse," XVIII (1858), 181-
       84 (natives in Australia).

1876   [Lang, John]. "The Abors," XVIII (1858), 204-05 (India).

1877   [Morley, Henry]. "British Columbia," XVIII (1858), 252-56.

1878   [Bourne, Henry Richard Fox]. "Hindoo Law," XVIII (1858), 337-41.

1879   [Martin, Miss]. "On the Gold Coast," XVIII (1858), 419-23.

1880   "Books for the Indian Army," XVIII (1858), 437-38.

1881   [Morley, Henry]. "Britannia's Figures," XIX (1858-59), 13-16 (imperial statistics).

1882   [Martin, Miss]. "King Cotton," XIX (1858-59), 38-40.

1883   [Thornbury, George Walter]. "Gib," XIX (1858-59), 42-47 (Gibraltar).

1884   [Gill, Charles]. "Sultry December," XIX (1858-59), 47-48 (colonial health in Victoria).

1885   [Morley, Henry]. "Perils in India," XIX (1858-59), 174-79.

1886   [Mitchell, Andrew]. "A Journey in Kafirland," XIX (1858-59), 193-97 (South Africa).

1887   [Bourne, Henry Richard Fox and Morley, Henry]. "Fire-Worshippers," XIX (1858-59), 286-88 (Parsees in India).

1888   [Thornbury, George Walter]. "Going to Africa," XIX (1858-59), 315-21 (military life in Gibraltar).

1889   [Martin, Miss]. "Bush and Beach," XIX (1858-59), 364-67 (Gold Coast).

1890   [Morley, Henry]. "A Group of Noble Savages," XIX (1858-59), 385-90 (British North America).

1891   [Lang, John]. "An Illustrious British Exile," XIX (1858-59), 454-56 (pickpocket in Australia).

1892   [Lang, John]. "A Special Convict," XIX (1858-59), 489-91 (Australia).

1893   [Martin, Miss]. "On the West African Coast," XIX (1858-59), 510-14 (Gold Coast).

1894   [Lang, John]. "Baron Wald," XIX (1858-59), 537-41 (special convict in Australia).

1895   [Lang, John]. "Three Celebrities," XIX (1858-59), 553-57 (bushrangers in Australia).

1896   [Lang, John]. "Kate Crawford," XIX (1858-59), 596-600 (special convict in Australia).

1897   [Thornbury, George Walter]. "My Farewell Dinner at
        Gib," XIX (1858-59), 602-05 (Gibraltar).

1898   [Lang, John]. "Bad Bargains," XIX (1858-59), 610-13
        (note on officials before competitive testing in
        India).

1899   [Lang, John]. "Miss Saint Felix," XIX (1858-59), 613-
        17 (convict in Australia).

HOWITT'S JOURNAL OF LITERATURE AND POPULAR PROGRESS

1900   Thompson, George. "The Raja of Sattara," I (1847), 46-
        48 (India).

1901   "Letter from South Africa," I (1847), 74.

1902   Howitt, William. "India the Preferred Salvation of
        England - Will We Have It?" II (1847), 228-30, 274-
        76, 329-33.

1903   "Thomas Clarkson, the Advocate of the Extinction of
        Slavery by means of India," II (1847), 338-39 (cotton
        and sugar).

1904   "Australian Life: Prospects for Emigrants," III (1848),
        384-88 (South Australia).

THE IRISH QUARTERLY REVIEW

1905   "Transatlantic Communication," I (1851), 268-301 (Brit-
        ish North America and Ireland).

1906   "Government Patronage at Home and Abroad," I (1851),
        485-507 (appointments of members of the Irish bar in
        the empire).

1907   "The English in America," I (1851), 523-48.

1908   "Emigration, Emigrants, and Emigrant Ships," IV (1854),
        430-71.

1909   "Convict Systems - Past and Present," IV (1854), 870-
        916 (transportation to Australia).

1910   "Convicts - Transportation and Reformation," VI (1856),
        559-86.

1911   G., N.J. "Steam and Telegraphic Communication," VI
        (1856), 586-600 (notes on the empire).

1912   "Recent African Explorations," VII (1857-58), 504-28
        (notes on all regions).

1913   "Livingstone's Travels and Researches," VII (1857-58),
        1165-216 (South and Southeast Africa).

1914   "The Irish Intermediate Convict System," VIII (1858-
        59), 1057-102 (notes on Western Australia).

1915   "Montalembert on England and India," VIII (1858-59),
        1381-420.

JOURNAL OF THE STATISTICAL SOCIETY OF LONDON

1916   Tulloch, Capt. A.M., F.S.S. "Sickness and Mortality
        among the Troops in the West Indies," I (1838-39),
        129-42, 216-30, 428-43.

1917   Rawson, R.W., Esq. "Emigration from the United Kingdom,"
        I (1838-39), 155-67.

1918   Christie, Robert, Esq., F.S.S. "On the Rate of Mortality
        amongst Officers Retired from the Indian Army," I
        (1838-39), 279-83.

1919   Bannister, Saxe, Esq. "Condition of the Population of
        New Zealand," I (1838-39), 362-76.

1920   Capper, John, Esq. "Commercial Statistics of Ceylon,"
        II (1839), 424-34.

1921   Committee of the Society. "Report on the Sickness and
        Mortality of Troops in the Madras Presidency," III
        (1840), 113-43; IV (1841), 137-55.

1922   Tulloch, Major A.M., F.S.S. "On the Sickness, Mortality,
        and Prevailing Diseases among Seamen and Soldiers,"
        IV (1841), 1-16 (notes on the empire).

1923   Burney, Lieut.-Col. H., Bengal Army, Late Resident at
        the Court of Ava. "On the Population of the Burman
        Empire," IV (1841), 335-47.

1924   Sykes, Lieut.-Col. W.H., F.R.S. "Civil and Criminal
        Justice in British India," VI (1843), 94-119.

1925   Everest, Rev. Robert, Chaplain to the East India Co.
        "Famines in India," VI (1843), 246-48.

1926   Maconochie, Capt. [Alexander], R.N., Late Superintend-
        ent. "Criminal Statistics and Movement of the Bond
        Population of Norfolk Island to December, 1843," VIII
        (1845), 1-49.

1927   Sykes, Lieut.-Col. W.H., F.R.S. "Population and
        Mortality of Calcutta," VIII (1845), 50-58.

1928   Sykes, Lieut.-Col. W.H., F.R.S. "Bengal Hospitals for the Insane," VIII (1845), 58-63.

1929   Balfour, T. Graham, M.D., Assistant Surgeon, Grenadier Guards. "Sickness and Mortality, Naval and Military," VIII (1845), 77-86 (notes on India).

1930   Sykes, Lieut.-Col. W.H., F.R.S. "Statistics of the Educational Institutions of the East India Company in India," VIII (1845), 103-47, 236-73.

1931   Balfour, Edward, Assistant Surgeon, Madras Army. "Health of Troops in Different Climates and Localities," VIII (1845), 193-209 (notes on the empire).

1932   Sykes, Lieut.-Col. [W.H.], F.R.S. "Mortality of the Madras Army; from Official Records," IX (1846), 157.

1933   Sykes, Lieut.-Col. W.H., F.R.S. "Statistics of the Administration of Civil and Criminal Justice in British India from 1841 to 1844, Both Inclusive," IX (1846), 310-38.

1934   Sykes, Lieut.-Col. W.H., F.R.S. "Government Charitable Dispensaries of India," X (1847), 1-37.

1935   Sykes, Lieut.-Col. W.H., Vice President of the Royal Society. "Vital Statistics of the East India Company's Armies in India," X (1847), 100-31.

1936   Sykes, Lieut.-Col. W.H., Vice President of the Royal Society. "Revenue Statistics of the Agra Government," X (1847), 243-51.

1937   Tulloch, Lieut.-Col. A.M., F.S.S. "Mortality among Her Majesty's Troops in the Colonies," X (1847), 252-59.

1938   Sykes, Lieut.-Col. W.H., Vice President of the Royal Society. "Prices of the Cerealia and Other Edibles in India and England Compared," X (1847), 289-316.

1939   Nelson, F.G.P., Esq., F.L.S. "Analysis of the Census of New South Wales," XI (1848), 38-54.

1940   Sykes, Col. [W.H.], Vice President of the Royal Society. "Statistics of Civil Justice in Bengal," XII (1849), 3-33.

1941   Balfour, Edward, Asst.-Surgeon, Madras Army. "Additional Observations on the Means of Maintaining Troops in Health," XII (1849), 33-42 (notes on India).

1942 Sykes, Lieut.-Col. W.H., Vice President of the Royal Society. "Mortality in the Jails of the Twenty-four Pergunnahs, Calcutta," XII (1849), 48-59.

1943 Danson, J.T., Esq. "Commercial Progress of the Colonial Dependencies of the United Kingdom," XII (1849), 349-439.

1944 Sykes, Lieut.-Col. W.H., F.R.S. "Statistics of Sugar Produced within the British Dominions in India," XIII (1850), 1-24.

1945 Danson, J.T. "Progress of Emigration from the United Kingdom during the Last Thirty Years," XIII (1850), 61-63.

1946 Finch, Dr. Cuthbert. "Vital Statistics of Calcutta," XIII (1850), 168-82.

1947 Porter, G.R., Esq., F.R.S. "Examination of the Recent Statistics of the Cotton Trade in Great Britain," XIII (1850), 305-12 (notes on the empire).

1948 Sykes, Lieut.-Col. W.H., F.R.S. "Expenditure in India on Public Works from 1837-8 to 1845-6, Inclusive," XIV (1851), 45-47.

1949 Sykes, Lieut.-Col. W.H., F.R.S. "Mortality and Chief Diseases of the Troops under the Madras Government," XIV (1851), 109-42.

1950 Thomson, Arthur S., M.D., Surgeon of the 58th Regiment. "Statistical Account of Auckland, New Zealand, as It was Observed during the Year 1848," XIV (1851), 227-49.

1951 "Statistics of New Munster, New Zealand, down to 1848," XIV (1851), 250-61.

1952 Balfour, Edward, Esq., Asst. Surgeon to Rt. Hon. Governor's Body Guard. "Men Discharged the Madras Service," XIV (1851), 348-56.

1953 Sykes, Lieut.-Col. W.H., F.R.S. "Mortality and Sickness of the Bombay Army, 1848-9," XV (1852), 100-07.

1954 Bedford, J.R., Civil Asst.-Surgeon. "Vital and Medical Statistics of Chittagong," XV (1852), 117-50 (Bengal).

1955 Farr, William, Esq., F.S.S. "Influence of Elevation on the Fatality of Cholera," XV (1852), 155-83 (notes on the empire).

1956   Grey, Rt. Hon. Earl. "Population of the Colony of
       British Guiana," XV (1852), 228-49.

1957   Sykes, Col. [W.H.], F.R.S. "On the Census of the
       Islands of Bombay and Colaba," XV (1852), 327-38.

1958   Sykes, Col. [W.H.], F.R.S. "Administration of Civil
       Justice in British India," XVI (1853), 103-36.

1959   Thomson, A.S., M.D. "Contribution to the Natural History
       of the New Zealand Race of Men," XVII (1854), 27-33.

1960   Cheshire, Edward, Asst. Secretary. "Statistics relative
       to Nova Scotia in 1851," XVII (1854), 73-80.

1961   Bell, G.M., Esq. "Historical and Statistical View of
       the Colony of Victoria," XVII (1854), 259-74.

1962   Valpy, Richard, Esq. "The Progress and Direction of
       British Exports," XVIII (1855), 160-73 (notes on the
       empire).

1963   Clarke, Robert, Surgeon, Colonial Medical Service.
       "Prevailing Diseases, Etc., in the Colony of Sierra
       Leone," XIX (1856), 60-81.

1964   Sykes, Col. [W.H.], F.R.S. "External Commerce of British
       India," XIX (1856), 107-26.

1965   Danson, J.T., Esq., Barrister-at-Law. "On the Existing
       Connection between American Slavery and the British
       Cotton Manufacture," XX (1857), 1-21 (notes on the
       empire).

1966   Bowring, Sir John. "The Population of China," XX (1857),
       41-52; with Postscript by S.W. Williams, 53 (see
       #2746).

1967   Sykes, Col. [W.H.], F.R.S., M.P. "Notes on Public Works
       in India," XXI (1858), 121-55.

1968   Hendriks, Frederick. "On the Statistics of Indian
       Revenue and Taxation," XXI (1858), 223-96.

1969   Sykes, Col. [W.H.], M.P., F.R.S. "Past, Present, and
       Prospective Financial Condition of British India,"
       XXII (1859), 455-80.

1970   Valpy, Richard, Esq. "On the Rapid Progress of British
       Trade with India," XXIII (1860), 66-75.

1971   Dassy, G.F., Constantinople. "Dassy ON THE COMMERCE OF
       THE RED SEA," XXIII (1860), 465-74 (trade using
       Suez route).

1972   Fenton, F.D., Compiler of the Statistical Tables of the Maori Population. "Fenton, REPORT ON THE MAORI POPULATION OF NEW ZEALAND," XXIII (1860), 508-41.

1973   Australian and New Zealand Delegates to the International Congress, 1860. "Statistical Phenomena in Australia, Consequent on the Gold Discoveries of 1851," XXIV (1861), 198-207.

1974   Farr, Dr. [William], F.R.S. "The Effects of Recent Measures for Improving the Health of the British Army," XXIV (1861), 472-84 (notes on the empire).

1975   Abstract of the Official Reports by the Governors. "British West India Colonies in 1859 (STANDARD, 10 October 1861)," XXIV (1861), 528-34.

1976   Sykes, Col. [W.H.], M.P., F.R.S. "Progress of the Trade with China, 1833-60," XXV (1862), 3-19.

1977   Mouat, Frederic John, M.D., F.R.C.S., Surgeon-Major Bengal Army. "Prison Statistics and Discipline in Lower Bengal," XXV (1862), 175-218.

1978   Merivale, Herman, Esq. "On the Utility of Colonies as Fields for Emigration," XXV (1862), 491-96.

1979   Levi, Leone, Esq., F.S.A., F.S.S. "The Cotton Trade and Manufacture as Affected by the Civil War in America," XXVI (1863), 26-48 (notes on the empire).

1980   Purdy, Frederick. "The Expenditure of the United Kingdom for Colonial Purposes," XXVI (1863), 359-83.

1981   Bird, James, M.D. "The Vital and Sanitary Statistics of Our European Army in India," XXVI (1863), 384-405.

1982   Chapman, H.S. "The Industrial Progress of Victoria as Connected with Its Gold Mining," XXVI (1863), 424-42.

1983   Hind, Henry Youle, M.A., F.R.G.S., Trinity College, Toronto. "The Commercial Progress and Resources of Central British America," XXVII (1864), 82-105 (Hudson's Bay Company territory).

1984   Tait, P.M., Esq., F.S.S., F.R.G.S., Director of Indian Business, Albert Life Assurance Co. "On the Mortality of Eurasians," XXVII (1864), 324-56 (India).

1985   Westgarth, William, Esq. "The Statistics of Crime in Australia," XXVII (1864), 505-19.

1986   Brown, Samuel, F.S.S. "On the Rates of Mortality and Marriage amongst Europeans in India, XXVII (1864), 566-79.

1987   Blakely, E.T., Esq., F.S.S. "On the Commercial Progress
        of the Colonies and Dependencies of the United King-
        dom," XXVIII (1865), 34-55.

1988   Mann, Horace, Esq. "On Public Schools and the Civil
        Service of India," XXVIII (1865), 150-69.

1989   Mouat, Frederic J., M.D., F.R.C.S. "On Prison Disci-
        pline and Statistics in Lower Bengal," XXX (1867),
        21-57.

1990   Sykes, Col. W.H., M.P., F.R.S. "On Charitable Donations
        by Natives of India," XXX (1867), 535-47.

THE LONDON QUARTERLY REVIEW

1991   "India under the English," I (1853), 233-74.

1992   "The British and Foreign Bible Society," I (1853), 353-
        93 (notes on the empire).

1993   "Our Australian Possessions," I (1853), 517-57.

1994   "Junction of the Atlantic and Pacific Oceans," II
        (1854), 172-85 (British North America and Central
        America).

1995   "The New Educational Measure for India," III (1854-55),
        159-80.

1996   "The British Government and Buddhism," III (1854-55),
        436-57 (Ceylon).

1997   "The West-India Question," IV (1855), 478-507.

1998   "Liberia," IV (1855), 507-20 (notes on Sierra Leone).

1999   "Canada, and the Far West," VI (1856), 143-64.

2000   "Christian Missions and THE WESTMINSTER REVIEW," VII
        (1856-57), 209-61 (notes on the empire).

2001   "Gold, in Its Natural Sources," VIII (1857), 50-76
        (notes on Australia).

2002   "Indian Missions - Martyn and Groves," VIII (1857),
        329-54.

2003   "Canadian Agriculture and Commerce," VIII (1857), 430-
        53.

2004   "The Sepoy Rebellion," IX (1857-58), 208-62 (India).

2005   "Dr. Livingstone's Researches in South Africa," IX
        (1857-58), 431-58 (also Southeast Africa).

2006   "Crisis of the Sepoy Rebellion," IX (1857-58), 530-70
        (India).

2007   "Christianity in India," X (1858), 1-32.

2008   "The Roman Alphabet Applied to Eastern Languages,"
        XI (1858-59), 143-56 (notes on Anglo-Indians).

2009   "The Southern Frontier of the Russian Empire," XI
        (1858-59), 233-74 (notes on Central Asia).

2010   "Fiji and the Fijians," XI (1858-59), 524-53.

2011   "The Serampore Mission," XII (1859), 249-70 (India).

2012   "Barth's African Researches," XIII (1859-60), 354-75
        (notes on West African trade).

2013   "Memoirs of Bishop Wilson," XIV (1860), 451-76 (India).

2014   "Recent Discoveries in Eastern Africa," XV (1860-61),
        30-63.

2015   "Russia in Asia," XV (1860-61), 439-54 (Central Asia).

2016   "Cotton," XV (1860-61), 459-519 (sources in the empire).

2017   "New Zealand," XV (1860-61), 519-52.

2018   "The Women of India and Ceylon," XVI (1861), 145-66.

2019   "The Chinese Insurgents, and Our Policy with respect
        to Them," XVI (1861), 222-46 (Taipings).

2020   "The Bible in South India," XVII (1861-62), 182-205.

2021   "Great Britain and Her West India Colonies," XVII
        (1861-62), 540-83.

2022   "Dr. Jobson's AUSTRALIA AND THE EAST," XVIII (1862),
        201-34 (Australia and Ceylon).

2023   "Trollope's NORTH AMERICA," XIX (1862-63), 234-58.

2024   "NOVA SCOTIA AND HER RESOURCES," XIX (1862-63), 478-91.

2025   "The Rejection of Fiji," XX (1863), 35-54.

2026   "The South Ceylon Wesleyan Mission," XX (1863), 113-30.

2027   "The Taeping Rebellion in China," XX (1863), 304-30.

2028   "The Jubilee of the Wesleyan Missionary Society," XX
        (1863), 471-92 (notes on activities in the empire).

2029   "Jurisdiction in Colonial Churches," XXI (1863-64),
        189-209.

2030 "Penal Servitude," XXI (1863-64), 271-99 (notes on
      transportation).

2031 "The Latest from New Zealand," XXI (1863-64), 437-57.

2032 "Captain Speke's JOURNAL," XXII (1864), 118-58 (notes
      on East African trade).

2033 "Gibraltar," XXII (1864), 337-75.

2034 "Our British North American Colonies," XXIII (1864-65),
      23-45.

2035 "Mr. Trevelyan on India," XXIII (1864-65), 169-97.

2036 "Abeokuta and Dahome," XXIII (1864-65), 452-83 (notes
      on Niger River).

2037 "The Judgment in Dr. Colenso's Case," XXIV (1865), 492-
      504 (religion in South Africa).

2038 "Livingstone's Expedition to the Zambesi," XXVI (1866),
      70-99 (notes on East and Southeast Africa).

MACMILLAN'S MAGAZINE

2039 Blakesley, Rev. J.W. "M. de Lesseps and the Suez Canal,"
      I (1859-60), 407-16.

2039a Ludlow, J.M. "Sir Charles Trevelyan and Mr. Wilson,"
      II (1860), 164-68 (government of India).

2040 Fawcett, Henry. "On the Social and Economical Influence
      of the New Gold," II (1860), 186-91 (notes on the
      empire).

2041 C., G.E.L. [Cotton, G.E.L.]. "Indian Cities - Benares,"
      III (1860-61), 58-65.

2042 Kingsley, Henry. "Travelling in Victoria," III (1860-
      61), 140-50.

2043 "The Chinese Capital, Pekin," III (1860-61), 248-56.

2044 McC., T. [McCombie, Thomas]. "New Zealand," III (1860-
      61), 328-33.

2045 Hare, Thomas. "On the Development of the Wealth of
      India," III (1860-61), 417-26.

2046 C., G.E.L. [Cotton, G.E.L.]. "Indian Cities - Lucknow,"
      IV (1861), 155-62.

2047 Ludlow, J.M. "The New Indian Budget: a Few Hints as to
      Men and Things," IV (1861), 201-05.

2048 An Ex-Competition Wallah [Boult, Swinton]. "The Indian
      Civil Service as a Profession," IV (1861), 257-68.

2049 [McTear, Robert]. "A Zulu Foray," IV (1861), 432-35
      (South Africa).

2050 Stewart, William J. "British Columbia," VI (1862), 29-
      33.

2051 A Professor of Political Economy [Leslie, T.E.C.].
      "The Wealth of Nations and the Slave Power," VII
      (1862-63), 269-76 (note on ex-slaves from United
      States in British Columbia).

2052 Broughton, H. [Trevelyan, G.O.]. "Letters from a
      Competition Wallah," VIII (1863), 80-87, 197-206,
      267-79, 341-53, 421-36; IX (1863-64), 16-31, 117-35,
      198-211, 288-304, 392-406, 482-95; X (1864), 1-17
      (Indian civil service).

2053 Martineau, Harriet. "Death or Life in India," VIII
      (1863), 332-40.

2054 Eyre, Major-General Vincent, C.B., Late Royal Artillery
      (Bengal). "Memorandum on a 'Story of the Great Muti-
      ny'," IX (1863-64), 445-48 (India).

2055 Maurice, F.E. "A Letter to a Colonial Clergyman: on
      Some Recent Ecclesiastical Movements in the Diocese
      of Capetown and in England," XI (1864-65), 97-112.

2056 [Hobart, V.H.]. "Charles Sturt: a Chapter from the
      History of Australian Exploration," XI (1864-65),
      204-17.

2057 Smith, Goldwin. "The Proposed Constitution for British
      North America," XI (1864-65), 406-16.

2058 Gorst, J.E. "Our New Zealand Conquests," XII (1865),
      168-75.

2059 [Yonge, Charlotte M.]. "CAWNPORE," XII (1865), 267-74.

2060 Cairnes, Professor [J.E.]. " 'The Negro Suffrage',"
      XII (1865), 334-43 (notes on West Indies).

2061 Kingsley, Henry. "Eyre, the South-Australian Explorer,"
      XII (1865), 501-10; XIII (1865-66), 55-63.

2062 Kennaway, John H. "The Camp in Canada," XIV (1866),
      69-73 (defense).

2063 [Bradley, G.G.]. "The Late Bishop of Calcutta," XV
      (1866-67), 102-11 (G.E.L. Cotton).

2064   "Home Defences," XV (1866-67), 277-94 (notes on the empire).

2065   "Dangers in India," XV (1866-67), 412-16.

2066   [Edwards, Edward]. "The National Rifle Association," XVI (1867), 177-88 (notes on colonial defense).

THE MONTHLY CHRONICLE

2067   [Bulwer, E.L.]. "Slavery and the New Slave Trade," I (1838), 126-38 (West Indies).

2068   [Bulwer, E.L.]. "Lord Durham's Mission," II (1838), 201-08 (Canada).

2069   "The Bayadères," II (1838), 476-80 (Indian dancers).

2070   [Fraser, James Baillie]. "Russia, Affghanistan, and India," III (1839), 422-29.

2071   "Colonisation of New Zealand," IV (1839), 110-23.

2072   "The War in the East," IV (1839), 139-48 (Afghanistan).

2073   A Resident Proprietor. "The Social Condition of Jamaica," IV (1839), 172-77, with a note by Robert Bell, 177.

2074   "Colonies and Emigration - South Australia," IV (1839), 193-208.

2075   [Hodgkin, Thomas]. "On the Practicability of Civilising Aboriginal Populations," IV (1839), 309-21 (British North America).

2076   "The War with China," V (1840), 415-26.

2077   Innes, Frederick Maitland. "The Convict System of Van Diemen's Land," V (1840), 431-49.

2078   [Innes, F.M.]. "Transportation," VI (1840), 159-62.

2079   [Hodgkin, Thomas]. "New Theory of Colonisation," VI (1840), 191-92 (South Australia).

2080   O.P.Q. [Chapman, H.S.]. "New Zealand," VII (1841), 148-53.

2081   [Chapman, H.S.]. "Australind," VII (1841), 385-405 (Western Australia).

2082   "Prospects of New Zealand," VII (1841), 500-10.

2083   von Hugel, Baron [Carl Alexander Anselm]. "The Valley of Kashmir," VII (1841), 551-55.

THE MONTHLY REPOSITORY

2084   [Martineau, Harriet]. "Van Diemen's Land," VI N.S.
       (1832), 372-80.

2085   [Martineau, Harriet and Fox, William Johnson]. "Rajah
       Rammohun Roy on the Government and Religion of India,"
       VI N.S. (1832), 609-17.

2086   T., W. [Turner, Rev. William]. "American Colonization
       Society," VII N.S. (1833), 153-60 (notes on West
       Indies).

2087   Junius Redivivus [Adams, William Bridges]. "On the
       Ministerial Plan for the Abolition of Negro Slavery,"
       VII N.S. (1833), 453-74 (West Indies).

2088   Author of the EXPOSITION OF THE FALSE MEDIUM [Horne,
       R.H.]. "Rationale of the 'Speech of Loo, Governor
       of Canton, in a Private Audience with Lord Napier',"
       IX N.S. (1835), 276-84.

2089   "Canada," IX N.S. (1835), 530-43.

2090   Chapman, H.S. "Canada," IX N.S. (1835), 614-21.

2091   "Recent Occurrences in Canada," X N.S. (1836), 106-22.

2092   "State of the Canadas - Recent Events," X N.S, (1836),
       265-70.

2093   [Hunt, Thornton Leigh]. "The Colonization of New
       Zealand," I 3S. (1837), 341-50.

2094   [Hunt, Leigh]. "Alleged Resignation of the Governor of
       Canada," I 3S. (1837), 369-72.

2095   [Hunt, Leigh]. "The New American War," II 3S. (1838),
       52-54 (Canada).

2096   A Correspondent. "Canada," II 3S. (1838), 54-56.

2097   [Hunt, Leigh]. "Canada," II 3S. (1838), 124-27.

THE NATIONAL REVIEW

2098   [Greg, W.R.]. "Secondary Punishments," IV (1857), 267-
       94 (transportation).

2098a [Martineau, Russell]. "Ancient India," IV (1857), 335-
       58.

2099   [Temple, Richard]. "The Military Revolt in India," V
       (1857), 440-86.

2100   [Greg, W.R.]. "Principles of Indian Government," VI
        (1858), 1-37.

2101   [Lathbury, D.C.]. "The Interior of British North Amer-
        ica," XIII (1861), 62-86 (Hudson's Bay Company
        territory).

2102   [Lathbury, D.C.]. "British Columbia," XIII (1861), 340-
        58.

2103   [Bullock, Henry]. "Bengal Planters and Ryots," XIV
        (1862), 114-34 (indigo).

2103a   "Health of the British Army at Home and Abroad," XVII
        (1863), 323-39 (notes on the empire).

2104   [?Greg, W.R.]. "Foreign Policy of the English Govern-
        ment and the English Nation," XVII (1863), 465-92
        (notes on China).

2105   [Campbell, George]. "The Administration of Justice in
        India," XVIII (1864), 136-68.

2106   [Harrison, Frederic]. "The Destruction of Kagosima,"
        XVIII (1864), 270-93 (notes on British military and
        commercial policies in the Far East).

THE NEW MONTHLY MAGAZINE

2107   "Narrative of a Settler in Canada," XXXIV (1832), 335-
        42.

2108   [Martineau, Harriet]. "What Shall We Do with the West
        Indies?" XXXIV (1832), 408-13.

2109   "Secondary Punishments: Report from Select Committee
        on Secondary Punishments," XXXV (1832), 125-28
        (notes on transportation).

2110   [Taylor, Philip Meadows]. "On the Thugs: Received from
        an Officer in the Service of His Highness the Nizam,"
        XXXVIII (1833), 277-87 (India).

2111   Martin, R. Montgomery. "The Financial State of Great
        Britain: Part IV - East and West India Interests,"
        XL (1834), 334-41 (cotton and sugar).

2112   Westmacott, Capt. "Summer in India," LII (1838), 507-
        08.

2113   Bluejacket. "A Night on the Table Mountain," LIII
        (1838), 170-76 (Cape Colony).

2114   Campbell, Major [Robert] Calder. "An Adventure in Ava,"
        LV (1839), 341-45 (Burma).

2115   Hood, Thomas, Esq. "The War with China," LX (1840),
        122-26.

2116   Tolfrey, Frederic, Esq. "A Winter and Summer in Canada,"
        LXI (1841), 382-88.

2117   The Editor [Hood, Thomas]. "News from China," LXVI
        (1842), 281-89; "More News from China," 422-31.

2118   The Old Forest Ranger [Campbell, Walter]. "Extracts
        from My Indian Diary," LXVII (1843), 99-110, 200-11,
        349-62, 481-95; LXVIII (1843), 81-92, 480-95; LXIX
        (1843), 265-71, 406-19; LXX (1844), 433-45.

2119   R. [Ridgway, Archibald R.]. "Letters from Hong Kong
        and Macao," LXX (1844), 153-72, 297-313, 353-84.

2120   Levinge, Capt. [R.G.A.]. "Echoes from the Backwoods,"
        LXXVI (1846), 33-49, 221-33, 267-80, 457-62; LXXVII
        (1846), 40-57 (New Brunswick).

2121   [Ainsworth, W. Francis]. "THE EXPEDITION TO BORNEO,"
        LXXVI (1846), 365-68.

2122   [Ainsworth, W. Francis]. "The Oregon Question," LXXVI
        (1846), 488-90.

2123   Butler, Capt. [Henry], 59th Regiment. "A Glimpse of
        the Frontier and a Gallop through the Cape Colony,"
        LXXVII (1846), 312-20, 457-74.

2124   "CANADA AND THE CANADIANS," LXXVIII (1846), 460-62.

2125   [Ainsworth, W. Francis]. "China: Its Present Condition
        and Prospects," LXXX (1847), 82-94.

2126   [Ainsworth, W. Francis]. "Sir George Simpson's NARRA-
        TIVE OF A JOURNEY ROUND THE WORLD," LXXX (1847), 219-
        41 (notes on British North America).

2127   [Ainsworth, W. Francis]. "ASSAM AND THE HILL TRIBES,"
        LXXX (1847), 308-12.

2128   Hamilton, George, Esq. "Fishing in South Australia,"
        LXXXI (1847), 160-65.

2129   [Ainsworth, W. Francis]. "James Brooke, Rajah of
        Sarawak," LXXXI (1847), 474-83.

2130   Napier, Lieut.-Colonel E. [D.H.E.]. "A Few Months in
        Southern Africa," LXXXII (1848), 21-30, 189-204, 301-
        08, 456-67; LXXXIII (1848), 51-63, 172-81, 301-08,
        497-507; LXXXIV (1848), 69-80, 215-26, 320-30, 480-
        95.

2131   [Ainsworth, W. Francis]. "HISTORY OF BARBADOS," LXXXII
       (1848), 80-87.

2132   [Ainsworth, W. Francis]. "Mr. Brooke's Latest Journals,"
       LXXXII (1848), 512-15 (Borneo).

2133   "The Kaffir War," LXXXIII (1848), 251-54 (South Africa).

2134   "The Question of General Emigration," LXXXIII (1848),
       523-26.

2135   [Ainsworth, W. Francis]. "Vancouver's Island," LXXXIV
       (1848), 161-68.

2136   "THE NEW ZEALAND QUESTION," LXXXIV (1848), 250-60.

2137   "Notes on Men and Things in the New World of Australia,"
       LXXXV (1849), 58-63, 159-64, 281-89, 489-96; LXXXVI
       (1849), 152-56.

2138   "The 'Rebel' Boers," LXXXV (1849), 74-78 (South Africa).

2139   Kinston, William H.G., Esq. "Colonies and Colonists;
       or, England and Her Offspring," LXXXV (1849), 354-70.

2140   "A Visit to the Ionian Islands in the Summer of 1848,"
       LXXXV (1849), 416-22.

2141   "The Red Men and the Trappers," LXXXV (1849), 436-40
       (Hudson's Bay Company).

2142   "New Zealand Cookery-Book," LXXXV (1849), 441-53 (Maori
       cannibalism).

2143   Sullivan, Capt. [B.J.], R.N. "The Falkland Islands,"
       LXXXVI (1849), 17-20.

2144   "The Ionian Islands in 1849," LXXXVI (1849), 105-12.

2145   Blundell, J.W.F., Esq. "Western Australia," LXXXVI
       (1849), 166-70.

2146   Wrottesley, The Hon. Walter. "Hints to Emigrants to
       New South Wales," LXXXVI (1849), 191-98.

2147   "Colonies and Constitutions," LXXXVI (1849), 335-41;
       LXXXVIII (1850), 376-82.

2148   Blundell, J.W.F., Esq. "The Emigrant in Western Aus-
       tralia," LXXXVI (1849), 359-66.

2149   "A Voice from Ceylon," LXXXVI (1849), 467-74.

2150   Blundell, J.W.F., Esq. "The Swan River - Fremantle -
       Perth," LXXXVI (1849), 475-83.

2150a   Charlton, Mrs. "The Mediterranean Stairs," LXXXVII (1849), 47-50 (Gibraltar).

2151   Blundell, J.W.F., Esq. "The Eastern Settled Districts in Australia," LXXXVI (1849), 84-93.

2152   Mackinnon, Capt. [L.B.], R.N. "Wild Sports of the Falklands," LXXXVII (1849), 139-56 (notes on possible immigration).

2153   Blundell, J.W.F., Esq. "The Canning River and Its Settlers, Western Australia," LXXXVII (1849), 195-205.

2154   Cooke, Henry. "An Excursion to Niagara and Canada," LXXXVII (1849), 358-68.

2155   [Ainsworth, W. Francis]. "Proposed Communications between the Atlantic and Pacific Oceans," LXXXVIII (1850), 172-93 (Central America).

2156   "The Colonial Reform Party," LXXXVIII (1850), 211-18.

2156a   [Ainsworth, W. Francis]. "THE SURVEY OF THE EUPHRATES," LXXXIX (1850), 122-28 (c. 1835-37 with notes on India).

2157   Hamilton, Dr. [William]. "On the Advantages and Practicability of Forming a Junction between the Atlantic and Pacific Oceans," LXXXIX (1850), 365-72, 444-51; XC (1850), 37-40, 167-79, 314-28 (Central America).

2158   [Ainsworth, W. Francis]. "The Boundary Commission in Canada," XC (1850), 41-51 (British North America).

2159   [Ainsworth, W. Francis]. "The Charms of an Australian Squatter's Life," XCI (1851), 215-23 (New South Wales).

2159a   "Major Edwardes's YEAR ON THE PUNJAB FRONTIER," XCI (1851), 475-79.

2160   [Ainsworth, W. Francis]. "The War in Kaffirland," XCII (1851), 271-81 (South Africa).

2161   [Ainsworth, W. Francis]. "Gold in Australia," XCIII (1851), 353-64.

2162   "Sir Charles Napier in Scinde," XCIV (1852), 144-54.

2163   "Recollections of the Last Caffre War," XCIV (1852), 313-19 (South Africa).

2164   "Hunting in South Australia," XCIV (1852), 362-71.

2165   [Ainsworth, W. Francis]. "The Burmah War," XCV (1852),
        360-78.

2166   [Ainsworth, W. Francis]. "Teas and the Tea Country,"
        XCV (1852), 439-54 (China).

2167   [Ainsworth, W. Francis]. "Digging for Gold," XCVI
        (1852), 76-89 (Australia).

2168   "The French in the South Seas," XCVIII (1853), 48-63
        (notes on East Indies).

2169   "The Chinese Revolution," XCIX (1853), 180-98 (Taipings).

2170   "HITHER AND THITHER," CI (1854), 301-08 (notes on
        Canada).

THE NEW QUARTERLY REVIEW

2171   "Kaye's HISTORY OF THE WAR IN AFGHANISTAN," I (1852),
        18-24.

2172   "Napier's Administration of Scinde," I (1852), 45-49.

2173   "FIVE YEARS IN THE WEST INDIES," I (1852), 264-66.

2174   "OUR ANTIPODES," I (1852), 268-69 (Australia).

2175   "The Great Canadian Railway," I (1852), 296-300 (Brit-
        ish North America).

2176   "India - the Trader Sovereign and the Hindu Slave," I
        (1852), 343-52 (see #2178 and #2179).

2177   "Indian Poets and Their English Translators," I (1852),
        363-66.

2178   "India - How the Hindu Thrall is Ruled," II (1853),
        39-51 (see #2176 and #2179).

2179   "India - the Anarchy of Thraldom," II (1853), 175-97
        (see #2176 and #2178).

2180   "THE COLONIAL POLICY OF LORD JOHN RUSSELL'S ADMINISTRA-
        TION," II (1853), 197-99.

2181   "THE SECOND BURMESE WAR," II (1853), 263-64.

2182   "Recent Discoveries in Africa," II (1853), 328-38
        (notes on Gold Coast).

2183   "Recent Progress of the Indian Question," II (1853),
        347-49.

2184   "AUSTRALIA VISITED AND REVISITED," II (1853), 366-68.

2185 "The Party of Progress in China," II (1853), 465-73 (Taipings).

2186 "A Few More Words on India," II (1853), 474-84.

2187 "Contributions to Indian History - Napier," III (1854), 28-31.

2188 "Travels," III (1854), 183-99 (notes on gold in Australia).

2189 "Travels," III (1854), 330-34 (notes on Punjab).

2190 "India - the Punjab and the Presidencies," III (1854), 429-34.

2191 "History and Biography," III (1854), 462-76 (notes on India under the Muslims).

2192 "The Land Question in Bengal," IV (1855), 145-46.

2193 "Polynesian Mythology, Etc.," IV (1855), 211-14 (New Zealand).

2194 "TRAVELS AND ADVENTURES IN THE PROVINCE OF ASSAM," IV (1855), 313-16.

2195 "THE FUR HUNTERS IN THE FAR WEST, ETC.," V (1856), 46-48 (Hudson's Bay Company).

2196 "EIGHT YEARS' WANDERINGS IN CEYLON," V (1856), 48-52.

2197 "Lord Dalhousie's Administration in India," V (1856), 470-81; VI (1857), 103-18.

2198 "LIFE IN ANCIENT INDIA," VI (1857), 48-55.

2199 "THE LIFE AND OPINIONS OF GENERAL SIR CHARLES JAMES NAPIER, G.C.B.," VI (1857), 189-97, 306-15 (notes on Sind).

2200 "Judicial Reform in India," VI (1857), 240-52.

2201 "A RESIDENCE AMONG THE CHINESE, ETC., ETC.," VI (1857), 297-305.

2202 "Land Tenure in India," VI (1857), 361-70.

2203 "VICTORIA AND THE AUSTRALIAN GOLD MINES, IN 1857," VI (1857), 408-19.

2204 "The Indian Revolt, Its Causes and Cures," VI (1857), 463-76.

2205 "The Double Government of India," VII (1858), 73-89.

2206 "TRAVELS AND DISCOVERIES IN NORTH AND CENTRAL AFRICA," VII (1858), 253-59 (notes on Niger River).

2207 "Free Labour Immigration and the Slave Trade: Letter and New Inquiry Instituted by the Emperor Napoleon III," VII (1858), 365-75 (West Indies).

2208 "Indian Heroes and Indian Reform," VIII (1859), 22-40.

2209 "The Administration of Justice in India," VIII (1859), 543-72.

THE NORTH BRITISH REVIEW

2210 [Dick, A. Coventry]. "Harris' HIGHLANDS OF ETHIOPIA," I (1844), 41-67 (notes on empire-building).

2211 [Wilson, John]. "Sacred Literature of the Hindus," I (1844), 366-97.

2212 [Cubitt, Mr.]. "Backhouse's Visit to the Mauritius and South Africa," II (1844-45), 105-35.

2213 [Robertson, T.C.]. "Thornton's HISTORY OF BRITISH INDIA," II (1844-45), 324-59.

2214 [Wilson, John]. "The Baron Hügel's TRAVELS IN KASHMIR AND THE PANJÅB," II (1844-45), 444-70.

2215 "Colonization and the Allotment System," III (1845), 406-43.

2216 "Australia," IV (1845-46), 281-312.

2217 [Kaye, J.W.]. "The War on the Sutlej," V (1846), 246-80 (Punjab).

2218 "China," VII (1847), 388-420.

2219 [Robertson, T.C.]. "Indian Politicals," VII (1847), 420-40.

2220 [Anster, John]. "Colonization from Ireland," VIII (1847-48), 421-64 (Australia and Canada).

2221 [Brewster, David]. "Mr. Brooke's JOURNALS OF A RESIDENCE IN BORNEO," IX (1848), 432-71.

2222 [Kaye, J.W.]. "The Fall of the Sikh Empire," XI (1849), 618-61 (Punjab).

2223 [Kaye, J.W.]. "The Romance of Indian Warfare," XII (1849-50), 193-224 (Punjab).

2224 [Kaye, J.W.]. "Christianity in India," XIII (1850), 583-620.

2225 [Bell, Robert]. "The Frontier Wars of India," XVI (1851-51), 230-58 (Afghanistan).

2226   [Mossman, Samuel]. "New Zealand," XVI (1851-52), 336-58.

2227   [Greg, W.R.]. "The Modern Exodus in Its Effects on the British Islands," XVIII (1852-53), 259-302.

2228   [Kaye, J.W.]. "The Government of the East India Company," XVIII (1852-53), 526-60.

2229   [Greg, W.R.]. "Our Colonial Empire and Our Colonial Policy," XIX (1853), 345-98.

2230   [Hill, Alicia with Whately, Richard]. "Free and Slave Labour," XIX (1853), 445-61 (cotton and sugar productions in the empire compared with those in the United States).

2231   [Kaye, J.W.]. "The Government of India - the New India Bill," XIX (1853), 552-82.

2231a   [Masson, David]. "Kaye's LIFE OF LORD METCALFE," XXII (1854-55), 145-78 (notes on India and Jamaica).

2232   [Freeman, E.A.]. "Mahometanism in the East and West," XXIII (1855), 449-80 (notes on India).

2233   [Muir, John]. "Indian Literature," XXV (1856), 205-32.

2234   [Kaye, J.W.]. "The Annexation of Oude," XXV (1856), 515-53.

2235   [Taylor, Isaac]. "The Trade in Opium," XXVI (1856-57), 521-58 (China and India).

2236   [Duns, John]. "Interior China," XXVII (1857), 75-105.

2237   [Kaye, J.W.]. "The Crisis in India," XXVII (1857), 254-76 (mutiny).

2238   [Chadwick, Edwin]. "Our Army in India," XXIX (1858), 211-43.

2239   [Duns, John]. "Fiji and the Fijians," XXX (1859), 44-68.

2240   [Tremenheere, J.H.]. "Indian Colonisation," XXX (1859), 441-66.

2241   "WANDERINGS OF AN ARTIST [Paul Kane] AMONG THE INDIANS OF NORTH AMERICA," XXXI (1859), 72-88.

2242   [Duns, John]. "Ceylon and the Singhalese," XXXII (1860), 188-222.

2243   [Tremenheere, J.H.]. "Sir Henry Lawrence," XXXII (1860), 345-65 (Oudh and Punjab).

2244 [Cunningham, Bruce]. "Australian Ethnology," XXXII (1860), 366-88 (natives).

2245 [Tremenheere, J.H.]. "Colonial Constitutions and Defences," XXXIII (1860), 83-113.

2246 [Kaye, J.W.]. "India Convalescent," XXXIV (1861), 1-32.

2247 [Tremenheere, J.H.]. "British Columbia and Vancouver Island," XXXV (1861), 61-81.

2248 [Greg, W.R.]. "Our Colonies," XXXVI (1862), 535-60.

2249 [Sellar, A.C.]. "Mr. St. John's Borneo," XXXVII (1862), 198-221.

2250 [Kaye, J.W.]. "Lord Canning," XXXVII (1862), 222-48 (India).

2251 [Patterson, R.H.]. "Syria and the Eastern Question," XXXVII (1862), 422-47 (notes on Euphrates Valley route).

2252 [Greg, W.R.]. "Convicts and Transportation," XXXVIII (1863), 1-35.

2253 [MacLennan, John F.]. "Hill Tribes in India," XXXVIII (1863), 392-422.

2254 [Smith, Walter]. "Christian Missions," XL O.S. and I N.S. (1864), 417-50 (notes on India).

2255 [Eastwick, E.B.]. "RAMBLES IN THE DESERTS OF SYRIA," XL O.S. and I N.S. (1864), 471-97 (notes on Indian defense).

2256 [Leslie, T.E. Cliffe]. "The New Gold Mines and Prices," XLII O.S. and III N.S. (1865), 300-26.

2257 [Mills, Arthur]. "Colonial Policy in the Government of Coloured Races," XLIV O.S. and V N.S. (1866), 388-410.

2258 [Hunter, W.W.]. "The Bengal Famine of 1866," XLIV O.S. and VII N.S. (1867), 242-76.

ONCE A WEEK

2259 Martineau, Harriet. "River Scenes in China," I (1859), 146-49, 176-78.

2260 Kaye, J.W. "Mountstuart Elphinstone: In Memoriam," I (1859), 502-04 (India).

2261   Scott, Ingleby. "Representative Men: the Missionaries -
        Martyn, Huc, Livingstone, Selwyn," II (1859-60), 26-
        30 (Persia, China, South and East Africa).

2262   Jager. "Catching Trout in Nova Scotia," II (1859-60),
        85-88.

2263   Scott, Ingleby. "Representative Men: the Knight Adven-
        urer - Rajah Brooke," II (1859-60), 364-69 (Borneo).

2264   "Last Week," III (1860), 220-24 (India); 501-04, 585-
        88, 669-72 (China).

2265   McDermott, E. "Telegraph Reporting in Canada and the
        United States," III (1860), 258-60.

2266   Scott, Ingleby. "Representative Men: Last Champions of
        Tribes - Cheetoo, Nana Sahib, Schamyl, Abd-El-Kader,"
        III (1860), 651-56 (notes on India).

2267   Swanwick, F. "Indian Juggling," IV (1860-61), 40-43.

2268   "Last Week," IV (1860-61), 54-56 (China); 418-20, 474-
        76 (India); 558-60 (British North America); 614-16
        (Bengal indigo); 670-72 (Queensland cotton); 722-24
        (China, India, and New Zealand).

2269   P. "The Fate of Tan-King-Chin, a British Subject," IV
        (1860-61), 95-97 (British response to kidnapping of
        local servant in China).

2270   "Recent Explorations in Australia by John Macdonald
        Stuart," IV (1860-61), 214-16.

2271   A[lexander], G.G. "The 'Outer Barbarians,' from a
        Chinese Point of View," IV (1860-61), 440-45.

2272   "Tartars and Taepings: a Personal Narrative of the
        Recent Expedition up the Yangtze Kiang," V (1861),
        121-25.

2273   W., A. "Cotton and the Cotton-Supply," V (1861), 212-
        18, 238-45.

2274   Aylmer, Isabella E. "The New Zealand Difficulty," V
        (1861), 348-49.

2275   "How the Rains Came upon Us in India," V (1861), 381-
        82.

2276   M., R.B. "The City of the Flying-Fox," V (1861), 639-
        44 (road building in Ceylon).

2277   Fiddes, Harriet Cawse. "My Arrival in Australia," V
        (1861), 707-11.

2278   "A Trip to the Timber Makers," VI (1861-62), 47-51
        (Canada).

2279   "The Victoria Exploring Expedition," VI (1861-62), 216-
        19.

2280   From the Mountain. "A New Britain in the West," VI
        (1861-62), 219-24 (British North America).

2281   "All down the River," VI (1861-62), 243-49 (Canadian
        timber).

2282   Prout, Skinner. "The Sketcher in Tasmania," VI (1861-
        62), 275-80, 304-08.

2283   Confutzao. "Chinese Dinners and Morning Calls," VI
        (1861-62), 417-18 (native manners).

2284   From the Mountain. "Where the Flags, There the Family,"
        VI (1861-62), 456-60 (need for women in colonies).

2285   "The English in India: as They Are, and as They Are
        Represented by One of Them," VI (1861-62), 484-88.

2286   F., D. "The New Zealand Census Returns, 1861," VIII
        (1862-63), 13-14.

2287   "Tapping for Toddy," VIII (1862-63), 139-40 (native
        use of coconuts in India).

2288   "From Rangoon," VIII (1862-63), 204-07.

2289   "Return of the Rival Explorers," VIII (1862-63), 347-
        49 (Australia).

2290   "Anglo-India from a French Point of View: a French
        Novel - LA GUERRE DU NIZAM par Mery," VIII (1862-
        63), 403-06.

2291   From the Mountain. "Old and New Fittings," VIII (1862-
        63), 508-12 (cotton and transportation in the empire).

2292   "An Australian Explorer," VIII (1862-63), 667-70
        (Francis Cadell).

2293   From the Mountain. "Old and New Times for the Hindoo,"
        IX (1863), 8-12.

2294   From the Mountain. "Florence Nightingale's Latest
        Charity," IX (1863), 205-09 (English troops in India).

2295   "Pathmasters and Road-Work in Canada," IX (1863), 402-
        05.

2296   From the Mountain. "Gold, Bread, and Something More,"
        IX (1863), 454-58 (British North America).

2297   "A Skating Rink in Canada," X (1863-64), 296-98.

2298   Chesshyre, Henry. "From Canada to Liverpool, with
       'Skedaddlers' from the Northern Army," XI (1864),
       340-44.

2299   M., J. "A Peep at Some of the Islands in the Western
       Pacific," XI (1864), 509-15 (notes on New Zealand).

2300   W., W.M. "Cashmere Shawls: of What are They Made?" XII
       (1864-65), 68-70 (notes on Indian trade).

2301   "Bootan and the Booteeas," XII (1864-65), 205-10 (sug-
       gestion of possible annexation to India).

2302   L., J.K. " 'How We Went to Fort Rupert,' and Made a
       Strange Purchase," XIII (1865), 19-22 (British
       Columbia).

2303   "A Virtuous Colony," XIII (1865), 147-53 (Pitcairn
       and Norfolk Islands).

2304   L. "The Maroons of Jamaica," XIII (1865), 707-09.

2305   "How I Liked Aden," I N.S. (1866), 263-66.

2306   Pringle, Chetwoode D. "A Visit to a Queensland Cotton
       Plantation," I N.S. (1866), 501-03.

2307   Cambalu. "On a River in China," I N.S. (1866), 632-37.

2308   P., J.J. "A 'Tangi' in New Zealand," I N.S. (1866),
       718-19 (Maori custom).

2309   Black, Simon. "Salmon in Australia," II N.S. (1866),
       716-17 (notes on gold miners).

2310   K. "A Cattle-Drive in British Columbia," III N.S.
       (1867), 39-42.

2311   W., A. "Indian Textile Fabrics," III N.S. (1867), 325-
       30 (cotton and other fabrics).

2312   "The Indian Museum, Whitehall," IV N.S. (1867), 246-50.

THE PENNY MAGAZINE

2313   "Van Diemen's Land," I (1832), 2-3, 10-11.

2314   "Emigration to the North American Colonies," I (1832),
       17-18.

2315   "The Seasons of the Antipodes," I (1832), 18-19 (cli-
       mate of Australia).

2316   "An Emigrant's Struggles," I (1832), 39-40 (Van Diemen's
       Land).

2317   "India," I (1832), 135-36.

2318   P. "The Cape Buffalo - Bos Caffer," I (1832), 137-38
        (notes on natives in Cape Colony).

2319   "Emigration," I (1832), 158-59 (Australia).

2320   "Condition of Convicts in Van Diemen's Land," I (1832),
        162.

2321   "British India," I (1832), 214.

2322   "Emigration," I (1832), 261-62 (British North America).

2323   "The Ostrich of South Africa," I (1832), 353-54 (colo-
        nial trade).

2324   "On Ancient India," I (1832), 354-55.

2325   "The Floating Gardens of Cashmere," I (1832), 365-66
        (notes on natives).

2326   "An African Judge and European Slave-Holder," I (1832),
        383 (South Africa).

2327   "A Party of Emigrants Travelling in Africa," II (1833),
        22-23, 28-29, 51-52 (South Africa).

2328   "Charmers of Serpents," II (1833), 49-50 (India).

2329   "The Hottentots," II (1833), 69-71 (South Africa).

2330   "The Pearl Fishery of Ceylon," II (1833), 174-76.

2331   "Old Travellers: Robert Knox," II (1833), 186-88, 198-
        200, 214-16 (Ceylon).

2332   P., T. "A Settler's Cabin in South Africa," II (1833),
        282-83.

2333   "Weaving in Ceylon," II (1833), 325-26.

2334   M., H. "The Cinnamon-Tree and Its Products," II (1833),
        402-03 (Ceylon).

2335   "Site of a Convalescent Establishment in the Himalaya
        Mountains," III (1834), 14-15 (India).

2336   "Gibraltar," III (1834), 19-23.

2337   "The East India Company," III (1834), 84-86.

2338   "The Parsees," III (1834), 138-40 (India).

2339   "Malta," III (1834), 151-52.

2340   "Life of an Indian Chief," III (1834), 282-84 (Canada).

2341   "Corfu," III (1834), 394-96.

2342   "Opium," III (1834), 397-99.

2343   "Indian Rivers," III (1834), 399-400 (irrigation).

2344   "North American Indians," IV (1835), 38-40, 53-55.

2345   "China," IV (1835), 297-99, 317-19, 332-34, 363-64,
       396-97, 424, 445-48, 486-87; V (1836), 50-51, 60,
       77-79, 120, 485-87.

2346   "The 'Pancha Tantra'," IV (1835), 358-59 (Indian
       fables).

2347   "Kingston, Jamaica," IV (1835), 373-75.

2348   "St. Helena," V (1836), 108-11.

2349   "Intellectual Progress of the Chinese," V (1836), 285-
       87.

2350   "A Brief Captivity among the Chinese," V (1836), 314-17.

2351   "Sugar Farm in Jamaica," V (1836), 348-50.

2352   "The River St. Clair and the Chippeway Indians," VI
       (1837), 153-54 (Canada).

2353   "Indian Fishing in North America," VI (1837), 193-94
       (Canada).

2354   "Fishing in North America," VI (1837), 209-10 (notes
       on natives).

2355   "The St. Lawrence and Quebec," VI (1837), 219-21.

2356   "Peculiarities of the Climate of Canada and the United
       States," VI (1837), 258-60.

2357   "Newspapers beyond the Ganges," VI (1837), 299-300
       (China and Singapore).

2358   "Fur-Trading with the Indians," VI (1837), 303-04
       (British North America).

2359   "Fish Poisoning in the West Indies," VI (1837), 370-
       72 (notes on colonists).

2360   "Adventures among the Indians of Guiana," VI (1837),
       486-87.

2361   "Canada, and the Other British Colonies in North
       America," VII (1838), 25-40.

2362   "Trade of the British North American Colonies," VII
       (1838), 46-48, 50-54.

2363   "The Tarai," VII (1838), 93-94 (India).

2364 A Correspondent. "Substitute for the Mulberry Leaves in the Leaves of the Ramoon Tree," VII (1838), 215 (trade in West Indies).

2365 "The Shawl-Goat in Europe and Australia," VII (1838), 266-68 (trade in New South Wales).

2366 "Neilgherry Hills," VII (1838), 271-72 (India).

2367 "Education in China," VII (1838), 286-87.

2368 "New Zealand," VII (1838), 325-27, 417-24.

2369 "Progress of African Discovery," VIII (1839), 41-43, 54-56 (Gambia and Niger River).

2370 "Malta and the Maltese," VIII (1839), 229-30, 241-42, 276-78, 297-98.

2371 "The Mogul Dynasty in Hindustan," VIII (1839), 237-40, 273-74, 286-88, 301-02, 307-08, 313-15, 345-47, 364-67, 398-400.

2372 "Barbadoes," VIII (1839), 329-30, 347-48, 354-55, 385-86.

2373 "Hyder Ali," VIII (1839), 409-11 (India).

2374 "The Mango," VIII (1839), 416 (use in liquor in West Indies).

2375 "The Canada Goose," VIII (1839), 448 (use as food).

2376 "Cultivation of the Tea-Plant in Assam," IX (1840), 59-60, 70-72.

2377 "Tea-Making in China and Assam," IX (1840), 75-77.

2378 "Opium Smuggling in China," IX (1840), 89-91.

2379 "The Observatory at Delhi," IX (1840), 217-18.

2380 "The North American Elk," IX (1840), 239-40 (uses by natives and colonists).

2381 "Sketches of the Coast from Singapore to Pekin," IX (1840), 245-47, 258-60, 286-88, 303-04, 311-12, 317-19, 326-28, 334-36, 358-60 (East Indies and China).

2382 A Correspondent. "Difficulties of Surveying and Allotting in North America," IX (1840), 298-300.

2383 "Alexandria," IX (1840), 460-62 (route to India).

2384 "The East India Company's Museum," X (1841), 207-08.

2385 "Port Lincoln, South Australia," XI (1842), 1-2.

2386   "Aborigines of Australia," XI (1842), 65-67.

2387   "The Polygars of Tinnevelly," XI (1842), 77-78 (India).

2388   "Ning-Po," XI (1842), 105-06 (China).

2389   "Natives of New Zealand," XI (1842), 132-34.

2390   "Singapore, or Sincapore," XI (1842), 140-43.

2391   "The Ganges," XI (1842), 165-67.

2392   "Aborigines of Van Diemen's Land," XI (1842), 195-96.

2393   "Sufferings of the Party Composing Captain Grey's Expedition of Discovery in Western Australia," XI (1842), 218-19, 239-40, 246-47.

2394   "Steam Communication with India," XI (1842), 225-26, 235-37 (notes on Suez).

2395   "Natives of Nootka Sound," XI (1842), 265-66 (Hudson's Bay Company territory).

2396   "Newfoundland," XI (1842), 289-90.

2397   "Afghanistan," XI (1842), 324-26, 361-63.

2398   "Kingston," XI (1842), 396-97 (Canada).

2399   "Hong-Kong," XI (1842), 500-02.

2400   "The Castes and Tribes of India," XII (1843), 9-10, 41-42.

2401   "The Niagara District, Western Canada," XII (1843), 17-18, 52-53, 85-86.

2402   "Shang-Hae," XII (1843), 81-83 (China).

2403   "The Tribes of India," XII (1843), 100-01.

2404   "Foo-Choo-Foo," XII (1843), 108-09 (China).

2405   "Amoy," XII (1843), 137-38 (China).

2406   "Scinde and the Scindians," XII (1843), 148-49.

2407   "On the System of Dawk Travelling in India," XII (1843), 156-58.

2408   "Indigo Planters and Plantations," XII (1843), 178-80 (Bengal).

2409   "Castes and Tribes of India," XII (1843), 188-90.

2410   "Tribes and Castes of India," XII (1843), 257-58.

2411   "Rise and Progress of the Seiks," XII (1843), 313-15 (Punjab).

2412   "Tribes and Castes of India - Cutch," XII (1843), 353-55.

2413   "Tribes and Castes of India - Rajpoots," XII (1843), 385-86.

2414   "Junction of the Atlantic and Pacific Oceans," XII (1843), 397-99, 404-06, 414-16 (Central America).

2415   "Tribes and Castes of India: the Rohillas," XII (1843), 429-30.

2416   "City of Caboul," XII (1843), 441-42 (Afghanistan).

2417   "Villages of North American Indians," XIII (1844), 109-10.

2418   "Gwalior, or Gualior," XIII (1844), 113-14 (India).

2419   "Cultivation of the Nutmeg in British Colonies," XIV (1845), 47-48 (Singapore).

2420   "Rain-Makers," XIV (1845), 182-84 (British North America and Ceylon).

2421   "The City of Benares," XIV (1845), 401-03 (India).

2422   "Native Indians of the Oregon Territory," I N.S. (1846), 141-44.

2423   "The Punjab," II N.S. (1846), 54-58.

2424   "The Oregon Question," II N.S. (1846), 139-44.

PEOPLE'S AND HOWITT'S JOURNAL

2425   "Emigration the Remedy," VI (1848), 125-26.

2426   Charlton, Mrs. "The Cholera Camp," VII (1849), 256-59 (India).

2427   "New Zealand," VII (1849), 289-91.

2428   "The First Bushrangers in Australia Felix," VII (1849), 367-69.

2429   "Emigration," VII (1849), 375-77.

2430   L., J.K. "The Punjab," I N.S. (1849), 39.

2431   Stewart, G.C. "A Day's Excursion in Van Diemen's Land," II N.S. (1850), 150-51.

2432   Allen, Nathan. "The Opium Trade," III N.S. (1850), 51-53 (China and India).

2433   C., F. "An Incident of Indian Life," IV N.S. (1851), 163-64.

2434   "An Emigrant's Trials," IV N.S. (1851), 362-64 (Victoria).

THE PEOPLE'S JOURNAL

2435   Wentworth, Mrs. "Glorious War!" I (1846), 230-32 (Punjab).

2436   Munro, Georgina C. "A Few Remarks on Emigration to the Cape of Good Hope," I (1846), 256-59.

2437   A Working Hand. "Life in New South Wales," II (1846), 74-78.

2438   Munro, Georgina C. "The Kafirs of the Cape of Good Hope; or, Scenes in Peace and War," II (1846), 100-04.

2439   Barmby, Goodwyn. "Military Agricultural Colonies," III (1847), 31.

2440   Dixon, Hepworth. "James Brooke, the Rajah of Sarawak," IV (1847), 347-50.

2441   Byrne, J.C. "Emigration and the Classes That Would Benefit from It," V (1848), 115-18.

2442   "The Landing-Place, Chandpaul, Calcutta," V (1848), 231.

2443   Saunders, John. "How and on What Principles Are We To Emigrate?" V (1848), 345-47.

THE PROSPECTIVE REVIEW

2444   "The Marquess Wellesley," III (1847), 370-95 (India).

2445   [Newman, F.W.]. "THE RACES OF MAN, AND THEIR GEOGRAPHICAL DISTRIBUTION," VI (1850), 48-59 (notes on Fijians).

THE QUARTERLY REVIEW

2446   [Milman, H.H.]. "Tod's ANNALS AND ANTIQUITIES OF RAJAST'HAN," XLVIII (1832), 1-39 (India).

2447   [Lockhart, J.G.]. "Earle's RESIDENCE IN NEW ZEALAND AND TRISTAN D'ACUNHA," XLVIII (1832), 132-65.

2448   "Steam-Navigation to India," XLIX (1833), 212-28 (Egypt and Euphrates Valley).

2449   [Lockhart, J.G.]. "M.G. Lewis's WEST INDIA JOURNALS," L (1833-34), 374-99.

2450   [Barrow, John]. "Free Trade to China," L (1833-34),
       430-67.

2451   [Barrow, John]. "Gutzlaff's VOYAGES ALONG THE COAST OF
       CHINA," LI (1834), 468-81.

2452   [Barrow, John]. "Burnes's TRAVELS INTO BOKHARA," LII
       (1834), 367-406 (Central Asia).

2453   "Bennett's NEW SOUTH WALES, ETC.," LIII (1835), 1-19.

2454   [Barrow, John]. "Emigration - Letters from Canada,"
       LIV (1835), 413-29.

2455   [Lockhart, J.G.]. "Pringle and Moodie on South Africa,"
       LV (1835-36), 74-96.

2456   [McNeill, John]. "SCENES AND CHARACTERISTICS OF
       HINDOSTAN," LV (1835-36), 174-94.

2457   [Barrow, John]. "The Foreign Slave-Trade," LV (1835-
       36), 250-85 (as related to sugar production).

2458   [Barrow, John]. "The Chinese," LVI (1836), 489-521.

2459   [Barrow, John]. "Travels and Adventures in Eastern
       Africa: the Manners, Customs, Etc., of the Zoolus,"
       LVIII (1837), 1-29 (South Africa).

2460   [Barrow, John]. "Travels in Ladakh, Kashmir, Bokhara,
       Etc.," LXI (1838), 96-122 (Central Asia and India).

2461   [Croker, J.W.]. "Canada," LXI (1838), 249-72.

2462   [Twiss, Horace]. "New South Wales," LXII (1838), 475-
       505.

2463   [Croker, J.W.]. "Political Affairs," LXIII (1839), 223-
       77 (notes on Canada).

2464   "State and Prospects of Asia," LXIII (1839), 369-402
       (India).

2465   [Croker, J.W.]. "Colonial Government - Head's NARRATIVE
       and Lord Durham's REPORT," LXIII (1839), 457-525
       (Canada).

2466   [McNeill, John]. "Russia, Persia, and England," LXIV
       (1839), 145-88 (also Afghanistan).

2467   [Broderip, W.J.]. "Sporting in Southern Africa," LXIV
       (1839), 188-232.

2468   [Head, Francis B.]. "British Policy," LXIV (1839), 462-
       512 (Canada).

2469   [Head, Francis B.]. "The Red Man," LXV (1839-40), 384-422 (British North America).

2470   [Barrow, John]. "Chinese Affairs," LXV (1839-40), 537-81.

2471   [Croker, J.W.]. "United States' Boundary Question," LXVII (1840-41), 501-41 (British North America).

2472   [Barrow, John]. "The Australian Colonies," LXVIII (1841), 88-145.

2473   [Milman, H.H.]. "Elphinstone's HISTORY OF INDIA," LXVIII (1841), 377-413.

2474   "Stephens's TRAVELS IN CENTRAL AMERICA," LXIX (1841-42), 52-91 (comments on British Honduras and possible canal).

2475   [Croker, J.W.]. "Treaty of Washington," LXXI (1842-43), 560-95 (British North America boundary).

2476   [Egerton, Francis]. "Simpson's NARRATIVE OF DISCOVERIES BY OFFICERS OF THE HUDSON'S BAY COMPANY," LXXIII (1843-44), 113-29.

2477   "Ecclesiastical State of the Colonies," LXXV (1844-45), 201-22.

2478   [Kinglake, A.W.]. "The 'French Lake'," LXXV (1844-45), 532-69 (Mediterranean with notes on Egypt).

2479   [Eastlake, Elizabeth]. "Lady Travellers," LXXVI (1845), 98-137 (notes on colonists in Australia and natives in India).

2480   [Brougham, Henry]. "Strzelecki on New South Wales and Van Diemen's Land," LXXVI (1845), 488-521.

2481   [Croker, J.W.]. "The Oregon Question," LXXVII (1845-46), 563-610.

2482   [Egerton, Francis]. "Borneo - Eastern Archipelago, Etc.," LXXVIII (1846), 1-23.

2483   [Gleig, G.R.]. "The War of the Punjab," LXXVIII (1846), 175-215.

2484   [Lockhart, J.G.]. "Captain Neill's Narrative - General Nott in Affghanistan," LXXVIII (1846), 463-510.

2485   [Lockhart, J.G.]. "HOCHELAGA and THE EMIGRANT," LXXVIII (1846), 510-35 (Canada).

2486   [Holland, Henry]. "Captain Blackwood's VOYAGE AND
        SURVEY - Darwin on CORAL REEFS," LXXXI (1847), 468-
        500 (notes on Australia and imperial defense).

2487   [Higgins, Matthew J.]. "The Friends of the African,"
        LXXXII (1847-48), 153-75 (notes on Sierra Leone and
        West Indies).

2487a   [Gleig, G.R.]. "Our Military Establishment," LXXXII
        (1847-48), 453-83 (notes on the empire).

2488   [Egerton, Francis]. "Borneo and Celebes," LXXXIII
        (1848), 340-59.

2489   [Young, G.F.]. "Free Trade," LXXXVI (1849-50), 148-83
        (notes on effects on the empire).

2490   [Owen, Richard]. "Mr. Cumming's HUNTER'S LIFE IN SOUTH
        AFRICA," LXXXVIII (1850-51), 1-41 (notes on natives).

2491   [Higgins, M.J.]. "The Mysteries of Ceylon," LXXXVIII
        (1850-51), 100-29.

2492   "Cheap Sugar and Slave-Trade," LXXXVIII (1850-51), 129-
        36.

2493   [Patterson, R.H.]. "Recent Travellers in North America,"
        LXXXIX (1851), 57-97 (Canada).

2494   [Bushby, Henry Jeffreys and Ludlow, John]. "Widow-
        burning - Major Ludlow," LXXXIX (1851), 257-76
        (India).

2495   [Greg, W.R.]. "Highland Destitution and Irish Emigra-
        tion," XC (1851-52), 163-205 (emigration).

2496   [Robertson, Thomas Campbell]. "Kaye's HISTORY OF THE
        WAR IN AFGHANISTAN," XCI (1852), 11-36.

2497   [Bowen, G.F.]. "Ionian Administrators - Lord Seaton and
        Sir Henry Ward," XCI (1852), 315-52.

2498   [Prinsep, Henry Thoby and Eastwick, E.B.]. "Sindh - Dry
        Leaves from Young Egypt," XCI (1852), 379-401.

2499   [Coulton, D.C.]. "Gold Discoveries," XCI (1852), 504-
        40 (notes on Australia).

2500   [Ellis, Henry]. "Indian Administration," XCII (1852-
        53), 46-76.

2501   [Merivale, Herman]. "The Missions of Polynesia," XCIV
        (1853-54), 80-122 (notes on Pitcairn Islanders).

2502   [Grant, Anthony]. "Religion of the Chinese Rebels,"
        XCIV (1853-54), 171-95 (Taipings).

2503   [Merivale, Herman]. "Christianity in Melanesia and
         New Zealand," XCV (1854), 165-206 (Fiji and New
         Zealand).

2504   [Bulwer-Lytton, Edward]. "The Disputes with America,"
         XCIX (1856), 235-86 (Central America).

2505   [Gladstone, W.E.]. "Prospects Political and Financial,"
         CI (1857), 243-84 (notes on Afghanistan and India).

2506   [Layard, A.H.]. "Persia," CI (1857), 501-41.

2507   [Gladstone, W.E.]. "The New Parliament and Its Work,"
         CI (1857), 541-84 (notes on China).

2508   [Elwin, Whitwell]. "Travels in China - Fortune and Huc,"
         CII (1857), 126-65.

2509   [Layard, A.H.]. "Communication with India: Suez and
         Euphrates Routes," CII (1857), 354-97.

2510   [James, Thomas]. "Indian Mutiny," CII (1857), 534-70.

2511   [Fergusson, James]. "Our Indian Empire," CIII (1858),
         253-78.

2512   [Milnes, R.M.]. "Personal Narrative of the Siege of
         Lucknow," CIII (1858), 505-26 (Indian mutiny).

2513   [Layard, A.H.]. "British India," CIV (1858), 224-76.

2514   [Elwin, Whitwell]. "Sir Charles Napier," CIV (1858),
         475-515 (Sind).

2515   [Gladstone, W.E.]. "The Past and Present Administra-
         tions," CIV (1858), 515-60 (notes on China and India).

2516   [Hayward, Abraham]. "Lord Cornwallis," CV (1859), 1-45
         (notes on India).

2517   [Ellis, William]. "The Islands of the Pacific," CVI
         (1859), 174-205 (notes on Fiji).

2518   [Tremenheere, J.H.]. "New Zealand - Its Progress and
         Resources," CVI (1859), 330-68.

2519   [Tremenheere, J.H.]. "The Australian Colonies and the
         Gold Supply," CVII (1860), 1-45.

2520   [Osborn, Sherard]. "China and the War," CVII (1860),
         85-118.

2521   [Tremenheere, J.H.]. "The Cape and South Africa," CVIII
         (1860), 120-62.

2522   [Tremenheere, J.H.]. "Canada and the North-West," CIX
         (1861), 1-37.

2523   [Tremenheere, J.H.]. "African Discovery," CIX (1861),
        496-530 (review with notes on Niger River and East
        and South Africa).

2524   [Macleod, John Macpherson]. "Indian Currency, Finance,
        and Legislation," CIX (1861), 566-607.

2525   [Tremenheere, J.H.]. "Russia on the Amoor," CX (1861),
        179-208 (China).

2526   [Tremenheere, J.H.]. "The Eastern Archipelago," CXI
        (1862), 483-516.

2527   [Macpherson, William]. "China - the Taeping Rebellion,"
        CXII (1862), 500-34.

2528   [Cecil, Robert]. "Four Years of Reforming Administra-
        tion," CXIII (1863), 253-88 (Ionian Islands).

2529   [Medlicott, J.G.]. "Industrial Resources of British
        India," CXIII (1863), 289-322.

2530   [Bayley, C.J.]. "Our Colonial System," CXIV (1863),
        125-51.

2530a   [Tremenheere, J.H.]. "The Nile - Speke and Grant,"
        CXIV (1863), 274-88 (notes on trade).

2531   [Brine, Lindesay]. "China," CXV (1864), 1-42.

2531a   [Tremenheere, J.H.]. "Captain Speke's JOURNAL," CXV
        (1864), 105-31 (East Africa with notes on natives).

2532   [Pollock, George David]. "Sanitary State of the Army
        in India," CXVI (1864), 413-19.

2533   [Smythe, Percy E.F.W.]. "Travels in Central Asia," CXVII
        (1865), 476-519.

2534   [Rawlinson, Henry C.]. "The Russians in Central Asia,"
        CXVIII (1865), 529-81.

2534a   [Tremenheere, J.H.]. "Livingstone's ZAMBESI AND ITS
        TRIBUTARIES," CXIX (1866), 1-26 (notes on natives
        and trade).

2535   [Maltby, T.]. "The Value of India to England," CXX
        (1866), 198-220.

2536   [Bayley, C.J.]. "Jamaica, Its Disturbances and Its
        Prospects," CXX (1866), 221-59.

2537   [Rawlinson, Henry]. "Central Asia," CXX (1866), 461-
        503.

THE RAMBLER

2538   J., F.W. [Jerningham, F.W.]. "Emigration; How Possible
       for the Poor," III (1848), 30-33.

2539   "THE CAPE AND THE KAFIRS," IX (1852), 410-20 (Cape
       Colony).

2540   "A Blue-Stocking in the Bush," X (1852), 322-26
       (British North America).

2541   "Mrs. Chisholm and Emigration," XI (1853), 148-66.

2542   "OUR ANTIPODES," XI (1853), 410-27 (Australia).

2543   "Emigration Considered with reference to Its Influence
       on the Spread of Catholicity," XI (1853), 456-74.

2544   [De Vere, Aubrey]. "Chinese Civilization and Christian
       Charity," XIII O.S. and I 2S. (1854), 552-57.

2545   [Simpson, Richard]. "Huc's CHINESE EMPIRE," XIV O.S.
       and II 2S. (1854), 331-44, 380-93.

2546   "The King of Oude's Private Life," XVI O.S. and IV 2S.
       (1855), 223-35.

2547   [Weld, Frederick]. "Christianity in the Pacific,"
       XIX O.S. and VII 2S. (1857), 202-12 (New Zealand).

2548   [Capes, Frederick]. "Chinese Life and Manners," XX O.S.
       and VIII 2S. (1857), 354-68.

2549   [Simpson, Richard and Grant, Thomas]. "Catholicity in
       India," XX O.S. and VIII 2S. (1857), 385-99.

2550   [Capes, J.M.]. "INDIA IN 1848," XXI O.S. and IX 2S.
       (1858), 249-67.

2551   [Capes, J.M.]. "India for Exeter Hall," XXI O.S. and
       IX 2S. (1858), 361-73.

2552   [Capes, Frederick]. "CHINA," XXII O.S. and X 2S.
       (1858), 345-56.

2553   [Arnold, Thomas]. "The Negro Race and Its Destiny,"
       XXVI O.S. and III 3S. (1860), 170-89, 317-37
       (slavery and its aftermath).

2554   W. [Simpson, Richard]. "Marshall on CHRISTIAN MISSIONS,"
       XXIX O.S. and VI 3S. (1861-62), 352-66 (notes on
       India).

2555   C., C. [Acton, J.D.]. "Colonies," XXIX O.S. and VI 3S.
       (1861-62), 391-400.

THE ST. JAMES'S MAGAZINE

2556   "The Defences of British North America," III (1861-62),
        217-22.

2557   "Popular Education in Bengal," V (1862), 483-88.

2558   "The Mission of Ticket-of-Leave Men," VI (1862-63), 163-
        67 (notes on Australia).

2559   P. "Blacks," VII (1863), 45-55 (West Indies).

2560   "Private Life of the Zulu Kaffirs," IX (1863-64), 335-
        42 (South Africa).

2561   Drayson, Capt. A.W., R.N. "Along the Coast of South
        Africa: from Cape Town to Natal," XII (1864-65), 80-
        86.

2562   "A New Gate for British Commerce," XIII (1865), 183-89
        (Peshawar).

2563   "Twelve Hours at Aden," XIII (1865), 449-55.

2564   Rees, L.E. "Hindoo Prejudices," XIV (1865), 377-86.

2565   "Jamaica of To-day," XV (1865-66), 59-69, 188-97.

2566   "Excursion to Pekin in 1861," XV (1865-66), 474-88.

2567   R., W. "A Street in Melbourne," XVI (1866), 196-201.

2568   "A Night in a Caffre Prison, and How I Came There,"
        XVII (1866), 231-44 (South Africa).

2569   C., W.S. "A Ride in Queensland," XVIII (1866-67), 365-
        72.

2570   V. "A Glimpse of the East," XIX (1867), 42-51 (notes
        on Gibraltar).

2571   P., J.J., An Army Medical Officer. "Stray Leaves from
        an Indian Note-Book," XIX (1867), 296-308; XX (1867),
        166-80.

SHARPE'S LONDON MAGAZINE (JOURNAL)

2572   "The Seiks and the Singhs," I (1846), 49-51, 66-70
        (Punjab).

2573   "The Australian Exploring Expedition," I (1846), 269-
        70.

2574   "DISCOVERIES IN AUSTRALIA," I (1846), 295-98.

2575   "Sir F. Head's EMIGRANT," III (1846-47), 120-24
        (Canada).

2576   "HOCHELAGA," III (1846-47), 237-39 (Canada).

2577   Kit. [Watkins, Kathleen Blake]. "Letters from New
       Zealand," V (1847-48), 180-84, 273-77; VI (1848), 76-
       79, 193-97; VII (1848), 91-96.

2578   Postans, Mrs. [Marianne]. "A Parsee Wedding," VI (1848),
       11-15 (India).

2579   "Scenes and Adventures in Borneo," VI (1848), 203-08,
       266-71.

2580   Postans, Mrs. [Marianne]. "Cocoa-Nut Day, and the Great
       Fair of the Temple," VII (1848), 32-37 (India).

2581   Traill, Mrs. [Catherine Parr Strickland]. "A Visit to
       the Camp of the Chippewa Indians," VII (1848), 114-
       18 (Canada).

2582   "The Tiger Hunt," IX (1849), 129 (India).

2583   "The Punjaub and Its People," IX (1849), 193-98.

2584   "The Church in the Colonies," IX (1849), 240-41.

2585   "Expedition into Central Australia," IX (1849), 249-51.

2586   "Montreal and the St. Lawrence," X (1849), 22-25.

2587   "Ceylon and Its Dependencies," X (1849), 57-59.

2588   "SKETCHES IN NEW ZEALAND," X (1849), 111-16.

2589   W., J.M. "A Few Words about Mr. Sidney Herbert's
       Emigration Scheme," XI (1850), 99-103.

2590   "EXCURSIONS IN SOUTHERN AFRICA," XI (1850), 120-25.

2591   "Pirates of the Indian Archipelago," XI (1850), 131-37
       (East Indies).

2592   Postans, Mrs. [Marianne]. "Notices on the Hindu Drama
       and Condition of the Women of India," XI (1850), 212-
       16.

2593   Postans, Mrs. [Marianne]. "Indian Railways," XI (1850),
       339-43.

2594   Postans, Mrs. [Marianne]. "The 'Sepoy': a Talbotype,"
       XII (1850), 137-41.

2595   "The English in Australia," XII (1850), 321-25.

2596   Traill, Mrs. [Catherine Parr Strickland]. "Bush Weddings
       and Wooings," XIII (1851), 90-93 (Canada).

2597   A Frenchman. "Malta," XIII (1851), 103-06.

2598   "Africa," XIII (1851), 129-33, 221-26; XIV (1851), 10-
        15 (South and West).

2599   "CHRISTIANITY IN CEYLON," XIII (1851), 315-20.

2600   "Major Edwardes on the Punjab," XIII (1851), 325-35.

2601   "Major Edwardes on the Punjab Again," XIV (1851), 18-
        23.

2602   "Letters from Australia," XIV (1851), 279-82 (from
        settlers of the continent).

2603   Traill, Mrs. [Catherine Parr Strickland]. "Female
        Trials in the Bush," XV (1852), 22-26 (Canada).

2604   Urquhart, Hugh John. "A Colonist's Story of Christmas
        Eve," XV (1852), 22-26 (South Africa).

2605   From the Diary of an Officer. "A Week in Jamaica in
        the Year 1841," XV (1852), 243-48.

2606   Traill, Mrs. [Catherine Parr Strickland]. "Female
        Servants in the Bush," XV (1852), 279-81 (Canada).

2607   "Recollections of a Quarantine Detenu," XVI O.S. and
        I N.S. (1852), 1-12 (notes on Malta).

2608   St. John, Horace. "The Birman Empire - the Seat of the
        War," XVI O.S. and I N.S. (1852), 42-45.

2609   "The Emigration Cry," XVI O.S. and I N.S. (1852), 352-
        61.

2610   "Hindostan: a Hindoo Woman - the Fan-Leaf Palm,"
        XVII O.S. and II N.S. (1853), 105-07.

2611   St. John, Horace. "An Indian Village," XVII O.S. and
        II N.S. (1853), 183-85.

2612   St. John, Horace. "The English Rajah in Sarawak,"
        XVII O.S. and II N.S. (1853), 228-33.

2613   "A Pirate's Life in Borneo," XVII O.S. and II N.S.
        (1853), 336-41.

2614   An 'Old Indian.' "The Thugs and Pindarries of Hindostan,"
        XVIII O.S. and III N.S. (1853), 76-78.

2615   "An Eastern Lunatic Asylum," XVIII O.S. and III N.S.
        (1853), 110-19 (Ceylon).

2616   "Recollections, Historical and Descriptive, of the Cape
        of Good Hope," XVIII O.S. and III N.S. (1853), 313-
        17, 367-72.

2617   N., E.D. "Two Days' Fishing in Nova-Scotia," XIX O.S.
       and IV N.S. (1854), 161-63.

2618   Ki-Ki. "A Colonial Village in New Zealand," XIX O.S.
       and IV N.S. (1854), 188-90.

2619   A Missionary. "A Visit to the Indians of Orialla,"
       XXIV O.S. and IX N.S. (1856), 99-103 (British Guiana).

2620   A Soldier's Wife. "A Word for India," XXIX O.S. and
       XIV N.S. (1858), 48-49.

2621   Arranged by Townbridge, Elizabeth. "First Glimpse
       of India," XXXI O.S. and XVI N.S. (1859), 242-47.

2622   Arranged by Townbridge, Elizabeth. "Some Adventures in
       India," XXXII O.S. and XVII N.S. (1859), 12-18.

2623   Arranged by Townbridge, Elizabeth. "Extracts from a
       Journal in India (Irregularly Kept from 1856 to 1859),"
       XXXII O.S. and XVII N.S. (1859), 174-81.

2624   Revised by Townbridge, Elizabeth. "A True Narrative of
       Emigrant Life in Australia from 1852 to 1860,"
       XXXIII O.S. and XVIII N.S. (1860), 186-96 (Victoria).

2625   Cartwright, John D. "Emigration, Emigrants, and Miss
       Rye," XXXVIII O.S. and XXIII N.S. (1863), 37-41.

2626   "English Naval Power and English Colonies: from an
       American Point of View," XXXVIII O.S. and XXTII N.S.
       (1863), 143-48.

2627   C., Mr. "A Glimpse of Vancouver's Island," XLIII O.S.
       and XXVIII N.S. (1866), 188-90.

2628   Viator. "Mauritius - a Sketch," XLV O.S. and XXX N.S.
       (1867), 54-55.

2629   Luxe. "At an Indian Railway Station," XLVI O.S. and
       XXXI N.S. (1867), 185-87.

2630   Luxe. "In the Jungle," XLVI O.S. and XXXI N.S. (1867),
       268-70 (India).

2631   Luxe. "Low Life in the East," XLVI O.S. and XXXI N.S.
       (1867), 294-98 (city life in India).

TAIT'S EDINBURGH MAGAZINE

2632   "True Causes of the Late Insurrection of the Slaves in
       Jamaica," I (1832), 81-90.

2633   "The Slave-Holders - the Missionaries - and Mr. Jeremie,"
       II (1832-33), 203-04 (West Indies).

2634   "Reforms in the British External Empire," II (1832-33),
        714-38.

2635   "British Commerce," III (1833), 169-82 (notes on the
        empire).

2636   "Whig Settlement of the 'Great Questions'," III (1833),
        649-55 (notes on emancipation of slaves and on India).

2637   "British Emigrant Colonies: No. 1 - New South Wales,"
        I N.S. (1834), 401-19.

2638   "The Emigrants of Glen-Lynden," I N.S. (1834), 458-67
        (Cape Colony).

2639   "Shirreff's Travels in Canada and the United States,"
        II N.S. (1835), 146-56.

2640   "Political State of Canada and Historical Retrospect
        of the Colony," II N.S. (1835), 439-50.

2641   "Politics of Upper Canada - Lord Stanley," II N.S.
        (1835), 663-67.

2642   "Anglo-Indian Society," II N.S. (1835), 683-93.

2643   "Slavery in British India," IV N.S. (1837), 185-88.

2644   Tait, W. "Affairs of Canada, and the Ministerial Bill,"
        IV N.S. (1837), 260-63.

2645   "Bacon's FIRST IMPRESSIONS IN HINDOSTAN," IV N.S. (1837),
        397-400.

2646   "WRONGS OF THE CAFFRE NATION," IV N.S. (1837), 515-23
        (South Africa).

2647   "The East India Company's Accounts," IV N.S. (1837),
        553-55.

2648   "Canada - Standing Armies," IV N.S. (1837), 709-14.

2649   "The Progress of Society in India," IV N.S. (1837),
        765-69.

2650   "Canada - Political Juggling," V N.S. (1838), 67-72.

2651   "White's VIEWS AND TOURS among the Himalaya [Mountains],"
        V N.S. (1838), 115-19 (India).

2652   "Abolition of Negro Apprenticeships - Sturge and
        Harvey's Tour in the West Indies in 1837," V N.S.
        (1838), 135-48.

2653   "Lord Brougham's Speeches on Slavery," V N.S. (1838),
        203-09 (West Indies).

2654   "Communication from Mr. Hume on the Causes of Canadian
       Discontents," V N.S. (1838), 265-69.

2655   "Benthamisms, No. 1: Emancipate Your Colonies," V N.S.
       (1838), 328-31.

2656   "The Winding Up of the East India Company's Commercial
       Affairs," V N.S. (1838), 429-34.

2657   "Howitt's COLONIZATION AND CHRISTIANITY," V N.S. (1838),
       527-34 (treatment of natives).

2658   "Steam Communication with India," V N.S. (1838), 571-
       78 (Egypt and Euphrates Valley).

2659   "Wild Sports of the Far West; or, a Few Week's Adven-
       tures among the Hudson's Bay Company Fur Traders, in
       the Autumn of 1836," V N.S. (1838), 648-55; VI N.S.
       (1839), 328-35.

2660   "Friendship in Trade; or, the Practical Results of the
       Protective System," V N.S. (1838), 701-04 (effects
       on the empire).

2661   "Alexander's Discoveries in the Interior of Africa,"
       V N.S. (1838), 727-39 (notes on South Africa).

2662   "The New Colony of South Australia, and the Penal
       Colonies," V N.S. (1838), 776-89 (also Van Diemen's
       Land).

2663   "Mrs. Postans' CUTCH; OR, RANDOM SKETCHES of Western
       India," VI N.S. (1839), 28-35.

2664   "Mrs. Jameson's WINTER STUDIES AND SUMMER RAMBLES in
       Canada," VI N.S. (1839), 69-81.

2665   "War in India," VI N.S. (1839), 82-86.

2666   "Australian Emigration," VI N.S. (1839), 168-76.

2667   "Steam to India," VI N.S. (1839), 293-96 (Egypt).

2668   "The War in India," VI N.S. (1839), 518-21 (Afghanistan).

2669   "The Rights and Duties of Nations, with reference to
       Passing Events," VII N.S. (1840), 726-31 (notes on
       Afghanistan and China).

2670   "Miss Roberts' Notes of an Overland Journey through
       France and Egypt to Bombay: with a Memoir," VIII N.S.
       (1841), 235-40 (India).

2671   Howitt, William and Richard. "Letters on Emigration to
       New South Wales, Etc.," VIII N.S. (1841), 270-72.

2672 "Catlin's Adventures among the North American Indians
      on the Upper Missouri," VIII N.S. (1841), 792-801;
      IX N.S. (1842), 106-17 (British North America).

2673 "Moffat's MISSIONARY LABOURS AND SCENES IN SOUTH AFRICA,"
      IX N.S. (1842), 528-44, 597-604.

2674 "Quaker Missions to Australia," X N.S. (1843), 218-24.

2675 "The Affghan War, and Lady Sale's JOURNAL," X N.S.
      (1843), 370-83; "Sir A. Burnes - the Retreat and
      Captivity," 456-69; "The Captivity of the English
      Officers and Ladies in Affghanistan," 512-21 (num-
      bered 421).

2676 "The Garbled Despatches of Sir Alexander Burnes," X N.S.
      (1843), 521-25 (numbered 421-25; Afghanistan).

2677 "THE CLOSING EVENTS OF THE CAMPAIGN IN CHINA," X N.S.
      (1843), 525-31 (numbered 425-31).

2678 "Hood's AUSTRALIA AND THE EAST," X N.S. (1843), 586-99
      (New South Wales).

2679 M'Combie, Thomas. "Australian Sketches," X N.S. (1843),
      605-10, 720-25; XI N.S. (1844), 95-101, 152-56, 308-
      11.

2680 "A SUMMER AT PORT PHILLIP," XI N.S. (1844), 213-18.

2681 "Godley's LETTERS FROM AMERICA," XI N.S. (1844), 317-
      20, 435-42 (Canada).

2682 "Quaker Mission to the Mauritius and South Africa,"
      XI N.S. (1844), 630-33.

2683 "British Aggression in Sinde," XII N.S. (1845), 385-89.

2684 "Recent Books on America," XII N.S. (1845), 593-604
      (Canada).

2685 An Englishman in America. "The Tariff and the Oregon,"
      XIII N.S. (1846), 273-76.

2686 "LIFE OF THE DOST MOHAMMED KHAN OF KABUL," XIII N.S.
      (1846), 596-99.

2687 Barmby, Goodwyn. "The Old Country and the New Country;
      or, Home Colonisation and Emigration," XIV N.S.
      (1847), 266-68.

2688 "The British Mission to Omar Ali, Sultan of Bruni -
      February, 1845," XIV N.S. (1847), 341-44 (negotiations
      by James Brooke).

2689   "Revolution in the Dekkan," XIV N.S. (1847), 554-59
        (India).

2690   "Descriptive Sketch of the Province of Bundelkund,"
        XIV N.S. (1847), 682-90 (India).

2691   "AUSTRALIA FELIX," XV N.S. (1848), 11-16.

2692   "Schomburgh's HISTORY OF BARBADOES," XV N.S. (1848),
        43-49.

2693   "Our Debt - Our Colonies - and Their Owners," XV N.S.
        (1848), 445-50.

2694   "Dangers of Our New Settlement in the Indian Archi-
        pelago," XV N.S. (1848), 650-58 (Borneo).

2695   "The Recent Emigration," XV N.S. (1848), 768-75.

2696   "English and Dutch in the Indian Archipelago," XVI N.S.
        (1849), 1-8 (East Indies).

2697   "The Colonial Question - Canada," XVI N.S. (1849), 141-
        47, 201-12, 282-88, 383-87.

2698   "Recent Australian Discovery," XVI N.S. (1849), 148-55.

2699   "Employment or Emigration," XVI N.S. (1849), 362-66.

2700   "Our Anglo-Saxon Empire," XVI N.S. (1849), 687-95.

2701   "The Position of the Colonies," XVI N.S. (1849), 752-
        59.

2702   "Original Correspondence of General Wolfe," XVI N.S.
        (1849), 804-18 (Canada).

2703   "British Policy in the Indian Archipelago," XVII N.S.
        (1850), 78-88 (East Indies).

2704   "How To Develop the Resources of British India,"
        XVII N.S. (1850), 201-06.

2705   "Peter against Paul: a Pig-Row at Malta," XVII N.S.
        (1850), 381-86 (religious conflict).

2706   "Sir James Brooke and the Pirates of the Eastern Archi-
        pelago," XVIII N.S. (1851), 607-15.

2707   "Plain Statement of the Origin of the Cape Difficulties,"
        XIX N.S. (1852), 22-27, 92-98 (South Africa).

2708   "Recent Discoveries in Southern Africa," XIX N.S.
        (1852), 419-23 (Southeast Africa).

2709   "California and Australia - Gold and Wool," XIX N.S.
        (1852), 425-26.

2710 MacGregor, John. "The United States and the British American Fisheries: to the Right Honourable the Earl of Derby," XIX N.S. (1852), 547-49.

2711 "Earl Grey's Colonial Policy," XX N.S. (1853), 230-34.

2712 "How To Lose a Colony," XX N.S. (1853), 275-79 (Orange River).

2713 M. "Canada and the Clergy Reserves," XX N.S. (1853), 297-302.

2714 "The South African Republic - How To Keep a Colony," XX N.S. (1853), 342-49 (Orange River).

2715 M'G. "India, Its People, and Its Governments," XX N.S. (1853), 484-88, 547-50, 609-14.

2716 "Recollections of Jamaica," XX N.S. (1853), 727-31.

2717 " 'The Legitimate Drama' on the Banks of the Ganges," XXI N.S. (1854), 428-30.

2718 "Who Are the Kings of the East?" XXII N.S. (1855), 747-54 (India).

TEMPLE BAR

2719 [Scoffern, John]. "Cotton," III (1860), 431-39 (notes on India).

2719a "Burke's Australian Explorations," V (1862), 43-52.

2720 [Hutton, James]. "Our Indian Newspaper," VI (1862), 502-11.

2721 B., S.L. [Blanchard, Sidney L.]. "The Bayard of India," VIII (1863), 215-35 (career of Sir James Outram).

2722 B., S.L. [Blanchard, Sidney L.]. "The Late Ameer of Caubul - Dost Mohammed Khan," IX (1863), 338-49.

2723 [Hutton, James]. " 'Young Bengal' as a Newspaper Correspondent," XI (1864), 295-303.

2724 "New Zealand: Past, Present, and Future," XI (1864), 397-405.

2725 B., S.L. [Blanchard, Sidney Laman]. "The Long-Bow in India," XI (1864), 409-22 (English in India).

2726 M., F. "Convicts at Swan River," XIV (1865), 50-53 (Western Australia).

2726a [Sala, George Augustus]. "The Streets of the World: Montreal, Canada East - Notre Dame Street," XV (1865), 43-50 (notes on HABITANTS).

2727   P., O. [Plunkett, Oliver]. "The Beautiful Prairie," XV
        (1865), 544-54 (Hudson's Bay Company territory).

2728   P., O. [Plunkett, Oliver]. "Among the Esquimaux," XVI
        (1865-66), 144-53 (Hudson's Bay Company territory).

2729   Morris, M. O'Connor, Late Postmaster of the Island.
        "Jamaica," XVI (1865-66), 209-18.

2730   [Lord, John Keast]. "From Vancouver Island to the Mound
        Prairies," XVIII (1866), 343-56.

2731   Marryat, Florence [Church, Mrs. Ross]. " 'Gup'," XIX
        (1866-67), 75-94, 395-404, 464-75; XX (1867), 463-72;
        XXI (1867), 66-77, 176-86, 338-48, 466-82 (officer's
        wife in India).

2732   [Slade, Alfred]. "A Bear Hunt in the Himalayas," XIX
        (1866-67), 229-37 (India).

2733   Fletcher, Lieut.-Colonel [H.C.]. "Winter Weather in
        England and Canada," XX (1867), 102-08.

2734   J., H. [Jepson, Henry]. "Reminiscences of Bush Life in
        Queensland," XXI (1867), 194-200.

THE THEOLOGICAL REVIEW

2735   D., S. [Davidson, Samuel]. "The British and Foreign
        Bible Society," III (1866), 486-501 (notes on the
        empire).

2736   Presbyter Anglicanus [Cox, G.W.]. "The Bishop of Natal,"
        IV (1867), 34-65.

2737   Osborn, R.D. "Missionary Work in India," IV (1867), 65-
        82.

2738   Bowring, John. "Rammohun Roy and Hindoo Theism," IV
        (1867), 182-207.

TITAN: A MONTHLY MAGAZINE

2739   "Notes on Indian Literature: Novels," I (1856), 108-17,
        "The Drama," 356-63; "Philosophy," II (1857), 23-32,
        "Law, Lawgivers and Law-Books," 507-19; "The Epos,"
        VI (1859), 203-14.

2740   DeQuincey, Thomas. "China," II (1857), 183-92, 343-55.

2741   DeQuincey, Thomas. "Hints towards an Appreciation of
        the Coming War in China," III (1857), 65-74.

2742   DeQuincey, Thomas. "Passing Notices of Indian Affairs,"
        III (1857), 504-11 (mutiny).

2743   "A Vocabulary of the More Common East Indian Terms,"
        III (1857), 557-61.

2744   "Indian Omens: a Retrospect and an Outlook," IV (1858),
        1-15.

2745   DeQuincey, Thomas. "Suggestions upon the Secret of the
        Mutiny," IV (1858), 88-94 (India).

2746   Bowring, Sir John. "The Population of China: a Letter
        Addressed to the Registrar-General, London," IV (1858),
        354-63; with Postscript by S.W. Williams, 364 (see
        #1966).

THE WESTMINSTER REVIEW

2747   "ADVENTURES ON THE COLUMBIA RIVER," XVI (1832), 130-45
        (Hudson's Bay Company territory).

2748   [Stephen, George]. "Jeremie ON COLONIAL SLAVERY," XVI
        (1832), 522-34 (West Indies).

2749   "Constitution and Government of India," XVII (1832),
        75-103.

2750   "Earle's NINE MONTHS RESIDENCE IN NEW ZEALAND," XVII
        (1832), 311-34.

2751   "Future Government of British India," XIX (1833), 107-
        46.

2752   [Crawfurd, John with Thompson, T.P.]. "Sugar without
        Slavery," XIX (1833), 247-62.

2753   "NOVA SCOTIA," XIX (1833), 300-12.

2754   "Kingdom of Greece; and the Ionian Islands," XIX (1833),
        493-516.

2755   [Crawfurd, John]. "Voyage of Ship AMHERST," XX (1834),
        22-47 (China).

2756   [Bannister, Saxe]. "Regency of Algiers," XX (1834), 132-
        41 (notes on Australian natives).

2757   [Richard, Thomas]. "Van Diemen's Land," XXI (1834), 18-
        52.

2758   [Crawfurd, John]. "Chinese Empire and Trade," XXI
        (1834), 221-56.

2759   [Crawfurd, John]. "New South Australian Colony," XXI
        (1834), 441-76.

2760   [Thompson, T.P.]. "Jacquemont's LETTERS FROM INDIA,"
        XXII (1835), 304-13.

2761   [Crawfurd, John]. "Tea and Tea-Trade," XXII (1835), 361-403.

2762   [Crawfurd, John]. "South Australian Colony," XXIII (1835), 213-39.

2763   [Roebuck, J.A.]. "Affairs of Canada," XXIII (1835), 269-91, "Postscript," 519.

2764   "Shirreff's TOUR THROUGH NORTH AMERICA," XXIII (1835), 319-33 (Canadas).

2765   [Bannister, Saxe]. "South Africa," XXIII (1835), 415-23.

2766   L., B. [Molesworth, William]. "New South Wales," I (LONDON REVIEW) and XXX (LONDON AND WESTMINSTER REVIEW) (1835), 25-47.

2767   H. [Buller, Charles]. "Napier on the Ionian Islands," I and XXX (1835), 295-316.

2768   R., J.A. [Roebuck, J.A.]. "The Canadas and Their Grievances," I and XXX (1835), 444-76.

2769   [Crawfurd, John]. "The Colonial Expenditure," XXIV (WESTMINSTER REVIEW) (1836), 1-31.

2770   L., B. [Molesworth, William]. "Sierra Leone: THE WHITE MAN'S GRAVE," III and XXV (LONDON AND WESTMINSTER REVIEW) (1836), 311-32.

2771   G. [Grant, Horace]. "Hottentots and Caffres," IV and XXVI (1836-37), 93-107 (South Africa).

2772   Omega [Chapman, H.S.]. "The Timber Monopoly," IV and XXVI (1836-37), 107-39 (British North America).

2773   R., J.A. [Roebuck, J.A.]. "ASTORIA," IV and XXVI (1836-37), 318-48 (notes on Hudson's Bay Company in Oregon).

2774   C., H.S. [Chapman, H.S.]. "Progress of Events in Canada," IV and XXVI (1836-37), 468-82.

2775   L., B. [Molesworth, William]. "Life in the Penal Colonies," V and XXVII (1837), 78-94.

2776   A. [Mill, J.S.]. "Lord Durham and the Canadians," VI and XXVIII (1837-38), 503-33.

2777   R., S. [Robertson, John]. "The Arctic Discoveries," VII and XXIX (1838), 373-92 (notes on Hudson's Bay Company).

2778   S. [Mill, J.S.]. "Penal Code for India," VII and XXIX (1838), 393-405.

2779   W., H. [Robertson, John]. "Sir Francis Head's Works,"
       VII and XXIX (1838), 461-67 (Canada).

2780   [Mill, J.S.]. "Lord Durham and His Assailants," VII
       and XXIX (1838), 2nd ed., 507-12 (Canada).

2781   A. [Mill, J.S.]. "Lord Durham's Return," XXXII (LONDON
       AND WESTMINSTER REVIEW) (1838-39), 241-60 (Canada).

2782   B., H. [Robertson, John]. "Canadian Affairs," XXXII
       (1838-39), 426-53.

2783   L., M. [Laird, Macgregor]. "Remedies for the Slave
       Trade: Foxwell Buxton - Turnbull," XXXIV (WESTMINSTER
       REVIEW) (1840), 125-65 (West Africa and West Indies).

2784   B., C. [Buller, Charles]. "The Boundary Question,"
       XXXIV (1840), 202-36 (British North America).

2785   T., P.P. [Thomas, Peter Perring]. "Early History of
       China," XXXIV (1840), 261-87 (notes on opium).

2786   C., H.S. [Chapman, Henry Samuel]. "Emigration: Compar-
       ative Prospects of Our New Colonies," XXXV (1841),
       131-87.

2787   X. [Bowring, John]. "Anglo-Turkish War: Egypt and
       Syria," XXXV (1841), 187-224 (Egypt and defense of
       India).

2788   E. [Hickson, W.E.]. "Catlin's LETTERS...ON...NORTH
       AMERICAN INDIANS," XXXVII (1842), 122-34.

2789   G. [Grant, Horace]. "Koonawur: Travels in the
       Himalayas," XXXVII (1842), 294-304 (India).

2790   N., S. [Sheridan, Charles Brinsley]. "The Ionian
       Islands," XXXVIII (1842), 413-29.

2791   [Buller, Charles]. "Lord Ashburton and the American
       Treaty," XXXIX (1843), 160-205 (see #2797).

2792   S., W.H. [Stowell, William Hendry]. "HISTORY OF THE
       BAPTIST MISSIONARY SOCIETY," XXXIX (1843), 407-12
       (notes on the empire).

2793   W. "Journals of Disasters in Afghanistan," XXXIX
       (1843), 475-90.

2794   E. [Hickson, W.E.]. "Buckingham's AMERICA," XL (1843),
       20-36.

2795   G., W.R. [Greg, W.R.]. "Resources of an Increasing
       Population: Emigration or Manufactures," XL (1843),
       101-22.

2796   E. [Hickson, W.E.]. "New Works on China, and the Late
        War," XL (1843), 123-41.

2797   [Buller, Charles]. "Sequel to the North American Bound-
        ary Question," XL (1843), 182-88 (see #2791).

2798   G., W.R. [Greg, W.R.]. "The Slave Trade and the Sugar
        Duties," XLI (1844), 486-515 (West Indies).

2799   G., B. "Affairs of India: Afghanistan and Scinde," XLI
        (1844), 521-52.

2800   P. [Harwood, Philip]. "Lord Stanley," XLII (1844), 275-
        317 (notes on the Colonial Office).

2801   I. "Proposed Railroad between Cairo and Suez," XLII
        (1844), 428-36.

2802   E. [Hickson, W.E.]. "Exploring Expedition of the United
        States," XLIV (1845), 469-96 (notes on Fiji, New
        Zealand, and Hudson's Bay Company territory natives).

2803   D., N. [Ward, John]. "Affairs of New Zealand," XLV
        (1846), 133-223.

2804   F., T. [Falconer, Thomas]. "The Oregon Question," XLV
        (1846), 418-54.

2805   C. [Cowell, E.B.]. "Indian Epic Poetry," L (WESTMINSTER
        AND FOREIGN QUARTERLY REVIEW) (1848-49), 34-62 (notes
        on culture).

2806   [Chapman, H.S. and a collaborator]. "Earthquakes in
        New Zealand," LI (1849), 390-408.

2807   "Freehold Assurance and Colonization," LI (1849), 408-
        19.

2808   "Extinction of Slavery," LII (1849-50), 202-05 (West
        Indies).

2809   "African Coast Blockade," LII (1849-50), 500-41 (notes
        on West Africa, West Indies, and sugar).

2810   S. "Junction of the Atlantic and Pacific," LIII (1850),
        127-44 (Central America).

2811   "Correspondence: India," LIII (1850), 249-52 (Elphin-
        stone Institution).

2812   C. [Cowell, E.B.]. "Hindu Drama," LIV (1850-51), 1-37
        (notes on culture).

2813   "Recent Campaigns in India," LV (1851), 49-69 (Punjab).

2814   E., W. "Extinction of Slavery," LV (1851), 329-45 (as
        related to sugar production).

2815   "Western Africa," LVI (1851), 1-26 (notes on Gambia).

2816   [Chapman, John]. "The Government of India," LVII O.S.
        and I N.S. (WESTMINSTER REVIEW) (1852), 357-405.

2817   [Chapman, John]. "Our Colonial Empire," LVIII O.S. and
        II N.S. (1852), 398-435.

2818   [Forster, W.E.]. "British Philanthropy and Jamaica
        Distress," LIX O.S. and III N.S. (1853), 327-62.

2819   [Chapman, John]. "India and Its Finance," LX O.S. and
        IV N.S. (1853), 177-99.

2820   [Martineau, Harriet]. "Rajah Brooke," LXII O.S. and
        VI N.S. (1854), 381-419 (Borneo).

2821   [Newman, F.W.]. "International Immorality," LXIV O.S.
        and VIII N.S. (1855), 37-73 (imperial misgovernment).

2822   [Martineau, Harriet]. "Christian Missions: Their Prin-
        ciple and Practice," LXVI O.S. and X N.S. (1856), 1-
        51 (notes on the empire).

2823   "Herat and the Persian War," LXVII O.S. and XI N.S.
        (1857), 173-98.

2824   [Lushington, Franklin]. "THE MYSTERIES OF CEFALONIA,"
        LXVII O.S. and XI N.S. (1857), 216-45 (Ionian Islands).

2825   "The Hindu Drama," LXVII O.S. and XI N.S. (1857), 364-
        92 (notes on culture).

2826   [Donne, W.B.]. "China and the Chinese," LXVII O.S. and
        XI N.S. (1857), 526-57.

2827   "QUEDAH; or, Adventures in Malayan Waters," LXVIII O.S.
        and XII N.S. (1857), 357-74 (East Indies).

2828   [Froude, J.A.]. "The Four Empires," LXVIII O.S. and
        XII N.S. (1857), 415-40 (notes on British imperial
        goals).

2829   [Lewes, G.H.]. "African Life," LXIX O.S. and XIII N.S.
        (1858), 1-28 (notes on South and Southeast Africa).

2830   "The Crisis and Its Causes," LXIX O.S. and XIII N.S.
        (1858), 154-79 (Indian mutiny).

2831   [Pelly, Lewis]. "The English in India," LXIX O.S. and
        and XIII N.S. (1858), 180-209.

2832   [Martineau, Harriet]. "China: Past and Present,"
        LXIX O.S. and XIII N.S. (1858), 370-401.

2833   [Newman, F.W.]. "Our Relation to the Princes of India,"
        LXIX O.S. and XIII N.S. (1858), 453-77.

2834   "Indian Heroes," LXX O.S. and XIV N.S. (1858), 350-75.

2835   [Chapman, John with Stanley, E.H.]. "The Government of
        India: Its Liabilities and Resources," LXXII O.S. and
        XVI N.S. (1859), 112-64.

2836   [Noel, Robert R.]. "Militia Forces," LXXII O.S. and
        XVI N.S. (1859), 313-53 (notes on Canada and Nova
        Scotia).

2837   [Wilson, H.B.]. "Ceylon," LXXIII O.S. and XVII N.S.
        (1860), 66-90.

2838   [Wilson, H.B.]. "Vedic Religion," LXXIII O.S. and
        XVII N.S. (1860), 333-63 (India).

2839   "The North American Indians," LXXIV O.S. and XVIII N.S.
        (1860), 333-54.

2840   "Canada," LXXV O.S. and XIX N.S. (1861), 57-89.

2841   [Drummond-Davies, F.M.]. "The Cotton Manufacture,"
        LXXV O.S. and XIX N.S. (1861), 419-57.

2842   [Maxwell, Peter Benson]. "Law in and for India,"
        LXXVII O.S. and XXI N.S. (1862), 1-30.

2843   [Call, W.M.W.]. "The Mythology of Polynesia," LXXVII O.S.
        and XXI N.S. (1862), 303-39 (notes on Fiji and New
        Zealand).

2844   "Lord Stanley," LXXVII O.S. and XXI N.S. (1862), 498-
        529 (notes on India).

2845   [Newman, F.W.]. "English Rule in India," LXXVIII O.S.
        and XXII N.S. (1862), 112-39.

2846   [Drummond—Davies, F.M.]. "GIBRALTAR," LXXVIII O.S.
        and XXII N.S. (1862), 370-94.

2847   [Goldstrücker, Theodor]. "The Religious Difficulties
        of India," LXXVIII O.S. and XXII N.S. (1862), 457-89.

2848   [Crofton, Walter F.]. "English Convicts: What Should
        Be Done with Them," LXXIX O.S. and XXIII N.S. (1863),
        1-32 (notes on transportation and Western Australia).

2849   [Newman, F.W.]. "Indian Annexations: British Treatment
        of Native Princes," LXXIX O.S. and XXIII N.S. (1863),
        115-57.

2850   [Markham, Clements R.]. "Resources of India," LXXIX O.S.
        and XXIII N.S. (1863), 396-428.

2851 [Goldstrucker, Theodor]. "The Inspired Writings of
     Hinduism," LXXXI O.S. and XXV N.S. (1864), 144-69.

2851a [Beke, Charles T.]. "The Basin of the Upper Nile and
      Its Inhabitants," LXXXI O.S. and XXV N.S. (1864),
      307-48 (notes on natives).

2852 [Carleton, Hugh]. "New Zealand," LXXXI O.S. and XXV N.S.
     (1864), 420-72.

2853 "The Canadian Confederacy," LXXXIII O.S. and XXVII N.S.
     (1865), 533-60.

2854 "The Principles of Our Indian Policy," LXXXIV O.S. and
     XXVIII N.S. (1865), 185-219.

2855 "Dr. Livingstone's Recent Travels," LXXXV O.S. and
     XXIX N.S. (1866), 178-210 (notes on Southeast Africa).

2856 "The Canadian Confederation and the Reciprocity Treaty,"
     LXXXVI O.S. and XXX N.S. (1866), 394-412.

2857 "Our North-Pacific Colonies," LXXXVI O.S. and XXX N.S.
     (1866), 429-45 (British Columbia).

2858 [Cheadle, W.B.]. "The Last Great Monopoly," LXXXVIII O.S.
     and XXXII N.S. (1867), 85-119 (Hudson's Bay Company).

2859 [Pringle, Hall]. "Jamaica," LXXXVIII O.S. and XXXII N.S.
     (1867), 189-225.

AUTHOR INDEX

This index refers by name to authors of
articles in Section II.

SUBJECT INDEX

This index refers by territory or topic to
articles in Section II. Persons named in titles
are not indexed.